The voice and the eye

*An analysis of
social movements*

Other works by Alain Touraine

published by Editions du Seuil

La prophétie anti-nucléaire, 1980
Lutte étudiante, 1978
La Société invisible, 1976
Au-delà de la crise (under the author's supervision), 1976
Lettres à une étudiante, 1974
Pour la sociologie, 1974
Vie et mort du Chili populaire, 1973
Production de la société, 1973
Université et Société aux Etats-Unis, 1972
Le Mouvement de Mai ou le communisme utopique, 1968
La Conscience ouvrière, 1966
Sociologie de l'action, 1965
Ouvriers d'origine agricole, 1961

by other publishers

L'Après-Socialisme, Grasset, 1980
Un désir d'histoire, Stock, 1977
Les sociétés dépendantes, Duculot, 1976
La Société post-industrielle, Denoël, 1969
L'Evolution du travail ouvrier aux Usines Renault, CNRS, 1955

The voice and the eye
An analysis of social movements

ALAIN TOURAINE

TRANSLATED BY ALAN DUFF

WITH A FOREWORD BY RICHARD SENNETT

CAMBRIDGE UNIVERSITY PRESS

Cambridge

London   New York   New Rochelle   Melbourne   Sydney

EDITIONS DE
LA MAISON DES SCIENCES DE L'HOMME

Paris

Published by the Press Syndicate of the University of Cambridge
The Pitt Building, Trumpington Street, Cambridge CB2 1RP
32 East 57th Street, New York, NY 10022, USA
296 Beaconsfield Parade, Middle Park, Melbourne 3206, Australia
and
Editions de la Maison des Sciences de l'Homme
54 Boulevard Raspail, 75270 Paris Cedex 06

Originally published in French as La Voix et le Regard by Editions du
Seuil, Paris, 1978, and © Editions du Seuil 1978.

First published 1981

Phototypeset in Linotron 202 Palatino by
Western Printing Services Ltd, Bristol, England
Printed in the United States of America
Printed and bound by the
Murray Printing Company, Westford, Massachusetts

British Library Cataloguing in Publication Data
Touraine, Alain
The voice and the eye
1. Social movements
2. Sociology
I. Title
303.4'84   HM101   80-41352
ISBN 0 521 23874 9 hard covers
ISBN 0 521 28271 3 paperback

to
François Dubet
Zsuzsa Hegedus
Michel Wieviorka
compagnons de travail

Contents

Foreword by Richard Sennett

Alain Touraine is a French sociologist whose works are becoming increasingly well-known among British and American readers. He is the originator of the phrase 'post-industrial society', and his writing may be said to be an attempt to create a 'post-industrial sociology'. That is, M. Touraine wishes to stop fighting the battles of the nineteenth century which so many other sociologists keep restaging in their work. He is not much concerned with drawing the lines of economic determinism; the relation of the social to the biological seldom appears as a theme in his writing; nor is the positivist's effort at a 'scientific' analysis of data of much interest to him. Above all, Alain Touraine seeks to break down the teleological thinking which infects so much twentieth-century sociology as a legacy from the nineteenth century. He rejects the view that society moves toward ends of which the members of the society are unaware; he rejects the notion that a human lifetime is merely an incident in the march of history. Rather, he espouses the view that society produces itself, that the goal of social action is social action. He takes seriously such experiences as commitment, the desire for justice, confusion, and disillusion in the formation and destruction of social groups. By eschewing fate as a sociological preoccupation, M. Touraine has widened the scope of sociology, has forced us to pay attention to forms of social life which have been neglected by others.

M. Touraine's sociological oeuvre consists of two parts. There are concrete studies of social movements, such as his analyses of the Chilean revolution, of the French student uprisings of 1968, and of the anti-nuclear movement in Europe during the last decade. These concrete studies are of social groups whose origins lie in spontaneous protests which in turn evolved into organized movements, then felt the trauma of confrontation with other organized movements and with the organs of established power, and were either destroyed or transformed as a result. M. Touraine's sensibility as an observer is drawn insistently to the relation between the spontaneous and the rigid in social life. What is distinctive in these studies is that he does not equate the spontaneous with the amorphous; he sees in the generation of spontaneous social movements a structure which is the key to understanding other kinds of structures in social life. For example, the nature of state bureaucracy is revealed by conflicts with small groups of protestors against nuclear power to have a character and a mode of activity which would not be revealed if the observer's attention were strictly focused on the state's formal relations to other established institutions like industrial management or union bargaining committees.

The second part of Alain Touraine's writing is an effort to articulate a theory of social movements based on these studies. In the past, his most comprehensive effort was *La Production de la Société*. This volume, *The Voice and the Eye* is M. Touraine's most important theoretical work since *La Production*.

The simplest way to suggest what M. Touraine is after in *The Voice and the Eye* is to make a contrast to Talcott Parsons. Both Parsons and Touraine are concerned with the 'glue' of social relations; both fall in the tradition of Durkheim in believing that the solidarity of society theory depends on how various social groups are structurally interrelated. But the meaning of the term 'structure' is very different for M. Touraine from what it was for Talcott Parsons; indeed, he uses the term in a way most English-speaking writers do not. For Touraine, structure is a property of activity. People do not act *in* a social structure, the structure of society is the structure of how a group moves; it has an identity only by virtue of its movement. In Parsons' work there is a repertoire of possible social actions; the actions take on different meaning, and acquire particular value, as they acquire a functional place in relation to other acts. Social structure is the architecture of these functions. Whereas in the writing of Alain Touraine there is no repertoire of action. We cannot say, people in this position make this kind of move because there is a functional logic compelling them to act. Action is continually creating a set of forms which have no meaning apart from a moment in time, a place. To the question: 'What is the structure of a modern trade union?' Touraine would respond, 'The question can only be answered by looking at what unions are doing: how they are acting and reacting, to other groups, at a given moment of their history, that is what they are.'

The drama of *The Voice and the Eye* is how the author seeks to rescue this theory of structure-as-action from ending up as pure empiricism, as simply a record of acts. There is a great emphasis in this book on conflict as a means of 'gluing' social life together. Touraine may be said to be seeking a choreography of conflict. There is also an emphasis of the relation between theory and action – an emphasis from which the book takes its title. Part of the life of a social movement is the effort to say what it is, to see its contours in order to speak in its name. In this desire to combine action and analysis, Touraine does align himself with a sociological tradition; it is that of active Marxism, of *praxis*. But it would be best to think of his sociology as radical rather than ideological; radical in its conceptual scheme, radical in its refusal to accord to mankind a destiny, radical in the responsibility it therefore places on human beings for the pains and freedoms in their lives.

Preface

This book has three aims: to present the general orientations of a *sociology of action* and to justify the crucial importance given by this sociology to the idea of *social movement*; then, in the second part, to develop a research method – that of *sociological intervention* – which would be the practice corresponding to the theoretical choices described in the first part; and finally to introduce a set of interventions focussing primarily on social movements or social struggles, in particular the intervention which has already been carried out on the student movement, the results of which have been published under the title *Lutte étudiante*.

This present work was written after the conclusion of the intervention on the student movement, at the beginning of the intervention on the anti-nuclear movement, and during the preparatory stages of the intervention to be carried out on the Occitanist movement.

In preparing this book, I have had invaluable assistance from the comments and observations – written and spoken – of the members of the research team engaged on these first studies. And it is to them that the book is dedicated.

I should also like to express my gratitude to Christiane Guiges, Annette Mont-Reynaud, Jacqueline Salouadji and Mireille Coustance for their aid in the preparation of the manuscript, and to Emmanuel Muheim whose hospitality at the Centre cultural de Sénanque enabled me to undertake the revision of the text in its initial state.

1.

vwvwvwvwvwvwvwvwvwvwvwvwvwvwvwvwvwvwvwvwvwvwvwvwvwvwvwvwvwvwvwvwvwvwvwvwvwv

Men make their own history

A. THE BACKGROUND

Directions

Men make their own history: social life is produced by cultural achievements and social conflicts, and at the heart of society burns the fire of social movements. My reason for writing this book was to set out the *principles* and the *method* of a sociology founded upon this idea: society is drama, it is a play not of situation or intent, but of social action and social relations.

Our study is a strange undertaking. Does it not already belong to the past, to the age of great social conflict in our industrialization, the conflict of the workers' movement against capitalism?

Is not Socialism today far more a type of state than a social movement? Much the same might be said of capitalism, which on the world scale is seen more clearly as imperialism dominating the dependent nations, or as a camp opposed to the so-called socialist camp, than as exploitation of the proletariat, which in many countries has won for itself the means of restricting the domination of the overlords and negotiating its working conditions.

And, while the old social forces have now become political forces – elements of the state apparatus or of doctrinaire ideologies – fresh upsurges are being felt, new thrusts forward, which have not yet been defined or which refuse to be defined by social relations: these include the rejection of an industrial society grown overwhelmingly crushing, the return to the lost great times of stability, the anguish of crisis and the fear of catastrophe, freedom movements of all kinds for the reassertion of identity but without clear definition of their opponents, and liberal or libertarian critiques of the state. Thus on one side we have the state and on the other the longing for liberation. Instead of a social battle we have the heartrending cry of a blind man imprisoned. Has not the time passed of social struggles, class relations, and social movements? Was not this no more than a brief lightning flash after

1

thousands of years of silence imposed upon the slaves, a silence broken only by their swiftly stifled cries, and before the battles between empires and the contradictions within a society that destroyed the nature of which it was part led to the quashing of the social struggles that had emerged during little Europe's short 'modern' era? For some, the social question is replaced by that of the state, for others by that of nature. Here I support a contrary view: not only do I believe that instead of allowing ourselves to be sidetracked by current changes we should set out to discover the new actors and the new struggles of the society taking shape under our very eyes, I also claim that it is only now that the social history of society is really beginning, a history that is no longer anything other than the entire accumulation of relations and conflicts, the stakes involved being the social control of a new culture, of society's increased ability to act upon itself. We are moving quite simply into a type of society in which no transcendence – be it of the gods, of man, or of evolution – will any longer force collective action to take on a meaning by which it is surpassed; we are entering a society which has neither laws nor foundations, which is no more than a complex of actions and social relations. Instead of abandoning the domain of society in order to move towards a break between an objective order and the subjectivity of need or desire, we should far rather recognize that this domain is of vast extension, that social conflicts, just like the creative achievements of culture, penetrate into many domains which were hitherto the preserve of the gods or of custom.

If the change society is undergoing calls for a wholly social, i.e. sociological analysis, the role of the sociologist is also to bring out the central social conflicts of the new society and to indicate what is at stake by going beyond the awareness of crisis, the doubt, and the resistance to change or rejection of it. The time of the utopia is drawing to its end. As in the mid-nineteenth century – but now going much further – the moment has come to make advances in the analysis of the relations, the action and the movements of which society is composed, and simultaneously to improve both knowledge and action.

A stage without actors

When one considers closely this idea that society is a system of action, i.e. of actors defined by cultural orientations and social relations, it seems newer and even more astonishing than it did at first. In fact, the most common portrayals of our society exclude the idea of action and leave only little room for the social movements.

Let us first examine our recent past.

2

Men make their own history

1. Capitalism, the first agent of the great economic and social transformations, brought about its changes by violence and by the spirit of enterprise, without leaving much place for social relations and political discussion. It developed by tearing apart and breaking up, by exploiting and conquering; and those who became proletarized by capitalism had great difficulty in organizing themselves and only gradually won their social and political rights. Peasants driven off their land, craftsmen ruined, workers – men, women and children – subjected to the most fearful conditions of exploitation, reduced to being nothing but a work force and a tradeable commodity: the history of capitalism is that of creative destruction, of misery and oppression exacerbated by the proud conviction of the overlords that their vocation was to dominate their people and the world. On top of this exploitation of the workers came the ransacking of the colonies, the destruction of societies and cultures, often reaching the proportions of genocide, and the imposition of an order. The workers' movement and the anti-colonial and anti-imperialist national freedom movements acquired extraordinary strength during the first half of this century; but how short their history seems, how difficult their birth, and how swift their transformation into industrialist and authoritarian states! The idea of conflict was less important during capitalist industrialization than was the idea of *contradiction*. For well over a century there had been belief in the progress of the Enlightenment and of the forces of production, and in the contrast between this and the self-centredness and the waste of private interest. It was in the name of nature and the development of nature that the battle was waged against the immobility of the established order, of law and succession. Between the difficult and restricted struggle of the exploited, confined inside capitalism, and the progress of history the intervening distance seemed too great to be spanned. Only political parties – here the Social Democrats, there the Communists – could be the agents of progress and of the reconciliation of social relations with forces of production. The whole period of capitalist industrialization was marked by the outbreaks of worker revolt, the refusal to work, or sabotage, and in particular there emerged a class awareness among the workers and a revolutionary trade-unionism battling for a society of producers freed from parasites and exploiters. But social repression and the colonial war had dominated capitalist industrialization to such an extent that the workers' movement had become almost wholly identified with the cause of *revolution* and the removal of social contradictions thus preparing not only for the movement's own destruction but also that of the capitalist class and all civil society, to the exclusive advantage of a post-

revolutionary and soon counter-revolutionary state. The idea of contradiction, which had been imposed by capitalist exploitation, did not
lead towards social movement but towards the *party*, and the party
became a *state*, which had established its power by elevating the nation
and the *order*. This was a necessary chain of effects, the implacable
logic of which no country in the world was able to disentangle.

2. Let us now consider the countries which came later and in a different
way to industrialization. They were dominated by states which went
about the modernization and industrialization of their country without
leaving any initiative to the national bourgeoisie; this occurred no
matter whether the states were communist, nationalist – post-colonial
and anti-imperialist – or counter-revolutionary in dependent societies.
  Wherever a ruling class is subordinated to the state or is no more
than an economic function thereof, how can the social conflicts
emerge, take shape, and occupy the centre of the stage? In the communist countries, the confrontations do not occur between the social
groups but between the state and its victims or those who defend the
freedoms and the autonomy of civil society in the face of omnipotence.
Where are the great social movements in a Latin America increasingly
dominated by a combination of state capitalism and multinational
companies? Suppression, as we know, is powerful there, but was it not
also strong in Paris or in Lyon after 1830? There, too, the chief problems are those of the state rather than those of class relations. From
bourgeois violence we have passed on to state violence, as though a
free space for social movements could never have existed.

3. We return at last to our modern societies. In the industrialized
countries, which have long been enriched and have enjoyed their
advantages, and where oppression is less severe – at least outside the
periods of crisis and political upheaval – the idea of a society enlivened
by social conflict would seem to have had considerable difficulty in
becoming entrenched. It is an idea overshadowed by two conflicting
images. For some people, society, like the sorcerer's apprentice, no
longer the master of its means, destroys the very conditions of its
survival and is borne towards catastrophe, famine, the spread of
nuclear weapons and the destruction of life. For others, we are living in
an increasingly restrictive and manipulatory social and cultural order,
which with growing repressiveness ensures the reproduction of privileges and inequalities. In either instance, society appears to be a solid
block. Workers' claims, movements and conflicts cannot penetrate this
block: it is one-dimensional, confined within its productivity madness
or the immobilism of the state ideological apparatus.

4. Even in the best of cases, the sphere of social relations and social action is no longer any more than a place for secondary negotiations, for reforms which are rather adjustments and which do not threaten the established power, or are themselves even instruments of manipulation: power, formerly concentrated in monumental institutions, now like a devouring enzyme pervades the entire social tissue. Social services of all kinds are no more than magnified social and cultural control agents.

What then remains of what was formerly called society? A social vacuum. The mass society has destroyed communities, disrupted social relations, and confounded roles and norms. Under the pressure of the great power apparatus all that have been allowed to survive are the fragments of society. Georges Friedmann* had already spoken of fragmentary labour; shortly after he was to begin reflecting on fragmentary culture. So why not add fragmented politics? It is this destruction of social relations, of society, that leads to violence. The infiltration of anomy into society was already noticed by Durkheim. Does not this anomy today create a feeling of vacuum, a lack of planning, with the corresponding urge to be filled by a sensation, an experience, or the liquid of an injection syringe for want of a social relation that can be lived through? Given this panorama of society, it is tempting to be mistrustful of a sociology of action and of a social movements. Does not such a sociology conceal a moralizing, a limited, timid humanism and reformism, and the hopes or the nostalgia of the middle class, on their way down or on their way up, but always unable to think of society in its entirety?

Thus the many years of effort that have gone into my attempt to construct a sociology of action – an endeavour I have taken up again in this book – and to invent a research method to fit its orientations, are by no means assured of success. One runs up against the doubt and mistrust of society which scarcely believes any longer in its power to shape the choice of its future through its own social battles and its internal political mechanisms. Have we not seen in France the political and social preferences expressed at the time of the Liberation crushed by the constraints of the cold war and the struggle of the empires? In spite of this, however – and without forgetting the growing importance of the state, of international relations and of new social control mechanisms, I shall here be supporting the idea that our type of society, more than any other, should be thought of as a complex of social relations and movements, cultural products and political struggles.

* Proper names followed by an asterisk are references to the list of works cited at the back of the book.

Programmed society

There are three kinds of change in our societies that justify the use of this term: (1) In the more industrialized societies, the conquering and entrepreneurial spirit and the mechanistic outlook are becoming increasingly replaced as the principal factors of power by human government, by management, i.e. by policy; at the same time, protest movements are also veering towards directly political struggles; (2) these societies are less and less societies of inheritance and reproduction, and more and more societies of production and change; (3) and, lastly, power in these societies is less unified than anywhere else, and the state is no longer the all-powerful god it was made out to be by certain great conservative liberals.

These changes reflect a social transformation – the appearance of a new societal type. This is an idea which emerged during the sixties, but which was generally too closely bound up with industrialist optimism not to be dropped when the social conflicts and cultural disputes reappeared and when growth became replaced by crisis. Today it is time we took up this idea again by associating it – as I have always endeavoured to do – with the analysis of the new conflicts and social movements.

1. *The first point* is the most important. The characteristic feature of post-industrial society – which I have described more exactly as *programmed society* – is that the central investments are now made at the level of production management and not at that of work organization, as is the case in industrial society. Like all historical societies, industrial society, which should be defined rather in terms of production relations than of techniques, is based on the hold exerted by the masters of industry over salaried labour; this is why the place where class awareness and class conflict is situated is the factory, even the workshop or work-place, all of these being situations in which the boss-organizer imposes production rates and methods on the workers. Whether the regime be capitalist or socialist, class domination in industrial society is always of the Taylorian type. By contrast, in programmed society class domination consists less in organizing work than in managing the production and data-processing apparatus, i.e. ensuring the often monopolistic control of the supply and processing of a certain type of data, and hence of a way of organizing social life. This is the definition of the technocracy controlling the running of management apparatus. Resistance to this domination cannot be limited to a particular sphere, any more than can the domination itself.

What is crucial now is no longer the struggle between capital and labour in the factory but that between the different kinds of apparatus and user – consumers or more simply the public – defined less by their specific attributes than by their resistance to domination by the apparatus. These are truly social struggles which bring a social relation into question because they are no longer able to support a profession or defend a status or a community. And they are general struggles because a rapidly increasing number of social activities is controlled by the great management and data-processing apparatus. Social struggles have for long been concentrated in the sphere of political and legal rights. In industrial society, they have been centred on the economic situation and labour relations; in programmed society, they emerge wherever a ruling apparatus is in equal control of demand and supply, and can thus shape social and cultural behaviour. This is why the defence against such apparatus is no longer carried out in the name of political rights or workers' rights but in support of a population's right to choose its kind of life and in support of its political potential, which is often called self-management. Political action is all-pervading: it enters into the health service, into sexuality, into education and into energy production.

2. *The second point* is the decline of inherited patterns and of social reproduction in these societies undergoing constant transformation. It becomes difficult to effect the transference of cultural capital when the tradition has developed into a negative value and when inequality is being radically altered by the economic and cultural changes. This gives growing importance to what I have deliberately called relations of production – class confrontations for the social control of historicity – as opposed to relations of reproduction, which set those who dominate the social order against those who are defending their professional and cultural autonomy. When the latter win the struggle, in dependent or autocratic countries for instance, society undergoes change through crises and upheavals, while when the relations of production predominate they are revealed through class struggles and political negotiations, in which the sociology of action is primarily interested.

This idea that we are entering into a society seeking rather to undergo transformation than to find its balance is one by which many feelings are upset. The new social movements often reject the cultural orientations of industrial society; nevertheless, they do not develop until they begin to struggle against the new forms of growth instead of calling only for the defence of their threatened balance. We are certainly increasingly responsible for the natural states of balance which our production disturbs and is in danger of destroying, but to contrast a society that accepts its corner in the ecosystem to a devastatory society would be artificial. All historical societies have transformed their relations with the environment: this is the very definition of their historicity. Likewise, they have all had to fit into the natural states of balance. Reconciling these two orders of behaviour has become a major political problem; this reconciliation requires deep thought and far-reaching decisions. Those, however, who would maintain that post-industrial society should be a post-historic society – i.e. one comparable to prehistoric societies – could be right only in a future very far beyond all that can be affected by our predictions and analyses. We are responsible for nature and must respect the inter-dependence of its elements; this is more difficult and must be done more conscientiously than in the past. We are also no less committed to the creation of a programmed society, one beyond industrial society, no matter whether we make our way into it by ourselves or, being unable to reach it or actually rejecting it, are brought in only as servants or the colonized subjects of new masters. The self-production of our societies through labour is – and continues to be – what is mainly at stake; this is why class relations and social movements must in-creasingly become the focus of our analysis. I feel closer to those who, like Marx, maintain that at the core of society lie the social struggles, in which what is at stake is society's self-production, than I do to those who seek to rediscover the lost balance or those who are aware of no other struggles than those of civil society against state incursion.

3. *The third point* is the separation of the various functions of the state in capitalist programmed societies. There is a growing distance between public companies forming part of the technocracy, administrative sys-tems which often represent sectional or corporate interests, the state as the maintainer of order and of the social hierarchies, and finally the state as the agent of development and international relations. There exists no power capable of uniting these four sectors, no force to play the role of the communist party or of any other one-and-only party such as may be found in many societies. Pierre Birnbaum* rightly reminds us that the ruling elites to an extremely large extent come from privileged social backgrounds, but this is not enough to prove that the decisions taken by the various sectors of the state are the reflection of a sole logic. The example of the communist states has led to the spread-ing of the idea that the state has become more and more completely dominant over society. As far as the capitalist industrial societies are concerned, this idea is false because, above all, the functions of the state are becoming less and less unified.

The growing role of the public sector in production should not conceal the decline of the old image of the sovereign. The state as an agent of development and international relations is, and continues to be, an essential agent in the transformation of societies, and even in Europe its role is increasing as the strength of the national bourgeoisies declines in relation to the power of the transnational companies. But this state-prince is becoming increasingly different from the technocratic state, which itself is becoming separated from the bureaucratic state, and even more from the conservative state. All of which gives the social relations of production growing importance and autonomy over relations between citizens and the state.

Altogether, these transformations govern the changes in the actors and in the focus of the chief social conflicts. We are living through the transition from industrial society to programmed society and hence experiencing the decline of a certain type of class relations and conflicts and the emergence of a new generation of social movements. It is this changeover that we wish to study in the research programme to which this book is an introduction. But the changeover is not effected simply: situations of transition, crisis and the breakdown of collective action intervene between two societal types. The aim of the sociological method of intervention presented in the second part of this book is to separate out these different directions in current social struggles in order to bring out in the most diverse areas the new social movement which tomorrow will take over the central role that the workers' movement held in industrial society.

A social movement of this kind, which cannot be reduced to the struggle against contradictions or to an action serving a natural and necessary development, sets up a self-managing determination against technocratic management, i.e. one project of society against another, instead of appealing during times of rupture to transcendence or to a post-revolutionary power. In a society which can for the first time be conceived as the product of its own action upon itself, social conflicts have no other basis and no other goals than the struggle of social forces for the control of historicity and of the action of society upon itself. For the first time, social movements are becoming the main actors of society; but this – as we must constantly remember – should not make us forget the ever essential importance of the problems of the state, development policies and international relations. In our type of society, social movements are more than ever the principal agents of history.

In a large part of the world, foreign capitalist domination and/or autocratic internal order have disrupted the social movements and have resulted in a merging of a struggle against deprivation and action against an autocratic state and/or foreign domination. This is the historical definition of communism.

9

By contrast, wherever the political system is democratic or where there is no direct dependence on a foreign state, and where economic exploitation dissipates into multiform technocratic domination, social movements emerge; and for these to be understood, a sociology of action must be formed, differing in principle from the analyses which reduce society to the mechanisms and laws of economic domination. Neither the idea of social movement nor the method of sociological action can be separated from this situation and from the new portrayal of society it requires.

B. FROM ONE SIDE TO THE OTHER

The new social movements do not emerge ready-armed from programmed society, nor does programmed society replace industrial society in the way that one stage backdrop can replace another. By the mid-nineteenth century some Western countries had already entered the phase of industrialization, but it was not until the second half of the twentieth century that they became industrial societies. Today we know that the economic success or failure of our society will depend on its capacity to produce and control the modern means of data processing, which will lead to the transformation of great sectors, particularly in the so-called tertiary activities; but the leading capitalist countries are sociographically still industrial societies, in which vast, pre-industrial, market sectors continue to survive and still exert considerable political influence.

This disjunction, then, explains why the transition from one type of social movement and conflict to another does not occur swiftly or easily. I shall outline the principal stages in the transition from the social movements of industrial society to those of programmed society: 1. the decline of the old social movements; 2. a more widespread cultural crisis, threatening the foundations of the past society; 3. the rejection of growth and the search for new forms of balance; 4. the liberal or libertarian criticism of the state, serving to replace a still confused social struggle; 5. rejection of the concentration of power and exchanges, which necessitates falling back upon primary groups and past experience; 6. the determination of the threatened categories to rediscover their identity while still accepting the change; 7. the emergence of new social movements.

The first three stages take us increasingly further away from industrial society; the last three bring out new collective actions. Sandwiched between these two contrasted and successive movements of decomposition and recomposition, is the moment we are now experiencing of pure rebuttal, of a call for liberation which simultaneously rejects a culture, a class, and the state, in the name both of modernity and of the revolution.

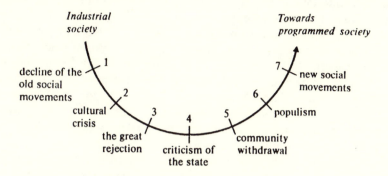

The decline of the workers' movement

1. Since our concern here is with the history of social struggles, it is from the *decline of the workers' movement* that one must begin and not from the industrial economic crisis. This expression may still come as a shock: what it means is that in a programmed society the chief conflict is not so much that which sets the worker against the head of the organization as that which opposes a population to the apparatus by which it is dominated. Industrial conflict has not, however, disappeared. The new social categories still fall under the domination of work organization and inhuman work norms. New regions are becoming industrialized; women and immigrant workers are being subjected to new assembly lines; office workers' jobs are becoming more mechanical; and the working conditions of many workers are deteriorating, particularly due to the rapid incursions of shift work: proletarization is forging ahead. Industrial class relations do not disappear with the emergence of the class relations of programmed society; merchant class relations retain their importance; and in agriculture and the handicrafts, the subordinate position of the producer in relation to the marketer becomes even more striking. But the conflicts which are specific to merchant society and to industrial society are gradually becoming institutionalized. One of the main transformations in post-war French society was the emergence of an influential agricultural trade-unionism matched by a defence movement on the part of the small producers and traders. Workers' trade-unionism won great political influence in most industrial countries, even in Italy, as a result of the state crisis which gave considerable political responsibility to employers and to the workers' trade union movement. France, which has consistently kept the trade unions remote from political influence,

has become the exception which cannot survive for long. Everywhere, the trade unions are becoming political actors, defined by their influence on decisions taken both at national level and within the company. They have not yet succeeded, particularly in France, in eliminating the most flagrant forms of worker exploitation in work organization; nevertheless, they have won guarantees and important negotiating power for the salary-earners, this being matched by increasing activity on the part of the authorities in the implementation of labour legislation and social policy. This institutionalization of the labour conflicts which transform the workers' movement into a truly political force has made it lose its role as a central social movement while at the same time increasing its importance in national life. There can therefore be no question of speaking of the disappearance of trade-unionism or of the working class; but it is becoming increasingly difficult for the workers to turn their past experience and their actual class-awareness into class action. Consequently, as at the early stages in the history of the workers' movement, this lends some importance in certain working sectors to the affirmation of pure class consciousness, which lies beyond the political parties or is even hostile to their intervention.

While this institutionalization of the trade unions has been taking place in the industrialized capitalist countries, the workers' movement has suffered far more drastic decline in the socialist countries, where it has become part of the state apparatus, in spite of certain short-lived efforts to establish workers' councils, and notwithstanding the important exception of Yugoslav self-management. This integration has become so complete that communist Europe has for the last thirty years been the focal point of workers' class struggles, which is only natural since those countries have undergone rapid industrialization and the workers have not been able to rely on the backing of political opposition forces.

Hungary and Poland have been the main centres of this class struggle; the absence of trade union representation and the presence of a dictatorial state have meant that the workers' movements have been expressed through uprisings, usually suppressed with violence; but these sporadic uprisings should not make one forget the importance of the everyday struggles, characterized by go-slows, absenteeism, theft, and sabotage. It is nonetheless true that in these countries the trade unions have lost almost all their importance by becoming merely a cog in the state machinery. The situation is comparable to that encountered in most nationalist countries, no matter of what colour they may be. Worker trade-unionism was controlled by the state in the Brazil of Vargas, the Mexico of Cardenas, and the Argentina of Peron as fully – or nearly as fully – as in the modern counter-revolutionary military

12

regimes of Latin America, or in the nationalist, socializing movements of Algeria, Guinea or Iraq.

Trade-unionism – on the one hand integrated into the state apparatus and on the other incorporated into representative political institutions – has ceased to be the focal point of social opposition, the chief agent in class warfare. Once again, however, this does not mean that exploitation of factory workers has disappeared or that the claim-making and negotiating role of the trade unions, at least in the capitalist countries, is not increasing in importance. Socialism, which used to be a social movement, has become above all a political force, to the point of sometimes being no more than a doctrine widely propagated by the university *establishment* in France and certain third world countries; it no longer represents the aim of the major social struggles. The new social movements, whose shaping we wish to follow and to accelerate, bear the mark of this situation.

These movements are not yet able to act as general political and ideological mouthpieces; the few attempts made in this direction have met with failure. What might potentially become a social movement can still emerge in no other way than as a pressure group, taking advantage of the elections to make itself known. On the whole, the new movements either fall back on past experience, sentiments, and a sense of spontaneity in their challenge to political institutions, or else become paralysed by the political or ideological categories of the old workers' movement which they continue to make use of although it no longer conforms to what they practise.

The crisis of industrial culture

2. This decline of the workers' movement, once it has become reformist or managerial, forms part of the far more general disintegration of the culture of industrial society. This breakdown is most apparent in the crisis of the industrial system of knowledge, for which history is led on by the laws of *evolution* towards greater complexity, rationality, and power over nature. This is a topic which is of present importance only in Soviet society, where faith in the scientific and technical revolution – the new name of progress – is still the official ideology. Man's knowledge used to be dominated by the historical method; within the space of a few years, economic history, like literary history or the study of 'primitive' mentality, was swept away and replaced by the marked progress of structural linguistics and anthropology, by textual analysis, and by a new generation of historical studies generated by anthropology. The interest that has been brought to bear on the societies that are historically and culturally furthest removed from our own has

occasionally been nourished, perhaps, by the desire to flee from weighty ideologies or shun the awareness of a social downfall – but this is not the crux of the matter. This long detour in time and space has made it possible for a new representation of society and culture to take shape. While the study of the contemporary world was sinking deeper into a popularization of evolutionism and a somewhat vague economic determinism, the attention focussed on societies controlled more by their functioning than by their development made it possible to come up with a representation of society in which the notions of system and structure replaced those of evolution and function. Maurice Godelier* has well demonstrated, in his critique of an economism handed down from industrial society, the extent to which anthropological discoveries have penetrated. Sociology, devoured on one side by this economism, and padded out on the other by structuralist thought, seems therefore to be on the point of vanishing. The great construct, over which Talcott Parsons took such determined charge during the fifties at Harvard, and which had such great success in the East and West alike, in societies eager to assert their superiority and confirm their stability, has been increasingly attacked and abandoned, to become a useless monument testifying more to the triumphant self-confidence of American society than to the progress of knowledge. The sociologist today must find his own path amidst these ruins of functionalism, economism, and evolutionism.

Is not this break with evolutionism contradicted by the already established idea of a transition, now in progress, from an industrial society to a programmed society that is post- and even hyper-industrial? Not in the least. Different societal types exist, defined by increasingly high levels of self-control, but it is only one of these types – industrial society – which represents itself by the place it occupies in an evolution it describes as progress. By contrast, when one reaches the highest level of historicity, the society's self-production, evolutionist representation becomes replaced by another form of knowledge, by the idea that society is a system capable of producing, of generating its own normative guidelines instead of having them passed down via an order or a movement that transcends society – no matter whether one call it God, Spirit or History.

In addition to the changes that have occurred in the form of knowledge and in the form of investment, there are those which have been produced in the *cultural model*, i.e. in the image a society forms for itself of its creative capacity, an image which becomes the basis of a morality. For industrial society, creativity remains transcendent: the forces of production develop above society. This society believes in progress, in the meaning of history, not as a product of social relations but as that which enables us to judge these relations. By contrast, our societies no longer believe in progress; they reject belief in science as the instrument of a liberating force, insisting instead on their responsibility, since they are just as capable of destroying themselves as they are of transforming and enriching themselves. They judge themselves in truly social and political terms. Socialism is never defined more seriously than by the society which has to come after capitalism, by superseding it. Whether one defends socialism or attacks it, one will define it in terms of self-determination, of democracy. This change in the representation of society is matched by an ethical transformation. The ethic of industrialization was based on what was known as the deferred gratification pattern: the recompense for effort and work had to be sought in a success or profit which would not come until later. Programmed society, on the other hand, views itself as a network of relations, and the forms of behaviour it rates highest are those which reinforce the ability to communicate more than the effort to save and invest. This transformation should not be confused with the simple disintegration of the old ethic in the interests of seeking immediate satisfaction and for the sake of consumption; but the transformation will not be able to emerge until the new ethic becomes incorporated in new forms of education. These new forms make their appearance with difficulty, particularly in France. The consequence thereof is a crisis in socialization, in the transference of a cultural heritage from one generation to another, a crisis that is all the more grave in that the family, the school, and the churches have most often been oriented towards a cultural model older even than that of the industrial culture. In becoming a centre of emotional relations, the family has passed through a crisis; in France, the Catholic Church has burst apart, becoming sometimes an organ of conservative moralizing and at other times a hotbed of eschatological movements, while the school, protected by its monopoly and by state power, remains the only institution apparently untouched – a great vessel carried by the flood. All these cultural changes have created an immense rift between a transformed culture and a society – including social ideas – neither of which yet exists as such. This is a rift which becomes manifest in what is known as a crisis of civilization. The channels of society no longer correspond to the cultural content they are meant to bear. Hence the personality crisis and the critique of power and of institutions which reach beyond politics and infuse the new social movements with a challenging power added to their already existing inclination towards protest and conflict. This crisis of industrial culture assumes a different form in each industrial country, but it is nonetheless general.

15

Men make their own history

The great resistance

3. This rift gives rise, primarily, to *great resistance*. The new adversary has not yet become clearly delineated: in face of this undefined threat, a community turns back upon its past, not in order to defend its former leaders, but in order to salvage a collective existence threatened with disintegration. This explanation given by Maria-Isaura Pereira de Queiroz* or Yves-Marie Bercé* of certain peasant uprisings or messianic movements may also be adopted for the self-protecting struggles of the middle or popular classes. But the messianic movements themselves are not only the defence strategies of a community: they are also a premonition of struggles which cannot yet assume an openly social form because the opponent is revealed only in the confused shape of economic changes. As in anarchy or Blanquism, this resistance is often buoyed up by confidence in the future and the determination to progress. Hence the resurgence today of anarchy, which rejects the institutional, established order and the state. This battle against social reproduction is clearing the way for the discovery of new relations of production by preventing the formation of a new ruling class sheltering under the order created by the class it has succeeded. It is an autonomous opposition which becomes all the more violent as state order sinks deeper into crisis and the political system offers still fewer alternatives. It is social resistance that can call upon only what lies beyond a particular society which is no longer regarded as a system of constraints or as an aberrant succession of scandals. In France, in 1968, the libertarian undercurrent surged powerfully to the surface. Later, it found expression only in small groups such as *Vive la Révolution*, although the influence it exercised was far more widespread: in Germany and Italy, it is still important among the autonomous groups. It has attracted the support of many intellectuals, most often ex-Marxists, who have replaced the idea of class warfare by a far more radical critique of society and culture aiming to uncover in the individual personality a power of substantiation or negation capable of overturning the barriers of the established order. This nihilism has been nourished by the great fear of catastrophe, the agonizing awareness of the limitations of a society that is moving more along the road towards self-destruction than towards self-reproduction. We have nuclear explosions, widespread famine, the deplenishment of primary materials – even the exhaustion of our oxygen – and the pollution of our seas and rivers: are we not close to the moment when this society is going to render life impossible? Attacking property or the ruling class is not enough; we must do away with conquistadorial and aggressive argumentation, with the illusions of growth and industrialization.

16

These feelings may represent a step towards new collective action, but they also lead directly towards the anguish of social vacuum and the sense of the destruction of social relations.

Liberation

It is easy to protect oneself against the illusion of taking this great resistance to be the social movement itself. Nothing could be more suspect than the all-round celebration of May '68 in France. These fine sentiments would be less widespread if the action taken in '68 had been socially and culturally more clearly directed. It is true that at the time a modernizing cultural critique – and hence one that suited the interests of the ruling elite, who were themselves new – became mingled with an archaic ideological way of thinking which was perpetuated, after the action had relapsed, by the most destructive form of sectarianism. This critique was also mixed up with the appearance of new social movements which took shape some years later only outside the universities. On the other hand, one should not be too hasty in swimming out from the trough of the wave and asserting too forcefully that new social movements have been formed. The great backlash is long-enduring: anti-intellectualism and the resistance so often exhibited by the feminist movements to over-ideological masculine thought also act as an instrument for the destruction of the progressivist ideology taken over from industrial society, inherited both from the workers' movement and from the action of the capitalists. For several years to come we shall be living through this destruction of an ideology which has gradually become crystallized into a doctrine at the same time as the social practice of which it was formerly an expression has been disappearing. Furthermore, historically we are not only experiencing the transition from one culture and one society to others but also witnessing the end of revolutions in our part of the world, the end of a connection between a social movement and a state crisis, and, consequently, the rejection of a Soviet-type revolutionary state and the quest for a new connection between a social movement and institutional democracy. This is a strategic change so fundamental that it requires us first to allow a new liberal current – that of the Rights of man and of the citizen vis-à-vis the state – to sweep away the degraded forms of revolutionary movements that have become more or less converted into totalitarian state-systems. This great resistance, together with the new liberalism, dominates our intellectual life today. I am not one of their flag-bearers, for I believe in the necessary reconstruction of social movements and conflicts, but I am also aware that this reconstruction will not be possible until we have cleared away the encumbering

17

rubble of the old social movements, and that for a while we shall have to live with cultural modernization movements linked to a liberal critique before we are able to assist the renaissance of social movements.

4. This libertarian reaction often infiltrates into a new *liberalism*, advanced particularly by intellectuals speaking and acting in the name of those who are prevented from speaking and deprived of the opportunity to act. This is why liberal campaigns are being stepped up against prison systems, the death penalty, and psychiatric wards, and in support of the cultural rights of minorities such as the homosexuals, or for respect for the opinions of conscientious objectors and draft-dodgers. Here too we encounter some of the features of the feminist movements. These are two-sided struggles: their call for liberty is meant to be anti-establishment, yet it is best heard by those at the top. These struggles are reminiscent of the campaigns in which Voltaire distinguished himself, fighting against prejudice and privilege, but more in the name of the up-and-coming, progressivist bourgeoisie than of the people. Today, too, these liberal campaigns tenuously attract those who are preparing the anti-technocratic struggles of the future, those who reject the institutions they consider to be a means of mass repression or manipulation, and also those who form the new ruling elite and who demand greater cultural liberty, just as the bankers and industrialists claimed greater economic liberty in the early days of capitalist industrialization. Soon these allies-of-a-day or comrades-of-a-demonstration will part ways, but for the present these liberal campaigns – even when they lump together a new bourgeoisie, new trade-unionists, and new anarchists – continue to be important because they are the answer to a moment in history when the rejection of the past is more clear-cut than the struggle for a different kind of future. The anti-colonial struggles demonstrated the vigour and confusion of these counter-state actions. This is why they represented the main field of action for left-wing intellectuals supporting anti-capitalist, anti-imperialist and anti-colonial action, who were at the same time liberals fighting against their own state in order to extend the realm of civil society and separate the powers as much as possible.

The community Utopia

5. The reverse side of rejection of the state, of the cultural crisis and the agonizing awareness of the social vacuum is the quest for personal and community identities capable of standing up against the ravages of history. Many communities have been created as a flight from indus-

18

trial and urban life, but rarely have they succeeded in remaining integrated and meeting the harsh demands of survival and difficult economic conditions. Most often they exhaust themselves trying to reduce their internal tensions. In a more diffuse way, the individual, exposed to an increasing number of stimulations, seeks to withdraw into a private realm, or rather to recreate for himself a private life as the traditionally private realms rapidly yield to invasion by the public domains of commerce or administration. Christopher Alexander,* developing the idea of the solitary crowd conceived by David Riesman,* speaks most appropriately of the 'retreat into autonomy'. But if Ivan Illich's* call for *conviviality* has been so widely heard, it is because he does not yield to the temptation of isolation or the rejection of modern techniques. Illich's thinking represents the great Utopia of our time; it spearheads the critique of industrial society in the name of science, nature, and at the same time morality; it is a call for the tool to be submitted to man, but it is also an attempt to discover the natural and hence scientifically definable limits to the use of certain forms of technology, whether it be a motor-car or hospital installations. Whoever finds himself indifferent or hostile to Illich will not discover the path that leads towards the new social movements of programmed society. But this cultural critique cannot yet be a social critique except when it is speaking out for a dominated third world, which is a different battle. It is not possible to identify the over-development of the technological *milieu* with a force of social domination. When Illich writes in *Tools for Conviviality* that the growing complexity of modern production systems endangers democratic participation he is introducing the myth of the transition from simple democratic societies to complex authoritarian societies, which is an inversion of the myth of evolution that gives it an even more arbitrary form than that of its customary formulation. The call for natural growth limits is even more dangerous, for if it were really heard it would make all social critiques unnecessary, and of its own accord it maintains the illusion of the naturalness of social organization. But what does it matter! Utopian thought is indispensable as a stage in the process of social and cultural change. It is a means of attacking, on their own ground, the evolutionist model, and the identification between the progress of production and moral and social progress advanced by most thinkers of the last century. The Utopia of the community appears at first to distance itself from the new social struggles, yet far more often it is actually paving their way. It is the camp of the ecologists that has been most ready to lend a sympathetic ear and to defend the appeals against technocracy, the concentration of power in giant systems, and the mystique of power itself. It is among the ecologists, too, that one encounters the simultaneous alliance and opposition of those who are seeking a new equilibrium – the subjection of society to the homeostatic mechanisms of the natural systems – and those who, like R. Dubos,* know that man is constantly altering the wholes into which he is integrated. In this place and at this time, the withdrawal towards a mythical past and the structuring of the social struggles of the future are so closely linked that one cannot yet know with certainty whether the ecological movement will become dissipated in contradictions, covering up the downfall of the old middle classes, or whether instead – as I am inclined to feel – it will tilt the scales towards the great battle against technocracy.

The populist hope

6. The *populist* movements are founded on the desire of social groups experiencing crisis to avoid splitting up and, by strengthening their collective identity, to succeed in regaining control over their own development. To avoid proletarization and uprooting, and to manage somehow to remain more and more the same while undergoing transformation – this is the populist dream that has coloured the great political myths of the Third World, from Latin America to Africa. If I place populism on the curve reaching back to the social movements, it is because it is progressivist. While movements of the Poujadist type are oriented towards the past, populism – which is one of the important components of regional movements – sets out to combat traditionalism and *passéism*: it is a modernizing movement, but it resists stoutly against the dispossession of peoples and territories dominated from afar by a distant master. It is not yet – but it may become – the antitechnocratic defence of a subjugated and alienated population; it is no longer the simple quest for an identity which might put a brake on change, but it is still close to being so. It has often drawn strength from religious aspirations, particularly in France, where Christianism has ceased to be incorporated within the Christianity of a society governed by the rules of the Church. Populism, therefore, is waging a social battle which is also conceived as a liberation from humanity's deeper needs. This Christian populism, reinforced by solidarity with the struggle of the Third World, is at the same time a vehicle for new aspirations, bearing the stamp of the progressivism of the last century and attached more to the issue of the fundamental contradictions than to that of the negotiable conflicts. It is a torrential stream in whose current the ideas of the past and of new sensitivities are tumbled and swept away.

Men make their own history

The anti-technocratic struggles

7. Social struggles do not reappear until a social category has defined the opponent against whom it is fighting. No real social relation is endangered by the call to creativity or individual desire against the established order, to liberation against the shackles of tradition and prejudice, or to nature against the excesses of technology. All movements whose rallying call is that of difference, specificity, or identity, dismiss only too easily any analysis of social relations.

It is for this reason that such movements, whatever may be their anti-establishment front, often become assimilated as elements in the ideology of the ruling elite, whose principle at heart is always to defend the freedom to innovate, to take initiative and thus dominate over all that resists to change or defends an acquired status and a work position.

At the half-way point between these elitist liberation movements and the new popular struggles one encounters the *denunciation of power*. This marks a decisive advance. The denunciation of power dismisses the image of society as a system, with its own language, or as an instrument of repression, and instead it chooses to set out from the event, i.e. the drama, the conflict, the clash of interests, and the sway of the dominator over the dominated who argues, resists, counter-attacks or negotiates. Those who, following the lead of Michel Foucault, have denounced power beyond the economic life to which it is still confined by so many thinkers, have greatly contributed to the revival of critical social thought. But is it possible to claim that power is ubiquitous, without making it difficult to define the relations of domination and particularly without levelling society with the state? Social domination is clearly to be seen in all spheres of social life, but if power is ubiquitous it must spring from somewhere, from the great technocratic apparatus, from the centres of domination made up by the ruling class. Only by locating and recognizing the power sources can one define and predict the areas of dispute and the fields of conflict. This is why the anti-nuclear protest has been picked out as the first important manifestation of the anti-technocratic movement, for here the opponent has been clearly marked out: the adversary is the great technico-economic apparatus, so powerful that it can impose even an energy policy which no scientific, technological, or economic argument could force one to recognize as being superior to any other policy. But this anti-technocratic struggle is never separated from other types of collective action ranging from populism to the great rejection of growth and of the industrial society. Sociological research, and the social struggles themselves, will gradually – but never completely –

21

sort out the elements that are jumbled together by history. The very word *self-management* – which is what is at stake in these new struggles, just as social justice was in the workers' struggles, and liberty in the fights against political and economic domination in the merchant societies – incorporates almost all these meanings. It is particularly important when it serves to designate the main adversary of the popular forces, i.e. technocratic management, and because it situates the struggles on their true ground. It is also important because it stipulates that social movements are capable of directing their own action, of managing themselves, instead of being merely a transmission or relay station in the service of political forces. But it also calls in a more reformist way for an enlargement of industrial democracy; and, finally, it often acts as a conveyer of the dream of community independence, of the dispersal of the forces of production, thus reviving the 'peasant' dream of a generalized middle class which would be both productive and managerial.

These anti-technocratic battles will be waged through a combination of two categories of actors. In the same way, the workers' movement drew its strength from the union of workers in a trade, defenders of productive labour against capital, with unqualified workers, who were more directly subject to exploitation by their employers and who were unable to ground their protests in the defence of a trade. In programmed society, it is a fraction of the *professionals* who perform the role that used to be played by qualified workers in industrial society. They speak in the name of knowledge against an apparatus that seeks to subject knowledge to its own interests, and they ally themselves with those who are forced to the sidelines by a central apparatus and submitted to its power. The union of these two protesting categories does not occur any more easily today than it did yesterday, and thus one of the most important features of the ecological movement is to have brought scientists into touch with groups from the public.

The formation of new social movements is not to be equated with the formation of new public causes, demands and disputes. Many public sensitizing campaigns can lead to changes in the law, only to vanish once this success has been obtained. In other instances, such campaigns are merely an accompaniment of social and cultural changes, on which they exert no real influence as their inherent function is quite different. In a society still in the process of formation, public causes initially take on the form of moral protests, of an appeal to principles or needs, to utopias. It is when they become more political, by seeking their way through the institutions, by joining up with other social forces and with representational agents, by showing an active awareness of the general problems of society – particularly those of society's

22

internal economic management and its international environment – that their social nature emerges.

The present, almost complete, rift between party policies and social movements or currents of opinion does not presage the coming victory of the latter but rather the beginnings of the reconstruction of political life. There seems to be an unbridgeable gap between the socially highly undefined liberation movements and the problems of a national society confronting the changes in international economic and political relations; yet no central social movement will come to exist unless this gap is to some extent bridged, unless the forms of political life are transformed by the new social forces, and unless these forces – by venturing away from the calm backwaters of specificity, identity and difference – become integrated, allied or combined with the coherent organizational plans of a particular society, even going to the lengths of concerning themselves with the problems from which they are furthest removed, i.e. state problems.

The nature of capitalist industrial societies, with their extremely large overall capacity for inventing institutional change mechanisms, makes it likely that social struggles will be accompanied by the appearance of new types of institutions, and mechanisms for decision-making and social intervention. The workers' movement, whether revolutionary or not, succeeded through the trade unions and through political action in creating and enforcing collective bargaining and labour legislation. One cannot help wondering what institutions – probably even *softer* ones than the contractual institutions – the new social movements will succeed in creating; and in the different forms of social work one must seek for something other than an instrument of control or a counter-deviation device, i.e. the embryo of the new institutions, in which dialogue, exchange, and the creation of an autonomous space will enable claims and disputes to gain strength and become politicized, instead of being crushed by repression or destroyed by *fidéism*.

It would be arbitrary to establish complete polarity between the formation of new social movements and the emergence of new mechanisms for the institutional treatment of social problems.

In other historical contexts, on the other hand, and particularly in countries dominated by a totalitarian state, one will need to follow the transformation of the new social movements into revolutionary action.

Our *plan of research* is now to concentrate on the stages that have just been outlined. We shall be studying the *workers' movement* in order to discover the changes that have occurred in what was the great social movement of industrial society, and still remains a political force of supreme importance; a *student battle* which will show the decline of

23

the old role of the intelligentsia while at the same time revealing the possibility of new conflicts – heralded by those of May '68 – over the social forms of production and the utilization of knowledge; the *women's liberation movement* which is seen particularly as a cultural liberation movement but which also encompasses a new type of social conflict; the *Occitanist movement*, which is a quest for a cultural identity, but also a populist breakthrough and a nationalist movement of the Third World type; and finally the *anti-nuclear movement*, located at the heart of an *ecological* movement which embraces nearly all these different tendencies at once, and which might easily provide the mould in which the main struggles that will later stir through history are to be formed. Once this research has been carried through, I shall collate the results to write the social history of tomorrow; but from the outset we needed to have an initial idea of where the phenomena to be studied are located. We needed, above all, to recognize that the capitalist industrial societies are not experiencing crisis or inner contradiction, but that they are living through the turbulent and dangerous transition from one type of society to another at the very moment when they are losing the world hegemony which for several centuries had aided their modernization.

One can now better understand, within this historical context, the practical aim of our research: to discover the social movement which in programmed society will occupy the central position held by the workers' movement in industrial society and the civil liberties movement in the market society by which it was preceded. No movement can be observed in its pure state: by indicating the various stages in the transition from one society to another, we have already established the forms of collective behaviour implicated in the social movement we are seeking to discover. In fact, this movement is all the more difficult to grasp because it is overlaid with layers of events, crises and conflicts of all kinds. This is why, before embarking upon research as a concrete whole, we must take a closer look at the methodological and theoretical research instruments that will enable us to extract the social movement from the admixture in which it is compounded with other types of collective behaviour. The purpose of this book is to present the different instruments, and to construct a theory and a method for studying social movements and, more generally, collective action. I shall now briefly outline the principal elements of this study.

C. THE GUIDING IDEAS

The principles for an analysis of the social movements to be studied in the first part of this book were elaborated before the development of the research programme, the method of which is to be presented in the second part. It is, however, our thinking on the present historical moment that explains why the main aim of this work is to establish a link between the theory and practice of the study of collective action. This present moment is a social one, marked by the appearance of new problems and new social movements which must be understood and which can no longer be explained by invoking another order of phenomena – the laws of capitalist development or the consequences of modernization. It is also an intellectual moment: in France, the disparity between doctrinal discourse, the belated product of the past action of the workers' movement, and the observable forms of collective behaviour has become all the more unbearable for giving rise to a division between an uprooted university world and the forces of change, and to the inability of the traditional left to understand social and political events.

Sociological thinking has been experiencing a lengthy crisis with the breakdown of the thought-patterns applied to the study of society, both those of conservative ideology and Marxist ideology alike. Our most urgent need is to learn how to name and analyse the new social practices and the new forms of collective action which are shaping the societies of today and tomorrow.

Analysis

The first part of this book describes the main elements for a study of collective action. Rather than attempt to summarize them in a few lines, I prefer to give the reader an advance review of the three most important themes he will encounter, those which have been the focal point of my thinking.

1. The first is that a society is a hierarchized set of *systems of action*, i.e. of social relations between actors who may have conflicting interests but who belong to the same social sphere and therefore share certain cultural orientations. A society is not founded upon its economy, nor upon ideas; it is not a combination of sub-systems or sub-levels. It has only two fundamental components: historicity, i.e. its capacity to produce the models by which it functions, and the class relations through which these orientations become social practices, still marked by a form of social domination. A society has neither nature nor foundations; it is neither a machine nor an organization; it is action and social relations. This idea sets a sociology of action against all the variants of functionalism and structuralism.

2. *Social movements* are neither accidents nor factors of change: they are the collective action of actors at the highest level – the class actors – fighting for the social control of historicity, i.e. control of the great cultural orientations by which a society's environmental relationships are normatively organized. The analysis of societies must bring out of hiding the antagonistic social movements and whatever they have culturally at stake together behind the false positivity of order, behind the categories of social practice, and behind the ideologies. It happens at times that social movements are weak or disorganized, but in the historical societies it never occurs that one cannot recognize the place of these movements at the centre of social life.

3. The functioning of a society is dominated by its historicity and by its class relations, and therefore by its social movements. But its change, in particular its transition from one societal type to another, requires another order of analysis, in which the *state* occupies central place. This separation – the limits of which we shall nevertheless have to describe – between the analysis of functioning and that of change, between *synchronic* and *diachronic* analysis, entails the abandonment of the evolutionist conceptions which claim that the functioning of a society can be explained by that society's place in an evolution leading, for instance, from the simple to the complex, from the transmitted to the acquired, or from the symbolic to the rational.

These three ideas look to one another for support in order to combat those which present society as a system governed by an inner logic, whether it be that of domination, reproduction, or adaptation. They establish an indissoluble link between the declaration that all social action is culturally oriented and the admission that no value or norm can be imposed on top of social conflicts. For some people, the very principle of society is torn apart by a contradiction; for others, the conflicts occur only within the cultural values which are directly imposed on the whole society. I favour the idea of setting these two conceptions aside, for the peculiarity of a social system is that its cultural orientations are never anything other than what is at stake in social conflicts, i.e. they never form the framework of social relations nor the ideology of a dominant actor. This representation of social action, added to the separation between synchronic and diachronic analysis, serves as the thread of Ariadne which must guide us in our study of social movements.

Method

The central importance given to the concept of action calls for a method to match. A conception of society is of no use unless it produces a sociological practice. This is why the second part of the book is devoted to sociological *intervention*, a method devised to meet the demands of a sociology of action, and one which will be used in the whole body of research on contemporary social movements (the research on the student struggle and on anti-nuclear movements has been published in *Lutte étudiante* and *La prophétie anti-nucléaire*). The method is based on three principles.

1. It aims to study collective action, and therefore approaches this action as directly as possible, that is, by studying a militant group in its militant role, in the name of which it accepts or demands intervention. The analysis bears neither on a situation nor on opinions, but on the *self-analysis* which militants perform upon their collective action.

2. As action is inseparable from social relations, this intervention places the author in a position of *interaction* with social partners, and what it provides as a basis for the group's work of self-analysis is not an ideological conscience but the content of these confrontations.

3. In these conditions, the *researcher* cannot be a distant observer. Such 'objectivity' would be contradictory to his recognition of the actor as such. Intervention requires that the researcher be an *intermediary* between the militant group and the social movement by which its action is conveyed. It is this new conception of the researcher as neither observer nor ideologist that most clearly distinguishes intervention from other methods. The question to which this intervention endeavours to reply is therefore: how can action be studied without being destroyed; how can social life be analysed without being 'naturalized'? This is why the principles of an analysis of social movements and the guidelines for intervention must be described and developed together, as an introduction to books which, by using the method of sociological intervention, will go on to analyse the social movements and collective struggles which are waiting at the very door of programmed society and proclaiming what will be the social history of tomorrow.

PART ONE

THE SOCIAL MOVEMENTS

Social movements are the expression of the collective will. Can we arrive at an understanding of them other than by identifying ourselves with them, by sharing what they reject and by joining in their expectations, i.e. by understanding them quite differently from when we explain social organization, institutions or power? These movements describe themselves as agents of liberty, equality, social justice or national independence, or even as appeals to modernity or to the liberation of new forces in a world of traditions, prejudices and privileges, and those who are interested in them feel themselves borne on by the same movement to besiege the established order. Should not the study of these movements come close to the epic, in which one sings the glory of the collective heroes of history who were most often condemned to repression or oblivion before being recognized – though not always – as exemplary?

One must, however, break away from this portrayal, not because it is too exalted but because it is too poor. Social movements are not exceptional and dramatic events: they lie permanently at the heart of social life. Those whose function is to maintain order agree – more or less grudgingly – to recognize that this is never absolute, that it is surrounded by innovation and by deviation, by refusal and by social movements. But this apparent concession is intended only to maintain the fictitious belief that order comes first – and this is patently false. What comes first is the work society performs on itself, by inventing its norms, its institutions and practices, guided by the great cultural orientations – pattern of knowledge, type of investment, and cultural model – which I have described as its *historicity*, but also dominated by this incessant conflict for the social control of historicity, i.e. the *class struggle*. Social movements are not a marginal rejection of order, they are the central forces fighting one against the other to control the production of society by itself and the action of classes for the shaping of historicity.

They are the fabric of society, the study of which is not a peculiar domain of sociology, a speciality. It is actually the banner of the entire sociology of action, which heads all other sociologies, for the other branches – no matter whether they study the inability to act, crisis, order and the maintenance of order, or social change – are dependent on the sociology of action.

This will explain to the reader why he will find himself flung apparently far from the specific theme of collective struggles right into the midst of general sociology. But it must be understood that sociology can only be constructed from the study of social movements which, alone, can save us from the vain search for the nature or essence of society and guide us towards an image of society as an ensemble of systems of action, as a drama in which the social movements play the main roles.

I am aware that this idea does not suit the tastes of today. The dominant strain in social thought speaks more readily of adaptation to change, while the strongholds of opposition wage all-out critical warfare on order and power in the name of forces or powers which seem to lie outside of society. Between the two, the concept of social conflict conveyed by the workers' movement and in particular by Marxism has practically disintegrated, since here it covers the most pragmatic reformism and the construction of a totalitarian state. We seem to have been overtaken by our history more than the authors of that history.

I should claim, nevertheless, that one must reconstruct a representation of society which would place in central position and give an entirely new definition to social relations, conflicts and movements. This is what is at stake not only in this book but also, with it, in all the research to which it provides an introduction by defining both new principles of analysis and a new method, a new sociological practice to enable us to arrive at a knowledge of social movements and conflicts.

The sociology of social movements cannot be separated from a representation of society as a system of social forces competing for control of a cultural field. It has split not only from analyses which reduce society to the internal logic of domination but also with those analyses which see sociology merely as the functional application of a means to serve ends defined by progress, modernity and reason. Far from the optimism of the Enlightenment and the pessimism of those who see only contradictions in society, this sociology of action ceases to believe that conduct must be a response to a situation, and claims rather that the situation is merely the changing and unstable result of relations between the actors who, through their social conflicts and via their cultural orientations, produce society.

vv

The birth of sociology

Action and relations

Sociology makes its appearance at the moment when the whole body of cultural orientations by which a community shapes its relationships towards the environment is no longer conceived as the expression of general principles or, on the other hand, of particular events, but as society's *working* upon itself. Human societies are able to produce and to change their models of functioning, i.e. concurrently to create knowledge of themselves, to invest part of the product of activity in order to change production, and to build up an image of their creativity. This first idea immediately calls forth a second. Society's triple action upon itself cannot be exercised by the entire community as a whole: the control and transformation of models of action and historicity on the one hand, and of social and cultural control on the other, require the concentration of this capacity for action inside a category of innovator-dominators. The *ruling class* is the group of innovator-dominators which becomes identified with this production of society by itself, with this historicity, which it in turn utilizes in order to legitimize its domination over the remainder of society, i.e. over the *popular class*, which is subjected to the ruling class but which also challenges its domination in order to win back historicity for itself. This interdependence between collective orientations and social conflicts constitutes the matrix of all social and cultural organization. A society is formed by two opposing movements: one which changes historicity into *organization*, to the point of transforming it into *order* and power, and another which breaks down this order so as to rediscover the orientations and conflicts through *cultural innovation* and through *social movements*. These movements are not a sign of crisis or of tension in a social order; they are an outward sign of the production of society by itself. There can, however, be no way of creating historicity which does not pass through class conflict. *A social movement is the collective organized action through which a class actor battles for the social control of historicity*

31

in a given and identifiable historical context. The social role attributed to conflicts and in particular to class conflicts and social movements – that of the ruling class and that of the popular class – is an indication from the outset that I am unprepared to consider any social category whatsoever, no matter how dominated it may be, as a non-actor. The working class is not a form of merchandise in industrial society; it is a historical actor, a suffering, fighting, thinking actor, powerless or rebellious, but always an actor. The history of our industrialization and the functioning of our industrial society are not controlled by mechanisms and laws but by social relations, and therefore by actions, by social movements of confrontation, e.g. between the bourgeoisie and the working class. The rest is all metaphysics.

The object of sociology

Those, in brief, are the *principles of analysis* of social action; we must now add a definition not of the approach but of the *object* of sociology. If analysis is governed by the concept of action, it is in terms of social relations that its object must be defined.

1. The object of sociology is the study of *social relations*. In making this statement, we are marking the boundaries of its domain and, in particular, excluding from the outset all futile discussion on the objective and the subjective. Explaining behaviour via a situation is an approach opposed to that of sociology, which instead reduces both the behaviour and the situation to social relations. This is why Durkheim's *Suicide* has remained a classic, even though his observations and conclusions have been called into question in numerous writings. To speak of anomy, for instance, is to indicate a state in the system of social relations and a breach between the relations and the actor. It is often vitally necessary to establish correlations between situations and forms of behaviour, but this is only a single step towards an analysis by which these words are transformed, as for instance in classical sociology, into roles and forms of status, which in turn belong to sociological analysis, because the one (status) designates the actor's position in a system of relations, and the other (role) defines the body of the legitimate expectations of the actor's partners, the actor being considered as having a particular status, i.e. it defines his relations. In the same way, I have studied class relations and social movements.

2. What then is a *social relation*? It is not merely any type of interaction. There can be no social relation unless the actors are operating in the same cultural field, for an action is social only if it is normatively

oriented by historicity while at the same time being situated in a social relation. A conflict which sets 'foreign' adversaries against each other – opponents not belonging to the same field of historicity – cannot be called social. To define class relations as relations of social warfare is so grave an error that it cannot but lead to denying the existence of a class action, of a significant social movement, and hence to adopting the point of view of a state militarily engaged in a war against a people or another state. But protests and strikes, like commercial competition, are both social and intersocial relations, i.e. relations between actors who do not belong to the same social field, and this is well demonstrated by the frequency of the military metaphors used. We shall find this language recurring in connection with social change and the state. The analysis of a social system is different, and it presupposes the existence of a field which is not merely a battlefield but also a social field.

3. What is a *social field*? It is a practical 'ensemble' built up through action by society upon itself. And to this one must immediately add that this action is always the expression of a *power*. This statement of the principles of general sociology should be concluded with the proposition: *all social relations are relations of power*. Allow me to explain these somewhat bald statements by means of a simple example, borrowed back again from the most classical sociology, that of social organization. The relation between the worker and the foreman in a factory is an interaction located in a field known as organization. This field is established by a power which defines a pattern of authority. The role of the worker or the foreman is defined by this pattern of authority, which is itself connected to the highest levels of social analysis, those of institutions, class relations and cultural orientations.

There exists no social relation that is based on equality or on a simple difference, for difference is nothing but the absence of relation. To say that women are different to men is sociologically meaningless, even if the sociologist knows what is intended by this formula: i.e., the desire to break off a relation of subordination which is itself real. If this desire does not lead to defining a conflict between real actors, it merely indicates the desire to dissolve the social category in question, for instance, in this case, to arrive at unisex by suppressing all discrimination and by establishing full equality between men and women. There is no third solution. An actor cannot be defined only by his identity, outside of any social relation; the resistance to subordination can lead ultimately only to the absence of social relations if it does not result in the open declaration of a more general conflict. If love has been accorded such great importance in our culture, it is because it is experienced as being opposed to a social relation, as being a choice or an encounter between individuals, as being desire and passion. Relations of equality have no other meaning for the sociologist than the adherence of several individuals to a collective actor who is himself involved in social relations – and hence unequal relations – with a partner or an adversary. This is well expressed in all the habitual demonstrations of comradeship and closeness. Thus a social relation immediately refers back to the whole body of social structure, and above all to the highest social field, that of historicity, which is formed by the opposition between class actors in a field of cultural orientation.

Turning backwards

It is difficult to understand this approach to social facts, not because it is any more complex than other approaches but for reasons of two kinds which are today combined, though less and less closely, in order to conceal the incursion of sociology.

1. The first of these is the attachment to the social descriptions of the past. We resist the idea of society being a set of systems of action if we have become accustomed to explaining social facts by placing them in time. For a long time, particularly in France, hostility towards sociology took this simple form: it enclosed itself in the present, forgetting the past, by which the present is illuminated. This is an objection which is all the more formidable in that is based on a sound observation from which an arbitrary conclusion is drawn. There is in fact nothing to justify the priority accorded to the present, and even less to justify a definition of the present such as the modern one, when the customs, rules, or forms of organization dating back several centuries or even millennia are more 'present' today than an event that may have occurred yesterday and which today is already part of the *de-passé* (past and outmoded). But the necessary enlargement of the object of knowledge, both in time and in space, has nothing to do with an explanation of social facts in terms of their place in an *evolution*; an explanation which is no longer sought by many of those who are called historians, and yet is one which indeed constitutes the definition of the historical method. Today, we no longer wish to set out from social evolution but rather from action.

2. The other way of avoiding what I have called a sociology of action is to conceive of society as a *person* guided by intentions, providing means to meet the ends which he has either chosen or which have been entrusted to him, and settling the problems and the conflicts of func-

tioning which arise in any complex ensemble. This is a *sociology of functioning* which is squarely opposed to the idea of the conflictual self-production of society. This sociology sets out from the most immediately observable, the categories of social practice, the forms of social and cultural organization and their rules, in order to discover their unity or interdependence. But should not work be organized, should not children learn from what the preceding generations hand down to them, should not there be criteria of social hierarchization, and sanctions against those who do not respect the norms established by the institutions? Here we have the key word. This sociology of *institutions* demonstrates how needs are interpreted by cultural values which give rise to norms, to forms of organization and to the definition of social roles in all the spheres of social life which work jointly for the maintenance, integration, and change of society, considered as a real entity. Everything relates back to the spirit and values of a society. This is a sociology of society which is opposed to the sociology of action; and the consequence of the idealism of this approach is the non-critical acceptance of 'reality'. The norm being what it is, the deviant is one who does not respect it; there is no point in trying to establish whether the deviant might not be a conquered opponent who has been 'reinterpreted' by his conqueror, for such an investigation would compromise the beautiful monumental unity of the conception of society which, more simply, represents society as the mansion of a sovereign bearing the mark of his every activity and every thought. It is primarily against this image of society – whether a person or a spirit – that I have had to struggle, because I began my professional life during the period of the hegemony of this sociology of institutions, which was particularly vigorous at that time in the United States. It was a sociology which reflected the ideas that a dominant society held of itself, sovereign ideas – both arrogant and liberal – and without the slightest misgivings as to their inherent values. They were the catechism of triumphant industrialization and capitalism.

A single thought is not sufficient to cause such a massive façade to crumble. But sociology must denounce the arbitrariness and the repressive character of this 'master-thinking', and be particularly attentive to the real forces which destroy the order of this thought, which reject the inferior position to which it aims to consign them, and which bring back to the surface the domination behind the values, the power behind the practice, the conquest behind the integration. And still today, now that this sociological idealism is in sharp decline in the United States, where it has assumed an intellectually acceptable form, and is disappearing shamefully wherever (as in certain Communist countries) it was no more than a propaganda apparatus, we must reject these social doctrines whose chief function is to legitimize the established order.

The critique of the categories of practice

The sociologist's first action is to dis-assemble the categories of social practice, to break down the ideologies and representations. What had formerly seemed to answer to a function or an intention now seems to be no more than a *compromise*, an *event* in which opposing forces or different ages are combined. Those who are described as historians often give proof of greater initiative than the sociologists in this work of critique. But often, too, sociology has come into being through criticism of the administrative or juridical categories which are put forward as being rational, or as meeting a general requirement for progress or justice, in particular by demonstrating the incoherence of texts or forms of organization in which different elements and influences are combined. Those notions which claimed to incorporate a historical ensemble in one idea are the first to fall beneath the onslaught of this critique. The spirit of the Middle Ages or the spirit of industrialization are among those idols which had to be toppled. The study of organizations is one of the domains in which this critical analysis has achieved the most remarkable results.

In the space of a generation, the idea that an organization is governed by norms which themselves represent general values was destroyed and replaced by the image of a complex of interlocking forces, demands, battles and negotiations leading to limited and temporary compromises which made it possible to exert control over a certain part of the behaviour in organizations. Likewise, those who have studied decisions have almost always experienced that the final result of the process of development corresponded only to a slight extent to the content of the decision, and that the outcome might have been different, on account of there being hidden oppositions, exclusions and rejections. Thus the unity of order breaks up and one gains a clear insight into the complex tissue of social relations and particularly the dimension of *power* which is ever present in them. This is the second stage of the ascent towards sociology. It is a stage accomplished by critical sociology, which in order sees only power, in the societal function only the service of the dominators' interests, in the categories of social practice only the work of the dominant class seeking to cover up the real social relations and its own domination. Those who have criticized the School and its claim to offer equal opportunities to all have demonstrated not only that the School perpetuated inequality but also that it actually established separation and set up barriers between children of different categories or social classes. They also sought to discover – behind the democratic formulae – the reality of the relations of domination. This critical sociology occasionally turns round against itself: for instance, when it causes the disappearance of the power relations it wishes to reveal beneath the yoke of absolute domination; when it reverts to a 'functionalist' representation of society by describing merely as domination whatever used to be called function, and power whatever used to be described as institution. Thus, the *One* rules again, and the action disappears from this society, which is once more portrayed as a mechanism driven by a central motor. This form of social thought is satisfactory only where there is an order imposed on all society, no matter whether one is concerned with dominatory values or with despotic power. But this critical sociology plays an essential role when it seeks out from behind the order the real conflicts which the dominators wish to rid themselves of. This theme of domination is just as indispensable for the construction of sociology as is that of social relations and interactions, for these are unequal exchanges, battles in which only one of the fighters has the choice of arms.

The social philosophies

Critical sociology, which enables us to sidestep institutional sociology and avoid its conformity, cannot by itself lead to the sociology of action, for it has not yet recognized that social behaviour is *normatively oriented*. And particularly because it does not see that the antagonistic actors – the dominating and the dominated – enter into conflict only because they belong to the same cultural field, because they have the same models in common: they are struggling for the social control of the field of historicity in which their relation is situated.

The recognition of the normative orientation of social behaviour came to sociology from that which preceded it and to which it also had to offer opposition, i.e. social philosophy, which sought to account for this normativeness by explaining social facts and relations in terms of a higher, transcendent, or more precisely *metasocial* order. This is what made it possible to place the conflicts at the centre: if the order were only an order of power, the dominators would be able to take it over in its entirety and to impose their own absolute order. On the other hand, the combats and the discussions remain open if the direction they take lies beyond the world of experience, with the result that power can never completely gain a hold over them. If, for instance, the direction in which a society is moving is towards the development of its forces of production, the ruling class cannot bring it entirely under its sway; in one way or another, natural progress outstrips the limits imposed by the relations of production. Even if the kings place themselves at the service of the Gods, the Gods are able to assert their sovereignty by overthrowing the kings. This approach, which is positive insofar as it recognizes the normative character of social behaviour, is at the same time contrary to the approach of sociology, since it seeks the explanation of social relations and actions outside of these relations and actions, in a metasocial order that transcends society. The explanations provided by the social philosophies always consist in defining social facts in relation to natural laws. These laws may be conceived as the expression of a *human nature* and of the passions of individuals or communities. Quite recently, we have been strongly exposed to the idea that the actors' behaviour must be related to the laws of *evolution*. All these areas in which direction is conveyed lie above social relations, with the result that we no longer know how to return to social relations except by invoking the theme of the Fall of Man, which divided men from one another, creating egoism, evil, and irrationality. Furthermore, this social philosophy cannot explain why this metasocial order changes, becoming deformed or transformed over time, for if it is recognized as being relative, and if it were no longer metasocial but social and historical, it would no longer be a principle of explanation and would itself have to be explained. It is this undertaking that is assumed by sociology in breaking away from the social philosophies. But the social philosophies have prepared the way for sociology by turning their backs on the naive definition of order and by discovering – even if indirectly – that society is created. Metaphysics lies closer to sociology than does sociology to the ideatic formulations which legitimize social order. To put it more exactly, sociology is the manner of regarding social action which is suited to a society aware of its ability to produce and to transform itself, just as metaphysics was the way of regarding social action at a time when this ability could not yet be recognized as social and had to be attributed to a transcendental principle. This is a principle of which the most recent reincarnation has been the idea of History and of Progress – metasocial order, but already in motion; human action, but already alienated from the categories of nature.

Sociology came into being by freeing itself from metaphysics and from the philosophy of history, and by establishing no other basis for the direction of action than historicity, i.e. society's self-production.

This brings us back then to our starting-point – there is no other. Sociology develops only by breaking with the naive definition of social facts by exposing, behind the outward appearances of established order, the heat of the combats, the tenuousness of the compromises, the changes in cultural orientation, and the dramas and longings with which society is fraught. It should not delay in devising a model, in admiring a balance or in listening to the formulation of an idea; it should strip society bare, expose its turbulent life, and learn to understand how society produces itself, materially and morally, through its conflicts and normative orientations.

3

Beyond sociology

Nothing more than change?

The image of society as being self-productive takes over from that of social organizations developing towards greater rationality with the gradual increase of their material strength. It is an image in which the vision of a social body integrating independent functions is consigned to the background. And, finally, it is the image farthest removed from the anthropologist's concern with investigating the conditions of survival and balance in a community or the cultural structures through which the laws governing the human mind are displayed. Although it does not gainsay the interest of such approaches with respect to other types of society or to certain aspects of our own, this is an image that consciously corresponds to contemporary societies which, after experiencing the upheavals of technical progress and revolution, are now rather turned towards the future than dependent upon the past, and are filled with both elation and anxiety by their almost unlimited capacity for acting upon themselves. Nevertheless, though we may recognize the claim that it is the industrial societies that have witnessed the emergence of sociology because their immense capacity for acting upon themselves has vastly extended the field of social action at the expense of a world that is on the one side metasocial and on the other natural, how can we greet such a statement today with the same positivist fervour as was shown in the last century? It will remain true that sociology is born with the idea – without which it cannot develop – that society is the product of its own works and that it has no definable essence or nature outside of a complex of relations between social actors. But has not this triumph of 'civil society' already brought about its own downfall? Are we not already beyond sociology? Can we still speak of social structures, of order and power, of social conflicts and movements? Do not these very words presuppose the existence of a society, a relatively stable whole, made up of cultural orientations and social conflicts? And today, in industrialized societies and even throughout the whole world, is not the whole movement towards development and change rather than – as earlier – towards order, structure, and reproduction? Has not the moment now come to view social life wholly in terms of change, i.e. in political and therefore particularly in statist terms? Look around: we have seen the idea of civilization vanish, to be replaced by that of society; and, today, societies are being replaced by *paths of development*. One-third of the world is communist. Can one speak in the Soviet Union or in People's China of classes, of class conflicts and social movements? In such instances, it would seem more important to speak of power and of the struggle for the rights of man. In the Soviet Union, and in the countries incorporated in its empire, the best observers – even the very ones who regard themselves as Marxist – define their society as state dominated. Their intellectuals are fighting for the human freedoms, as will always occur when despotism reigns rather than capitalism, and a type of state rather than a ruling class. In the Third World, i.e. in countries dependent on the world capitalist system, populism – in its more revolutionary and more moderate forms alike – has wished to entrench the rights and the independence of national societies in the face of foreign domination; yet everywhere populism is being driven back and put to rout. States everywhere have assumed direct command of society and almost everywhere silenced the social movements, even when they paid lip-service to these as being the movements from which the state first emanated. Finally, in the capitalist industrial societies, where the state's central role is relatively weaker, is it not more and more a global strategy of change that has become the stakes of political life, thus depriving class conflicts of the crucial importance they had in the last century and up to the beginning of the period of accelerated growth following the Second World War? Is not a sociology of action already an outdated ephemeral idea which emerged between the old form of analysis, which subjected social life to a higher order, and the new, which can no longer be called sociological because it is wholly analysis of change?

This general critique also bears more specifically on the concept which I have made the focal point of the analysis of society: the concept of historicity. If one is to speak of historicity, and therefore of the production of history, is not one introducing the idea of a society wholly defined by its capacity for change? And does not this idea run counter to my determination to continue speaking of culture and of classes and to define society as a system of action? Here I am, then, isolated and even accused of standing outside of reality – as if nothing existed between the social philosophies I no longer accept and the new political science of change created today by the analysts of the state, of domination and liberation. These second thoughts on sociology are further accentuated by the political and intellectual happenings that dominate the exact period and the region of the world in which I am writing. Our social life has been dominated by the political and social practice born of Marxism and for the past fifty years inseparable from the entrenched opposition between the capitalist and socialist worlds. Now, however, after a long drawn-out illness, exacerbated by the revelations of the XX Congress of the Communist Party of the USSR, by popular revolts against communist regimes, and by the spread of dissidence, the image of socialist societies has succumbed, its demise opening the way for the figure of the totalitarian state to appear. It is because thinking on society has for so long been placed at the service of state propaganda and of the outside agents that so many political philosophers, young and old, in order to save themselves from mendacity or from their own past excesses, refuse to speak any longer of society – in the East and West alike – and instead identify themselves with an intelligentsia struggling against despotism; now, in the name of concepts of liberty ranging from conservative liberalism to libertarian revolt, they will admit of no other adversary than the state.

I am just as aware of the moment and the place in which I am writing as I am of the criticisms that are met by sociology. I know that I must fight on two fronts: on the one, I must reject social philosophies and all forms of the submission of social life to a higher order, particularly if this is conceived as being the order of economic laws, and on the other front I must likewise reject the idea that the analysis of social structure must disappear to make way for the analysis of change. I shall even declare my counter-attack: I plan to construct the theory of new social movements, in the conviction that my theoretical work will have the reflex effect of helping these collective actions to take shape, and that these actions will in fact constitute the struggle of class actors for the social management of a field of historicity. What I wish to analyse is not change but the type of society into which we are moving, its structure and functioning, its cultural orientations and its social conflicts. But let us not rush ahead too fast, as though we had to dash through a blazing screen. Indeed, we should deliberately go more slowly in order to let the flames burn away that in us which belongs to the past. Let us reflect more attentively on the ideas of change which purport to replace the analysis of the social systems. The reduction of the problems of the social system to the problems of change takes on two main forms. The first of these stipulates that everything goes back to the study of the forms of reaction to a changing environment, a response which is differently expressed depending on the type of society under consideration: in the dominant capitalist societies one can speak of adaptation or better of strategies; in the other societies, of voluntarism and the quest for a specific, national, path of development. The second form is a reinterpretation of the internal problems of a society in terms of power, of the state, and hence of change or counter-change. This reinterpretation entails either the setting at the heart of social life of modernization and the progress of the forces of production – the generating force behind social contacts and institutions – or else the display of the absolute power of an order resistant to change. In either case, society emerges as subjected to a central principle and not to social relations.

There are therefore *four obstacles* preventing the emergence of a sociology conceived of as an analysis of the social dramas and the cultural orientations through which a society forms its practices. It is relatively easy to dismiss pre-sociological thinking and all forms of idealism; but it is certainly more difficult to defend a sociology of action against those who speak only of power and politics, of the state and change.

My doubt is not feigned: do not the analyses which would have society based on a culture and on class conflicts actually belong to the extremely restricted times and places of the liberal capitalist societies? And was not one of the attributes of their past hegemony to have considered themselves as pure societies? Is not the world today dominated by voluntarist liberation and development movements and by the battle against foreign domination and imperialism, all of which would call for an economic and geopolitical analysis of the world system and not for a sociological analysis of social forces and movements that exist no longer except in the collective memory of the leading capitalist countries? Has the time not come for these very countries to recognize that the class struggle has long since been replaced by the opposition between order and that which is excluded by order, powerholders and those who are culturally so completely dominated that the only choice left to them is between integration and non-submission, without their being equipped for active resistance? These are the issues disputed in the great debate of current social thought: should we have a political science of order and change, of the state and manipulation, or a sociology of classes and social movements? I declare my support for the latter, but I should first like to hear all the arguments raised in favour of the former.

Strategies

The first form of the process by which a society is reduced to its changes is that in which all society is made the battleground of a fight between the living and the dead, between fixed rules or principles and innovators or active campaigns which struggle to improve adaptation to a changing environment. Woe to all absolutes – values, beliefs, revolutionary movements or general theories – to all that attempts to halt the course of change by inventing an end to history.

Change of necessity entails the adaptation of the social organization to a constantly changing environment and the elimination of all reference to metasocial principles, which are replaced not by new values but by rational and instrumental behaviours.

This concept of change inveighs against all the impediments that may arise either from social mechanisms, as Michel Crozier* believes, or even from a general cultural orientation, as Alain Peyrefitte* has suggested. Whence springs this resistance to change? To put it down to a national character is little short of tautological or, conversely, of insisting upon the impossible claim that a society is wholly in a state of continual blockage, which would long ago have caused it to expire.

We must then – as Michel Crozier has long since done – contrast instead the poor, defensive strategies of those on the bottom rung of the social ladder with the highly diversified offensive and inventive strategies of the entrepreneurs, who can choose not to put all their eggs in one basket and who can afford to take risks, since these may well be more limited and better calculated. In his observation of bureaucratic society suffocating under its rules, the same author gives a more restrictive and pessimistic turn to his thought. Areas of uncertainty still exist, even where the rules are most highly formalized and detailed; these areas can be formed by the influence of the environment, particularly by the effect of the market, by the appearance of new techniques, or merely by the occurrence of accidents or breakdowns. Power belongs to those who can control these areas of uncertainty, take the initiative, study innovations, and place themselves beyond reach of the rules: in short, those who form the elite. Power is no more than the ability to introduce, govern and exploit change. In reply to this reasoning, which is the ideology of all ruling elites, ready to quash any resistance to change that may be set up to counter their innovatory undertakings and conquests, it must first be said that the entrepreneurs – the heads – are not only agents of movement but that they also create an order, together with its protective barriers. The author I have selected knows as well as anyone that: 'the power of those at the top is, in the long run, the power to create rules which they will later be able to manipulate in order to obtain from their subordinates the behaviour they consider "desirable"' (*L'Acteur et le Système*, pp. 76–7), but this he swiftly forgets, for if this statement were to be upheld it would undermine the superb self-confidence of the rulers, turning upon them the heavy eye of the dominated in denunciation of the irrationality, the waste, the repression, and the immobilism of those who hold the power and expend it. Society is reduced to its process of change only because it is first reduced to its ruling elites and because they are defined only in terms of their innovatory battles against tradition, custom, established order, and dogma of all kinds. This is a Voltairean theory of society which emerges during the rise of a new ruling class impatient to triumph over the closed, decadent world of traditions and privileges; but well before anything else it is an ideology of the ruling class. Today, it is no longer the ideology of the business-minded bourgeoisie, but that of technocracy. Its weakness lies in the complete dissociation it makes between the power of innovation and social relations of domination. In a single blow, social relations disappear and social life becomes reduced to a battle of light against dark. It is the peculiarity of ideologies to recognize a social relation only from the point of view of one of its terms, here the dominant one. The end of triumphal growth has caused this ideology of the ruling elite to make its withdrawal, but it will reappear in other forms and will always be one of the chief obstacles to sociological analysis, because it is one of the most immediately ideological images of society.

States

The withdrawal of this elitist ideology of change is also linked to the end of the hegemony long imposed by the great industrial capitalist powers over almost the entire world. In almost all continents the will towards development has risen up to counter outside domination or an internal order. Almost everywhere the state proclaims a national project of development, which it often describes as socialist, when it wishes to stress the break with outside capitalist domination.

This phenomenon of state-planned development is so immense that if one is to look at the world today it would seem that 'societies' – social systems that can be defined outside of state action – hardly exist at all outside the hegemonistic capitalist countries, as though these could experience no form of autonomous social life but by exporting their state in the form either of colonial imperialist domination or of international rivalries. In the communist world, post-revolutionary society was very rapidly submerged beneath the all-powerfulness of a state forging its national way of development by setting out from the past and yet also breaking with it. In what is known as the Third World, after short, feeble liberation movements, the state once again imposed itself almost everywhere, creating national development models.

Though an agent of social transformation, the state forbade regarding society as a network of social relations; proud of its sovereignty, the state did not wish to compromise it by being forced to recognize the presence of conflicts and the need for interests to be represented.

The rule of these states does not contradict only the principles of a liberal society, it is equally opposed to the action and ideology of social movements. Why should one continue to call the workers' movement *socialism*? On the world scale this acquires an inferior meaning, for the socialist states will bring out more soldiers and activists than the socialist movements will produce militants and protestors. The sociologist, who most often belongs to one of the countries which have long held world hegemony, feels himself profoundly challenged by this state power which imposes categories of analysis and action and stimulates reactions quite foreign to the categories to which civil society refers its knowledge, those of class, domination, movements institutions, and conflicts.

The strategic theory of change isolates the dynamic entrepreneurs from the rest of society, which is supposedly amorphous. The statist vision of development assumes charge over all society as a block, for the proper function of a state is to rule over a nation, a community, a concrete group defined by its relations with the other states and by its path of transition from a past to a future. It rejects all that escapes its hold. For the state, society is no more than an organization – hierarchized and militant – which becomes all the more integrated as the connection between the national culture and the will of the states becomes more direct and less encumbered by the socio-cultural or political intermediary bodies. Hence the triumph of historicism, for, unlike evolutionism, it does not insist on the change which leads to greater complexity, more liberty and initiative, but rather on the mobilization of a communitarian culture against internal and external obstacles through the creation of a national way of development. In the year in which this book appeared, the International Sociological Association selected 'The paths of development' as its main topic. Does not this use of the plural, and the importance given to development, seem to exclude the study of society and of social structure, a study undertaken by thinkers in the last century and one which sociologists of the same times endeavoured to develop?

Has not the most painful rift in social thought been produced by the terrible discovery that one could not, in the strict sense, speak of a socialist society but only of a regime, i.e. of a state, a socialist state, and of a certain way in which the state holds sway over cultural and social organization? The denunciation of Stalinism and the revelation of the mass deportations in the Gulag would have carried less weight had they not destroyed the most important image of a new society. In many of the modern Latin American countries, are there any more important actors today than the state and foreign capitalism? Is it still possible to apply notions we believe to be those of sociology? Not only have the sociologists been driven away almost everywhere, but even the very object of their work seems to have disappeared. It is plainly evident that these ways of development are an object of study as important as the internal life of the social systems; why then should one not acknowledge that the greatest social problem of our times is the development and transformation of societies which – each in its own way – plunge themselves into the construction of an industrial society? But must one agree to reducing a society to its state, and its social relations and movements to state-directed behaviour? Man's life is not merely History: Princes make History, peoples are subjected to a society and its domination. The worker is not only caught up in industrialization, he is also dominated by those who hold the power of investing, of controlling the work of others, and of exploiting the products of collective labour.

And if the state is the sole entrepreneur, it is then to the state as a ruling class and not to the state as an agent of development that the worker is subjected.

It would be erroneous to seek, from among the diversity of regimes, for the purity of a basic class struggle. I recognize that such a struggle is crucial only in the hegemonic capitalist societies, but one should nonetheless reject the idea of society's absolute subordination to a state or to outside domination. This mistaken idea has led to the death of many Latin-American revolutionaries deluded by the superficial theory of dependence. In another context, in the communist countries we are learning slowly to discover the existence of social forces, protest and opposition movements, which are not only political but which also fight against privileges and social barriers, exploitation and contempt. It would be a serious mistake to fight the authoritarian state only on its own terrain and to accept its restrictions on observing society. It is the sociologist's duty to mistrust the state's totalitarian thought processes, to free himself from doctrines and ideologies, to seek out the conflicting interests, to reveal the domination imposed, and the revolt when it breaks out, in which hope or defiance are almost always to be found. This he must do, not by contrasting the superiority of liberal society, in which power is controlled by the ruling classes, with societies held beneath the sway of the state, but by searching for all the social forces which tend to shape and express themselves in a social register and not solely on the state-controlled scene. It is not our job to condemn these states; our concern is to reveal the social forces which these states suppress – no matter whether they be authoritarian or popular states – and to make an analysis of them which will enable them to develop.

Forces of production

Let us return to our industrial societies: they are still sufficiently strong not to be reduced to the action of a ruling elite and to the battle against the past. But when we examine them, are we not also drawn towards an analysis purely in terms of change, and hence of the state? This *non-social analysis of society* takes two constrasting forms. The first portrays society as being led on by the force of change, the advancement of the forces of production; the second, by contrast, reflects society as an order, as the expression of a ubiquitous power, a multifaceted system of social and cultural control.

The most direct way of preventing a social representation of society is to claim that society is subject to technological determinism, that the forces of production determine a certain form of social organization and that, furthermore, they always sweep away the barriers set up to resist their onslaught by the old forces of social domination and organization. This is a concept that in numerous ways runs counter to the strategic theory of change of which I spoke at first, and yet is also comparable in that as a concept it is also the ideology of a ruling elite. It is, however, associated with an elite which does not believe in the adaptability of institutions, and which therefore regards itself as being entrusted with the task of freeing and organizing these new forces of production in order to create a society more efficient than the last, thanks to growth and the increasing diversification of its technological methods. This difference is limited. There is no great distance between the Soviet propounders of the *scientific and technical revolution* and the Western strategians of pragmatic change: both alike, good ideologists of the ruling elites, define society only in terms of resistance to change, as a body of traditions hostile to the innovation introduced by the elites. Let us draw out the consequences of this critique. One must dismiss every form of technological determinism and recognize technical methods as means, as forms of organization produced by a state of historicity and as class relations within an institutional system. This is something not done, for instance, by those who accuse nuclear industry of leading us towards an authoritarian society, while solar energy, which is being spread so forcefully, would lead us towards a decentralized, self-managing society. These are groundless judgements and ones which dangerously exclude political analysis, for if the policy of nuclear energy must be resisted it is not because it produces a ruling class but because it is imposed by a technocratic ruling class whose power it serves to strengthen.

The more one represents society as being built up through its work upon itself, the more one distances oneself from all forms of technical and economic determinism. The idea of the production of society is contrasted to that of the society of production. It is not material activity that determines what happens to the remainder of society, primarily because technology forms part of a culture instead of being simply a material fact, and secondly because, in industrial society and even more so outside it, technology is losing its autonomy. In industrial society, technology is subordinated to the organization of labour and hence subjected to the sway of the ruling class over the workers. In post-industrial societies, it is the product of scientific and economic policies, hence of the action of technocracy and of the opposition encountered.

Society is not a political and cultural building erected on material foundations; indeed, the architectural image would be totally misplaced, since nobody looking at the foundations of a building can imagine how the apartments will be furnished. It is, in fact, the reverse, for it is our knowledge of society's mode of self-production, its historicity – its cultural orientations and class relations – that explains its institutional manner of functioning and its cultural and economic organization. And as for the idea that it is the forces of production that develop prior to the other aspects of collective life, this is disproved by the historical role of the industrialist states and ideologists. One must abandon the metaphor by which society is depicted as a train – with the technical or economic engine drawing the coaches – or as a car, with the engine moving the pistons and this motion being transmitted to the wheels by means of the piston-rods and the gears. These mechanical metaphors are outworn.

Order

The final obstacle to sociological analysis is the image representing society as an ordered system in which everything is a sign of power and an instrument for the reproduction of power. I am examining this image of society last because it is the one which is least external to the sociologists' work: they have themselves created such an image. Ultimately, for historical reasons as well. After a long period dominated by the ideologies of a new ruling class – the calls for a liberalizing changeover or for modern, rational forms of production – the critique of the social order began to make its reappearance a decade or two ago. But because the new social forces and conflicts had not yet taken shape, this critique was brought to a standstill before the analysis of social relations. It then withdrew into the rejection and denunciation of the social order. This was done not in the name of a specific social actor but rather for the sake of non-order, or whatever is wild, plebeian, spontaneous, whatever resists the performance of rituals, the operation of any form of inequality, and the exercise of power. The actors' indecisiveness is the reverse side of the idea that power lies everywhere, and that society is unidimensional, to borrow Marcuse's expression. Behind these words, there are three ideas fighting to come to the fore.

1. The first of these ideas recognizes that power is not only political, that it is to be found wherever social behaviour is organized from a decision-making centre, and this holds true not just for manufacturing producers but also for television services, hospitals, municipal organizations or universities. It is an important idea and one which does not break with the great preoccupations of industrial society, but which generalizes them while at the same time freeing them from presentation in economic terms. It is an idea that I myself support.

2. The second maintains, in a far more disputable way, that the spread of power has put a stop to conflict and that the unidimensional whole has replaced the dominating centre. To start with, I reject the idea that power lies everywhere. The multiplication of the centres of power is quite another matter, and it leads rather to the multiplication – and perhaps also the dispersal – of the conflicts; the more self-producing society is, the more numerous are the conflicts it experiences. But nothing can be further removed from this self-production of society than the image of a society of *reproduction*. Our societies are reproducing themselves less and less; instead, they are acting upon themselves, imposing powers and suppressing movements opposed to this domination; They are also increasing the number of centres for negotiation and institutionalization. I should not speak like this were I not convinced that we are witnessing before our eyes the shaping of the conflicts and movements that will enable us at last to understand our society. The observable facts already belie the image of the unidimensional society, as the Paris students of May '68 observed to Marcuse, whom they had just discovered. These students were not outsiders, but rather inheritors (to use Pierre Bourdieu's* expression); yet their barricades were erected in the heart of Paris and their revolt shook the regime. How far we were away then from the image of a unidimensional society which could no longer be challenged except by its outcasts and self-exiled outsiders.

The image of a society drawn forward by its forces of production belongs to the social philosophy of the industrial age; and the image of a society dominated by an order, by an omnipotent, omnipresent cast of thought, is the result of the breakdown of this social philosophy. This image no longer corresponds to the bygone battles and former practices, yet it prevents us from becoming aware of new practices and fresh battles.

In societies in a state of turmoil, upheaval, and uprooting, where political and intellectual discussion is open, where discrimination and segregation have become everywhere visible, and where the established order is shaken by conflict, the pride of the new leaders is allowed to make its impression upon this image. Perhaps this strange aberration – which led to one of the most civil of societies being described in terms of state ideological apparatus – of a society overturned by its transformations in reproduction terms, derives from the isolation of French universities, sealed off as they are by their own esprit de corps and unable to try to link themselves with society as a whole except by conceiving of it as expressing thought that is as full and as unidimensional as university rhetoric. This was an extreme and temporary dissociation of social practice and thought by the epigones of Marxism, who retain only one of Marx's theories, emptying it of its historical reality and of its power to analyse economic and social practices.

As the workers' movement no longer has the strength to stand up against the whole social order, because in a large part of the world it has actually become an agent in the maintenance of order, the historical scene appears empty to those who think only through their memory. This is a curious reversal of Marxist thinking, which speaks so much of economy and of the classes and which, having been reduced to servitude by the social philosophers, seems no longer concerned by anything but the state and ideology. The notion which had become more widespread than any other is that of *dominant ideology*. This notion performs the function of a myth. Wherever practice does not match the image one wishes to impose upon it, the myth of the dominant ideology is cast into the chasm of the unintelligible: and are the dominated not reduced to the role inflicted on them by the dominators? This is a theory that cannot be verified because it cannot be falsified, because it is truly mythical.

Domination is not a service of the established order controlling all categories of social practice, nor are these categories merely the signs of an exercised power. Domination is exercised today by the apparatus of production and management, just as in the society we are now leaving behind it was exercised by those who organized the work –

whether they were socialists or capitalists – and still earlier by those who controlled produce and its circulation or those who owned the land. It was in opposition to these people that there came the uprising of those who suffered this domination, and of whom I shall speak at greater length. Social practices as a whole are today no more integrated into an order than they were in any other historical society, apart from those in which the state and not a ruling class was all-powerful and totalitarian. Social practices are a manifestation of an ideology of the *system*, an ideology created and manipulated for the benefit of the ruling class; but they are also a reflection of the acting potential of the powers of opposition and also of the autonomy of the cultural stakes involved in their struggle and in that of the institutions in which the social forces are represented and in which a compromise is negotiated between the conflicting interests. I fail to see, in the school or in the process of urbanization, the absolute stamp of domination by the state ideological apparatus.

What I see are historical groups, patched together and marked by class domination but also by popular pressure, by a political process, an intervention specific to the state, by the action of professional groups. This *space between social domination and state order* is essential because it is here that the conflicts, movements and negotiations occur.

Our society is not unidimensional; it is not a pure expression of the power mentality; on the contrary, it is more open to confrontations, conflicts and negotiations than those societies governed by a voluntarist state.

3. The *third* idea has been best expressed by Marcuse* himself. The end of transcendence, he says, entails the end of negative thought, of the idea of contradiction, enclosing us in the present-Being, the pleasure principle, or what David Riesman has called other-directedness. It is true that domination may wish to be taken as complete by calling upon pleasure and personal consumption; but domination has always leaned towards totality, towards the reduction of social life to an absolute order, and it is in particular not true that our society is bent upon pleasure and the instantaneous. No society in the past has saved or invested a greater proportion of what it produces. We are living in a world of atomic weapons and of prodigious military expenses just as much as we are living in a consumer society. We are a society of production, not only that of goods and services, but also of all society by itself. The gap between the dominators and the dominated is not being reduced, and the attachment of conflict by which they are linked cannot be broken to the advantage of a general dominating order. Transcendence is disappearing, not to the advantage of the social order

but to that of historicity. And wherever the order is imposed, as we said at the start, it is not as a form of reproduction and social control but as an instrument of the voluntary transformation of society to the advantage of an increasingly active and despotic state.

Social relations or relations of power

These four obstacles, these four masks which prevent us from seeing properly, are not all of the same size and shape to each of us, but all those who have explored sociology will have encountered them.

After a brief indication of the principles by which the analysis of society should be directed, I wanted – instead of immediately drawing the consequences for the study of social relations and movements – to pinpoint these obstacles so that everyone would be alerted to them whenever they cropped up in a sentence or page. To conclude, let us return to what unites these obstacles and opposes them to sociology. All alike dismiss the idea of social action, choosing to see in society only a process of change, or what is opposed to change, i.e. established order. This corresponds to the apparent absence of great historical struggles in the industrial societies, where the workers' movement is entering into its decline and the new social movements are still confused, while elsewhere in the world the policies of development and state powers are triumphing. But although this historical situation may explain these deviations in social thought, it drives one – if one analyses it instead of subjecting oneself to it – towards very different reflections. If the analysis of society can be made only by contrast with the analysis of change, and therefore of the state, it is because the separation of these two areas is the main outcome of the disappearance of the metasocial guarantees of social order. As long as societies remain subordinated to a metasocial order, their nature and their future state will be confused. The further one moves away from societies of strong historicity the more established order in the world will directly govern human history, until the time when our microcosm seems to be completely integrated into a macrocosm. The sacred order is therefore the one which gives social phenomena their meaning, i.e. their sense and direction. This is what was still thought by social philosophy of the industrial era, which believed in the meaning of history: this philosophy held that the metasocial order had been set in motion, and evolution was both human history and the law of nature. The state, then, is both an agent of social transformation and the guarantor of order, just as Jesus was both the central agent of the divine history of humanity and the founder of a morality.

By contrast, at the moment when social life no longer appeared natural but historical, produced by society's work upon itself, the metasocial order crumbled, and at the same time the problems of the change and transformation of societies became separated from the problems of their internal functioning. This is a split whose consequences affect the entire life and thought of our society. This idea should enter at the beginning of an analysis of social action, not merely on account of its own importance but particularly because it runs against the tendencies of social thought I have just mentioned, and even against our most immediate experience. Are we not speaking every day of development and of the state, while to speak of the bourgeoisie or the proletariat would seem to be making use of an outmoded ideological language? Has not the great discussion at present on energy policies and particularly on the electro-nuclear industry demonstrated most forcefully that our social life is directed by a project for the future introduced by the industrializing state, which is at the same time responsible for national independence? Are not the most original studies on our society being made on educational inequality, the mechanisms of exclusion and confinement to prisons or psychiatric wards (particularly thanks to Michel Foucault*), or on urbanization, all of these being areas in which the state is the main actor, particularly as one draws further away from market production? Should not one acknowledge this replacement of *social* forces by *political* agents? The state as producer and redistributor has taken on such great importance that one must ask: has not the image of a face-to-face confrontation between the bourgeoisie and the proletariat become archaic? One can now better understand the direction of my questioning: would not the death of sociology mark the end of societies? The sociologist may wonder, at the moment when he believes himself to have triumphed over the old social philosophies, whether he is not in turn being drawn back into the past. And taking over his place can one not see a political science, a knowledge of power relations instead of one of relations which deserved to be called social because they were located in a field, i.e. among the cultural orientations shared by the actors who were struggling socially amongst themselves for control of the field?

What I am defending here is not the idea of the dissolution of social relations within power relations but, on the contrary, of the *growing separation between two orders, that of the social system and that of change*, particularly of the transition from one societal type to another. But I am also aware that this position can be adopted only towards societies which move on without a sudden break into a new system of historical action, and that in the greater part of the world it is indeed the mechanisms of development which govern social practice. This is why these two claims are contrasted: the problems of change, particularly of deliberate change, are most evident in countries struggling for their own development and liberation. But in thinking of these countries, as of those which enter without break into a new type of society, one must also consider the relations, and the social conflicts and movements specific to societies which have a far greater capacity for self-production than industrial societies.

Is not our main task now – as it always was – to resuscitate social relations, opposition, defiance, struggle and hope wherever they have been crushed, distorted or stifled by order, which is always the order of the state? It is not enough simply to denounce the order; one must show that it is not all-powerful, one must rediscover the spring hidden beneath the cement, the word beneath the silence, the questioning beneath the ideology. This is what is at stake, and if we are to lose we shall have to give up believing in social movements and even in what we call society; we shall have to admit that there are no longer any citizens, only subjects, no longer class actors, only victims. Subjugation and exile are everywhere to be found, but I have undertaken this research into social movements to show that they do exist in spite of the subjugation and exile. I realize that I am no longer witnessing the equivalent of the workers' movement at the high-point of its historical action, but I am led on by the desire to reveal, behind order and crisis alike, the new conflicts, the new actors and the new stakes in the social struggles, first in France but then also in those parts of the world where state dictatorship seems to have most completely reduced society to an order.

4

vvvvvvvvvvvvvvvvvvvvvvvvvvvvvvvvvvvvvvvvvvvvvvvvvvvvvvvvvvvvvvvvvvvvvvvvvv

The historical actors

These forms of social thought, which all reject a sociology of action out of preference for a study of change or anti-change activated by material forces or governed by states which are themselves an embodiment either of the desire for historical change or, conversely, of the principles of order and reproduction, have one thing in common: they all relegate social relations to the background. Indeed, they even break down these relations, because as forms of thought they function both as actors and as the field, i.e. the system, while purely political analyses see only actors without a system, or systems without actors.

Actors or a system

A strategic concept of change entails the reduction of society to relations between the actors and particularly to power relations, detached from any reference to a social system.

To put it more precisely, power is never defined here as appropriation but rather as pure domination. There are no stakes in the social relation, and there is no field other than the relation itself. Conversely, this system is recognized universally by those who see society strictly as a dominating order and who cause the actors – manipulated, alienated, or subjugated by domination – to disappear.

On the one hand, the system becomes dissolved in the relations between the actors, while on the other hand the actor is made to vanish, overwhelmed by the laws of the system and its structure. On the one hand all is change, on the other all is order. The two positions are equally unacceptable. Those who see only the order disregard the pressures, the claims, the negotiations and conflicts, the whole political life whose vigour and swiftness invalidates all expatiations on the immobility of order and all-powerfulness of the mechanisms of reproduction. Those who see only the movement 'forget', in a truly ideological way, the shackles by which most movement, planning and enterprise is impeded.

A further common link between these two concepts is that they define the social situation outside of action and social relations. For the one group this situation is a market or battlefield, i.e. a domain within which one must act; for the other, it is a set of mechanisms within which the actor is enclosed.

Historical analysis has often accepted the terms of this discussion, either by adopting the viewpoint of the protagonists and debating the great schemes of an Alexander, a Napoleon, or a Stalin, or else by bounding the individual actor with the constraints of a collective situation, an economic and cultural 'framework'. This leads to the actor being placed on the surface of things and to greater importance being accorded to whatever is furthest removed from the will of the individual. One of the oldest forms of this approach consisted in explaining away the actors and the events in terms of economic crisis. As a young history student and attentive follower of Ernest Labrousse, I was sensitive to all that distanced one from the narrow search after the intentions and personal initiatives of the actors in seeking to discover the nature of the economic and social system which functioned through them. The sociologists took their side in the battles fought and won by the good historians of the first half of the twentieth century following on from François Simiand and continuing into the break with factual history. They followed Fernand Braudel* when he shifted the emphasis from Philip II of Spain to the Mediterranean.

It is Marxist thinking, however, that has moved furthest away in going beyond the search for the geographic and economic substrata of politics, for it has not disregarded social relations in preference to mechanisms and situations that are always artificially isolated. On the contrary, it has placed social relations at the centre of its analysis, but without introducing the actors' normative orientations.

The rejection of sociology is incorporated here in the idea of *contradiction*. The social system must be defined outside of the actors' orientations because it is the field where the contradictions arise between the actor and his works, the worker and the product of his work, and between demand and supply. History is the analysis of these contradictions and of the evolution which must finally lead to the triumph of the positivity of progress over social contradictions and over the social relations impeding its advance, until the day comes when humanity makes its entry, if it has not already sunk into barbarism, into post-history, into the world of liberated and self-governed needs. But let us leave aside this distant limit of evolution. At present, it is still the logic of contradiction, and particularly the law of profit, which governs historical situations; as a result, no actor can escape from the situation in which he is placed: his revolt may cause the contradiction to explode but *no social movement* can transform society. Only history, i.e. progress, can explode the social order, provided there is intervention by a knowledgeable and organized avant-garde capable of understanding the laws of historical development and of transforming the crisis of a social system undergoing revolution, that is, in the process of forming into a more natural order.

Is it not paradoxical that a thought which had been shaped to become the theory of the workers' movement should ultimately lead to dismissal of the idea of social movement by arguing simultaneously for historical necessity and political voluntarism? The experience of the international workers' movement and particularly of the Soviet revolution caused this paradox to come to a head and transformed it into tragedy. The Marxist parties have engendered modernizing states – with or without revolution – and tyrannical states, while in the industrial states workers' trade-unionism has to a very large extent shifted away from this voluntarism, but only in order to transform itself into a powerful force of reformist pressure.

At present, there is almost no link between the policy of the Marxist states and parties and the workers' movement. Today, it is with this failure that one must begin in order to consider the principles upon which the analysis of society should be based, so as to allow for the establishment and encouragement of the link between conscience and class action.

A sociology of action should first of all refuse to seek for the natural laws of a social system, since the system is no more than the product of social relations and, at the same time, of historicity. It is impossible to speak at the same time both of the contradictions of a system and of social action. It is readily recognized that class domination has a logic of its own and that the capitalists, for instance, are motivated by profit-seeking. Likewise, that a dominant class endeavours to create the forms of social and cultural organization that protect its interests and enable it to reproduce its privileges. But I should categorically deny that a social situation could be *reduced to the internal logic of domination*.

For a social situation is also based on a *culture*, i.e. on the construction of the norms which determine the relations between a community and its environment and which, instead of representing the ideology of the dominator, actually define a social field; at the same time, a social situation is activated by social struggles which challenge, restrict or overthrow this domination and the repression it inflicts.

In practice, the latter point is the most important. *A choice must be made between a philosophy of contradiction and a sociology of conflicts*, and it is only by choosing the second of these that one can reject the role which the new Prince, the interpreter of the laws of history, wishes to assume. Those who want nothing to do with a sociology of action either proclaim the morals of anti-power or else undertake to become the servants of the ideocracy which sets itself up as the exclusive interpreter of the laws of history.

It is extremely difficult to maintain such representations of the social system in a society in which the social movements, the representative institutions and the intellectual debates play such an important role that many Marxists, like Nicos Poulantzas,* have had to devise more moderate versions of this conception. But this opening out has more inconveniences than advantages, for it causes the idea of determination through the economy to lose its force, without however allowing for a truly social analysis. What use is there in recognizing that the political system is subordinated to the economic system, but that it still enjoys a certain autonomy? Such a proposition is too vague. In practice, this has led the open Marxists to alternate between 'hard' analysis, in which social facts are explained in terms of economic facts, and 'soft' analysis, in which political forces representing social interests are seen to make up an ensemble that is sufficiently autonomous to provide a satisfactory explanation for important historical events.

The system of action

Much confusion has arisen from the fact that the concrete – individual or collective – actor has been contrasted with a system more abstractly defined as a set of relations between social positions, thus ensuring the triumph of the system over the actor and the event. It is time to have done with this imbalance and define the actor in quite another way. The idea that represents the starting-point of the sociology of action I am presenting here is that human societies have the capacity not only to reproduce themselves or even adapt themselves through mechanisms of learning and political decision-making to a changing environment, but also – and especially – to develop their own orientations and to alter them: *to generate their objectives and their normativity.*

This springs from the reflexive capacity of human societies, from their ability to turn in on themselves, to work upon themselves by creating a *symbolic representation* of experience, by affecting their economic activity through accumulation and *investment* and by representing this production of themselves in the form of *cultural legitimization* of their self-generating activity. But this self-production of society through language, accumulation or religion, or any other form of what I have called the cultural model does not occur without disruption of the community. *A society's work upon itself is inseparable from social division*. A society of identity, pleasure and consumption is a community; it does not produce historicity. All distancing of the self from the self, of the viewer from the viewed, of the word from the object, of investment from consumption, of God from man, presupposes the *destruction of the community*, the formation of a group which becomes identified with viewing, accumulation, values, and what I refer to as the *ruling class*. As I said right at the beginning, *historicity is inseparable* from class relations. Historicity, which implies knowledge, investment, and a cultural model, comes into effect only through class relations. These relations establish a polarity between the ruling class, which identifies itself with historicity and in turn identifies historicity with its own domination interests, and the people or the popular class, who come by their own historicity only through the domination imposed by the 'master', yet who seek to regain this historicity by destroying the dominator. One can imagine a classless society only by accepting a society without historicity, wholly preoccupied with the quest for its own equilibrium and reproduction. Social struggles occur within a field of historicity, a type of accumulation, of knowledge, and a form of cultural model. The struggle of the dominated classes does not build up the society of the future. When a certain moment of historicity is replaced by another, the classes and the class struggles which provided the underlying impetus disappear together with it; a new ruling class often speaks in the name of those who were downtrodden or swept aside by the old class, but this new class must be judged not by its own historical justifications but by the domination it inflicts on the popular forces, which are defined in a new fashion. I use the term *historical actors* to define the classes and class actors engaged in the battle for the control of historicity. Actors of this type are far removed from those that the old historiography accepted or attempted to destroy. The latter type of actor was defined only in history, in the ever-tangled web of behavioural forms or social 'structures' through which the evolution of societies progressed. The actor I have in mind is, by contrast, conceived and shaped on the basis of a portrayal of society as a self-productive system. Here it is that the sociologist's work becomes involved in the appearance of a new paradigm of knowledge which in all domains substitutes a systemic mode for an evolutionist mode of knowledge. Edgar Morin has well illustrated this indispensable change of reference. The actor is not someone swimming along with the stream of evolution; he is not defined by the direction in which the current carrying him flows; he is defined, rather, by the social relations of which he is one of the terms. He holds a social position in a system of social and cultural organization which functions in accordance with certain rules and fulfils instrumental functions; he participates less individually in the mechanisms by which society adapts to changes of internal or external origin; and lastly, he participates even more collectively in the dramas of history, in the multifaceted struggle for the control of historicity, for society's self-production. One must reject with the same force the reduction of the system to the actor, the actor to the system, and the division of the one from the other. Above the doorway of sociology should be inscribed the concept of a *system of action*. A society is a hierarchized system of systems of action. *Action is the behaviour of an actor guided by cultural orientations and set within social relations defined by an unequal connection with the social control of these orientations.*

Any action, no matter at what level it occurs, is defined by this double reference to cultural orientations and social relations.

– At the *organizational* level, where a social system functions according to rules and norms, the cultural orientations appear to be detached from social relations. The relations of authority – some would say of power – appear to correspond to models of human relations independent of the economic and social system of production. A rationalized industry would function according to general cultural norms, as Weber has suggested; authority in this case could be more or less concentrated, more or less widespread, depending for instance on the cultural context concerned. Followed to its extreme, this argument would lead ultimately to a complete separation between a culturalist analysis of the national character and a socio-economic study reduced for instance to a declaration of the principles of work organization in firms. At this level, the sociologist's task is to narrow this gap, to re-establish the link existing between organizational norms and forms of authority, while still bearing in mind – beyond societal types – the historic ways by which these types are formed.

– At the level I described as *institutional* or political, social relations are defined by the influence exercised on decisions taken in the collective or community, and the cultural orientations are legally – and in particular constitutionally – defined by a connection between a form of historicity and a form of class domination.

– Lastly, at the level of *historicity* itself – the level with which I began – I shall state again that the cultural orientations are inseparable from the class relations.

Hitherto, I have been speaking of actors and of social relations. Action is the kernel concept of the analysis; it is the social relation that defines the object upon which the analysis bears. These two are linked by a third element: *work*. Sociology is the study of working society, of society's work upon itself.

In dealing with individual studies, one can speak of the sociology of work as one speaks of the sociology of education or administration. But here my position is at a different level of thought, the level at which Claude Lefort* was also operating when he wrote: 'It is once an activity becomes converted into work that it establishes its meaning, achieves the dimension of objectivity and externality by making tangible in itself the interconnection between an intention and a result, and finally breaks away from discussion focussed on the relation between man and man in order to bring to the surface a finality which was not entailed by their mere coexistence. In other words, work presupposes a *detour* in behaviour, a kind of distancing of others, or again a respite in the clash between men, a rest which makes it possible to develop something new, which in itself conveys a neutral relation.'

Nowadays, society's work upon itself is no longer carried out only in the economic order but in almost all the domains of culture. Sociology is therefore the study of all aspects of the production of society by itself, of its work – yes – but of its work upon itself, and this precludes any appeal to a metasocial order and any separation between actor and system, thus enclosing us in social action by reducing all the categories and all the objects of practice to the composite and changing expression of social relations and systems of action.

The social classes

Once again we must reply to the question: why should one continue using this word – class – when it has been identified by usage with economic categories, defined by the ownership or non-possession of capital, either in a precise form or through mixing this analysis with the simple recognition of inequalities and of social stratification? I use it because I propose to return to what is best in the heritage of social thought from the last century, and particularly the thinking of the theoreticians and practicians of the workers' movement. I no longer agree to defining class relations within a strictly economic mechanism, and intend instead to portray society as a cultural field torn apart by the conflict between those who take over historicity for themselves and those who are subjected to their domination and who are struggling for the collective reappropriation of this historicity, for the self-production of society. To place class relations and historicity at the centre of the analysis of societies is to proclaim a double refusal.

1. *Firstly, the refusal* to believe that a society is guided by *values* which are specified in terms of norms in each institutional domain, and then in terms of status and role. There exists no direct link between these values and norms, for class relations are *interposed* between them.

62

Consequently, the establishment of the categories of practice is just as fundamentally marked by class domination as it is by cultural orientations. The values presuppose a conscience and an actor; they are therefore ideological formulations and should be defined as class interpretations of cultural orientations. Values are always class values, while cultural orientations, although torn apart by class conflicts, nevertheless do have an autonomous existence.

In other words, the values govern the social conduct of a real – individual or collective – actor, while the cultural orientations are located in a field of historicity as constructed by analysis. For instance, the belief in progress, the cultural model of industrial society, becomes a value only by imposing the acceptance of industrialization within its real social framework, or, alternatively, by challenging a form of social domination regarded as an obstacle to progress.

Here lies the uncrossable boundary-line separating the analysis presented here from that of Talcott Parsons and his school.

2. *Secondly, the refusal* to believe that a society can be reduced to the domination of *a ruling group*. The popular class, particularly in the case of industrial working class society, is not just a dominated class, it is also a class of producers. The worker is not only the proletarian who has been deprived of his property and become the property of his master; he is also the worker, the one whose energy transforms nature and makes progress possible. Without this double definition of the working class, the workers' movement could not be understood.

The ruling class no longer acts according to a single principle – the maximization of profit – a principle which holds that the worker is motivated, as Taylor thought, only by rational calculation, by the desire to improve his salary while also reducing his work-load. Such statements are never completely false but they suffer from the insufficiencies of a purely instrumentalist analysis of behaviour, one which disregards all social relations. Just as the workers offer resistance to the employers by collective slow-down, individual absenteeism and organized union claims, so too the action of the employers or any other ruling class cannot be reduced to managerial psychology and must take into consideration class relations, political relations and the internal problems of the organizations. Taken on its own, the top class is simultaneously following at least three kinds of logic: the reference to historicity, the quest for domination, and the perpetuation and reproduction of this domination. These three forms of logic do not combine simply, but generate a great variety of policies. One tends to speak too hastily of laws and trends of capitalism. Profit rates cannot be separated from the state of class relations and from the political influence of the various social groups. This rejection of a purely economic theory does not in any way – it must be said – diminish the role of economic reckoning and analysis. In the same way, historiography has not been impoverished by the loss of an evolutionist explanation and by the introduction of economy and sociology into its reasoning. The discussions on investment, inflation and unemployment seem to me to have already indicated the superiority of political and sociological analyses over those which close themselves in upon the alleged internal logic of the system of domination.

I realize, as I conclude these opening remarks, that today all words are difficult to use. I cannot prevent the word 'class' from carrying with it the idea of a certain domination by the economic and therefore of a subordination – against which I *fight* with all my strength – of the social to the economic, an idea which reintroduces the almost pre-sociological ideas of metasocial guarantees of the social order. Would it then be preferable to speak of power? Yes, in order to indicate that any analysis takes place within the system of social relations but that power is then likely to be identified with an order, with a body of reproduction mechanisms, with a state and its ideological apparatus. This is a concept which is today recovering its strength at the very moment when the workers' movement is so often itself being transformed into state power; but it is a concept to which I am nonetheless vigorously *opposed*, in that I refuse to confuse class relations with the social order and class domination with state power. This is why I have chosen to continue the analysis in terms of classes, while stressing that I cannot define classes outside of class relations and hence class actions. Consequently, what I have made the focus of sociology is neither the notion of class nor that of power but that of *social movement*. This means that one is required to redefine classes by setting out from movements, i.e. from class action.

This leads us then to the notion of a *double dialectic of social classes*. The *ruling* class identifies itself with historicity, over which it assumes control, particularly in directing investment; but it becomes *dominant* through the reverse movement which forces it to change this direction in order and in the mechanisms of reproduction and the protection thereof. The popular class is *dominated* insofar as it must not only follow the direction but also submit to the domination of its adversary; it is also *anti-establishment* in that it resists this order as much for the sake of historicity itself as for its own liberation.

It is essential to add that this sytem of social relations is not self-contained, for the governing actor and the dominant actor are not perfectly matched, any more than the dominated class and the anti-establishment class are two sides to the same figure. The relationships of production, which set the rulers against the anti-establishment class, do not entirely overlap with the relationships of reproduction, which are those of the dominators and the dominated. A dominant class does not construct or impose an order except in a specific historical community, by forging an alliance either with the former dominant classes, with the categories of support, or particularly with the state apparatus. This leads to the creation of a *dominant bloc* which is more conservative than entrepreneurial. Similarly, a popular class – and even the working class – in the most agitated period of the capitalist industrialization, is not, *as a dominated class*, defined only by its submission to the control of its adversary. In itself, it protects a culture and social practices which belong partly to another historical field – just as the Irish workers retain their Catholic religion while living on Clydeside. *The disjuncture permits no confusion between class domination and social order*. It reintroduces history into sociology, change into functioning. This disjuncture must, therefore, be recalled because it is the point at which the analysis of change becomes rooted in the analysis of the social system and of its functioning.

Classes and culture

The second main group of analyses of social classes concerns the relations between classes and historicity, i.e. the cultural field that represents the stakes in cultural relationships. Does this field enjoy an autonomous existence, or can it be grasped only through the disruption of class values in conflict?

Initially, it is the infiltration of the social relationship into the cultural order which must be examined in order to dispel any illusion of separation between two orders of practice. Michel Foucault* in delineating the features of sexuality in industrial society has provided an excellent example of such an analysis. Wherever procreation is defined as an energy drive towards the advancement of the species, class domination emerges, at the level of public morality, as an opposition between the bourgeois man, capable of submitting to the long-term imperatives of production, and the 'hysterical' woman, the masturbating adolescent, or the 'pervert' who is a threat to the reproduction of the species. These moral categories reproduce the relationships between social classes. A second way of determining cultural categories through class relations, described some while ago, applies to those classes whose function is to discount these relations or to deflect attention from them. Manuel Castells* was right in thinking that the study of urban life was often a way of masking the study of economic relations between the social classes, and Alain Cottereau* has recently extended this idea to include the nineteenth century, when slum-dwellings or alcoholism were blamed for the spread of tuberculosis in order to avoid facing up to the effects of the unmentionable working conditions in the factories.

But these offshoots of the social critique of culture cannot go as far as a Manichean vision which would reduce all social life to a confrontation between two class ideologies. A society's cultural orientations have an existence of their own in what I have called the historicity agencies, which are most often controlled by intellectuals. This does not however prevent us from saying that these agents are constantly undermined by the ideology, provided we add that its penetration is still limited.

These spheres of cultural production can be reduced to ideological state apparatuses only in instances when an absolute state imposes its order on the whole society, leaving no autonomy whatsoever either for cultural creation or for class relations. The situation is conceivable, but certainly not in societies in which the ruling class dominates the state, or at least is not subject to the state. In the capitalist societies, cultural innovation most often occurs far from the main class battleground, both in the 'marginal' artistic circles and under the protective umbrella of the institutional guarantees to universities. *A society is not made up only of social domination. Of equal importance to society are, on the one hand, class struggles and, on the other, the cultural orientations which are at stake in these struggles and which develop in the historicity agencies.*

But what best confirms the interdependence between class conflicts and a cultural field is the fact that a class can never be defined in purely economic terms. *The historical actors are determined as much by a cultural field as by a social conflict.* If the metasocial guarantee is political, as it is in merchant societies, the social classes are simultaneously political actors and economic agents. It is only in industrial society that the metasocial guarantee of social order is the progress of the forces of production, and is therefore economic, and that the shortlived *illusion* that classes are of a purely economic nature is for a while entertained. It is high time to rid ourselves of this illusion if we wish to understand the class struggles of today, for these struggles set in action classes which are defined in relation to historicity itself and therefore in relation to a cultural model. They are therefore simultaneously cultural and economic actors. In speaking of social classes, one must therefore construct a general theory of classes, in which the ideas of industrial society, born in Scotland in the eighteenth century and diffused throughout Europe in the nineteenth century, represent no more than a specific aspect. Yet again, one must refuse to give the role of an infrastructure to an order of social facts. What forms the substratum of social life is neither the economic system nor political or moral ideas, but a system of action which is shaped by historicity and class relations and which includes some elements which can be labelled as economic and others which certain people refer to as ideological, a term that serves here only to obscure and slow down the analysis.

These all too brief observations have concentrated far more on class relations than on classes, which accords with the general definition of sociology as an *explanation of the behaviour of actors through the social relations in which they are involved*. It is pointless to break down society into a certain number of classes. Picking out socio-professional categories or establishing levels of income, prestige or education may be useful for non-sociological studies, just as sociology may make use of notions which the economists would consider insufficiently integrated into their system of thought. It is nevertheless difficult to confine oneself to the opposition between the ruling class and the popular class. In a concrete historical situation one must combine categories belonging to different societal types, but within a single type one must also distinguish not so much class fractions as *levels of class affiliation*. Underneath the bourgeoisie – if this is the label one attaches to the ruling class – there lies what may be called the petty bourgeoisie, which does not directly participate in social domination but does share in its *influence* in all spheres of decision-making and participates with the *cadres* by whom *authority* is exercised in the dominators' name. The bourgeoisie is situated directly at the level of the classes, while the petty bourgeoisie acts only at the institutional level, and the cadres only at the organizational level. Among the popular classes in industrial society there also exist, alongside the workers who depend on a pattern of work organization controlled by the ruling class, those who simply have no *influence* at all and those who, even more simply, are subjected to an *authority*, a very wide-reaching definition which is adopted by Ralf Dahrendorf* to define the working class in terms not of class relations but of relations of authority.

An individual or a group, therefore, is not determined by a single social situation. It should finally be mentioned, too, that there are always middle classes, the classic example being the peasants in a merchant society, since these producers also have direct access to the market. In industrial society, one likewise finds worker-organizers, for instance control agents of the first level.

In post-industrial society, the works of John Galbraith* and others have stressed the role of the technostructure, which has considerable influence and decision-making ability and yet cannot be confused with the technocratic controllers; it is therefore the new petty bourgeoisie beneath which there lies a body increasingly made up of all those whose authority derives from the control of certain information. This differentiation within each class in no way diminishes the crucial importance of the class conflict which in every type of society sets one *class* against *another*, the rulers against the dominated. The complexity of historical situations cannot serve as an argument against the prime importance accorded to this principle of analysis.

Class consciousness

There can be no social role without awareness of this role. *There can be no class without class consciousness.* A sociology of action cannot think otherwise, since it rejects the division between situation and behaviour. A class is a class actor: it is impossible to separate class, class consciousness and social movement, i.e. class action. A complete break must be made with the approach, still so frequently encountered, which sets out from the description of an objective situation – primarily an economic one – before seeking to discover its effects as manifested in collective behaviour, as though action were a means of serving 'objective' interests. Analysis must focus on class relations, not situations, relations which cannot be defined outside of the confrontation between actors for the control of a field of historicity and hence for the management of a society. To state that a class may exist without class consciousness would be tantamount to saying that this class can, and therefore should, be introduced from without. This separation – characteristic of a predominant aspect of Leninism – between the workers' limited awareness and the form of class consciousness introduced and evolved by revolutionary intellectuals represents the counterpart of a social philosophy which still submits society to the laws of a metasocial order, i.e. the dualism which dominated the entire thinking of the nineteenth century. On the one hand we have the workers, defending themselves or revolting within the confines of the iron circle of capitalist domination, from which they cannot escape; and, on the other hand, the intellectuals and the revolutionary party, who do escape because they are the interpreters of a natural evolution, that of the forces of production. And it is they who must break down the social barriers in order that society may escape from the general crisis and from barbarism.

The suppression of recourse to any metasocial guarantee leads conversely to the termination of the central role of the party and the revolutionary intellectuals and to the recognition that the class bears its own consciousness and can direct its own action. This then means opening the way for social movements – an idea and a reality which do not hold a central place in nineteenth-century social thinking and particularly in Marxism. The reader may hesitate to follow me here. Even though in principal he may accept my approach, he will ask with astonishment how one can support such an extreme claim: no class without class consciousness. Is it not plain to see that the workers do not always have consciousness of their situation and of their class relations, whether it be because they have been deluded, alienated, or simply confined to a horizon so limited that they can go no further than making purely defensive economic claims?

There is a double objection. First, I am being faced with the limitations of workers' consciousness and then by their alienation, i.e. the reduction of the dominated to the image of himself imposed on him by the dominator. The first objection is the most general and the easiest to submit to the test of verification. I hold that it is false. To say that the workers in a capitalist regime have not by themselves outstripped trade-unionism and the limited protection of their salaries and working conditions is false. The survey I myself carried out in the early sixties into the class consciousness of workers in France revealed the powerful presence of such a consciousness, in particular the recognition of the idea that technical progress – regarded as positive in itself – was being exploited by the employers in their own interests and against the interests of the workers. The study revealed in particular that this consciousness increased the closer one came to the heart of industrial society. In manufacturing centres where the labour of the professional work-force falls under the domination of the lords of industry and the organizers in their service, and that it was particularly strong amongst the qualified workers engaged – most often as toolmakers – on the mass production lines. Workers' class consciousness does exist and it has a history. But it should be added straight away that members of a class do not have merely class consciousness: a worker is defined not only by the class relations in which he is involved but also by many other situations and social roles which affect his attitude to work. I studied, for instance, the case of workers from agricultural backgrounds who were straining for upward social mobility, remaining on the sidelines of workers' collective action and manifesting firm belief in their expectations of breaking free from their salaried positions in order to branch out on their own. Numerous studies carried out on immigrants – in the United States for instance – have reached similar conclusions, and further observations of this nature can easily be furnished. But they do not run counter to my central statement. Saying that there is no class without class consciousness does not mean saying that workers' attitudes must be reduced to class consciousness. For a group of workers is not defined only by its class situation or by its place in a production system; it is also involved in a national, political, religious etc. situation; it is in a favourable or an unfavourable economic situation, and its class position is not always what matters most to a given group.

The idea that domination destroys class consciousness is one which deserves closer attention. The unskilled or semi-skilled worker tends to behave only as an exploited person; he cannot oppose his own work, his skill, to the domination it suffers through the organization of labour. This explains why, until very recently, and still to this day in most countries, trade-unionism has been primarily the concern of the skilled workers. This limitation of class consciousness is a real one. All the more reason, therefore, for not confusing it with simple economism. Whoever is thereby reduced to making immediate and limited claims at the same time rejects the system of domination imposed on him, either by escape or by revolt, and whenever possible endeavours to re-establish worker control over production, particularly by means of collective slowdown. Was it not in recognizing this fact that industrial sociology was born? This defensive class consciousness still retains a powerful hold in East and West alike – as many studies have shown – over the collective behaviour of workers at work.

The idea of *alienation* goes very much further. It claims that class consciousness is not only limited by but also destroyed by domination. This is an idea that has often been propounded in the vaguest of ways. It would be arbitrary to speak of alienation whenever a dominated class fails to fight for its liberation; conversely, it would be erroneous to assume that domination is always so complete that it destroys the ability and the urge to fight. The use to which the notion of alienation can be put is more limited and more demanding. The popular class can be described as alienated when it experiences the contradiction between its class consciousness and its submission to an order dominated by the higher class, or, more precisely, the contradiction between its class behaviour and a general social order.

But one must still demonstrate directly how this disorganized contradiction makes personal or collective behaviour incoherent, as has been shown by the regrettably few studies or accounts – such as that of Douassot* – which describe the self-criticism of workers who attribute their difficulties to jealousy, idleness, and lack of professional conscience, and who go so far as personally to accuse themselves of these defects or to ruin their own hopes of success. This is an important phenomenon and one worth describing, although it assumes that workers are defined as much by a form of participation in social organization as they are by a work situation. Class consciousness also deteriorates when another mode of production becomes dominant, a mode other than that to which the class belongs. Workers' class con-

sciousness grows weaker in societies in which the main relation between the classes is no longer that which sets the master-organizer
against the salaried workers in the industrial firm but that which is
peculiar to programmed societies, i.e. the relation between the production apparatus and the users, who are subjected to the domination of
this apparatus in various spheres of social life.

These reservations by no means undermine the importance attributed to class consciousness, but rather assist us to understand the
obstacles which prevent this consciousness from becoming easily elevated to *class action*. The gap between class consciousness and class
action is due to other reasons as well: *political action* can never entirely
be class action.

Occasionally, class action is directed by truly political agents operating within representative institutions; in other instances, it is oriented
and even dominated by agents of historical transformation, and
therefore by forces within the domain of the state far more than by
those within the sphere of social relations. Pure political class action
does not exist because there is never a social situation that can be
reduced to class relations. One is faced with the constant presence of
the other systems of action, the other levels of the functioning of
society and the mechanisms of historical change. Hence the complementarity and the permanent conflict of class consciousness and, in
consequence, the disparity between social movement and political
action in all its forms.

Class consciousness is most often allied to other types of behaviour.
The trade-unionists are well aware of this. Their activity is less concerned with changing class consciousness and class action than with
extracting class consciousness from limited claims, strategies, negotiations or the forms of crisis behaviour or rejection behaviour with which
this consciousness is involved.

There is therefore no continuity between class consciousness and
political action: it is never possible to accept the formula of the working
class and its party.

Classes and power

Class relations permeate the entire body of society. Historicity does not
drift above them, even though it is not absorbed by the opposition between two class ideologies. Institutions and organizations are not only
specific systems of action, they are also dominated by class relations.
Systems of action do not fit neatly into one another like Russian
dolls. The higher system describes the field in which the lower system
is situated. Class domination controls institutions just as institutional

decisions control organizations. But the fact that society as a whole is marked by class relations and class domination does not mean that society becomes dissolved in the omnipresence of power relations or in a total order which, in the final count, would be that of the state, i.e. a model of interaction outside of any system. *Class relations have their effects everywhere; nonetheless, they also have their own locus.* In society today, this locus has been displaced and extended; but this historical observation – no matter how important it may be – should not overshadow the permanence of a sociological analysis of class relations, particularly today, when the representation of a society peculiar to the industrial era is beginning to disintegrate, and the image – both too vague and too general – of an omnipresent power deriving from nowhere is spreading out to fill the void thus created. The locus of class relations, consciousness, and movements continues to be that of the social control of historicity, and not that of institutions or organizations, the state or the process of historical change. What we refer to as power is merely the hold of class domination over the other systems of action. On the other hand, nobody speaks of *power* without introducing the state, i.e. without associating an analysis of the functioning of society with that of its transformation. This makes it even more difficult to retain the concept of class relations as the focal point in the study of social systems without its being confused with the power that continues to be exerted in a concrete historical ensemble.

As soon as there occurred a weakening of the old representation of society, which portrayed society as being subjected to a metasocial economic order and in which the image of classes and class struggles relating to this society became visibly distanced from observable reality, it was natural that an awareness of inequality and domination should tend to become detached from any specific conception of the social system and be spread throughout society. Does not the same occur whenever the historical scene changes? At the beginning of the industrial era, power was identified with money, whose kingdom was universal and whose domination absolute. It was only later that this idea of the power of money was replaced by that of the relationships of production and that the concentration of capital emerged from behind the ubiquity of money. A similar effort must be made in order to discover behind the ubiquity of power the concentration of management apparatus and the locatable presence of the centres of technocracy.

Dead 'factors'

Historicity, the system of action and classes – these are the instruments which serve to build up our knowledge of society and to prepare the discovery of the social movements at the heart of social life. The approach thus defined is the opposite of an architectural description of society, so much so that it is difficult to make the mental shift from the idea of society as a construction to that of society as action. Nevertheless, the first of these ideas – contrasting infrastructure and superstructure – does exist, and is even frequently encountered. One must attempt to discover its *raison d'être*. I can see main reasons, which have in common the fact that they are opposed to sociology. The first and most evident reason is that this image corresponds to the experience of actors in the very specific type of society in which sociology was born – that of liberal capitalism. What is most important here is also that which is least controlled: economic forces overthrow cultural traditions and political barriers; social ideas seem to be no more than the reflection of this economic evolution. This is why past generations have constructed models of societies by piling politics onto economics and placing culture on top. The other, more acceptable, reason is that pre-sociological thinking caused the social phenomena to be governed by a metasocial order which was initially cosmological, then became political, then economic, and that the range of factors or levels was more than the ensemble of non-social explanations of society. But let us leave aside economics, politics and ideology, for these words are utterly devoid of meaning; in society there are no factors or levels. It must be mentioned here that the Marxists – or at least some of them – by no means hold a monopoly over this representation of society, which encumbers the pages of so many history books. A society is not made from the combination of categories of facts, any more than it is made from a block of institutions each of which would answer a fundamental need. Society is above all a system of action, a mode of social self-production, and historicity is formed from a model of knowledge, a model of accumulation and a cultural model: knowledge, economics and ethics are all incorporated in it. Similarly, class relations are both economic conflicts and cultural designs at the same time. There exists a hierarchy of systems of action, but none corresponds to a category of social facts, since they define orders of social *relations*.

The systems of action

Lying beneath historicity, and governed by it and by class relations, is the *institutional* system of action which produces legitimate decisions; these decisions in turn impose a mode of authority on *organizations*. Are these decisions economic? They always have economic functions; they should not, however, be understood by their content but by their functioning as specific systems of action. For over a century, sociologists have been patiently advancing their knowledge of these systems of action. Why then should there still subsist the archaic image which reduces an organization or an institution to the service of interests, as though neither had any internal logic, as though they had been created by some diabolical spirit to fulfil functions in the service of a sovereign whom some call the bourgeoisie, others the state or the social order?

I purposely attribute to the word *institution* a meaning that is not traditional. I have previously mentioned the customary meaning given by classical sociology to the study of institutions, i.e. the study of the rules for dealing with certain of the needs of social life and, more exactly, of the reproduction of the social order: the punishment of delinquents, the education of children, the recognition of values, the devising of rules for collective life, etc. In adopting the outlook of the self-production of society, I would by contrast describe an institution as a system of social relations which produces decisions considered legitimate by the community which institutes the social organization. I do not refer to a *lycée* as an institution, because it decides on practically none of the aspects of its activity: it is an establishment. By contrast, the reform of university life in 1968 should be understood as a limited effort towards the institutionalization of higher education. In this instance, the word institutionalization – which is at present over-fashionable – is used to signal the appearance of a political function in an organization. But it also has another, equally important meaning: that of the descent of the field of historicity towards the political field. It is in this sense that one speaks of the institutionalization of industrial conflicts, to the extent to which negotiations develop between firms and trade unions, with or without the direct intervention of the state. An institutional system of action is not entirely bounded by limits set by the state of historicity and class relations, for it is located in a political society, and therefore in an ever-complex social formation in which the systems of historical action inter-relate with relations between different classes.

An *organization* is governed by institutional decisions which authorize and regulate a certain type of authority. The social relations within an organization are controlled by hierarchization, but they are not governed solely by the rules it produces. Whenever they are so governed, the organization becomes a *bureaucracy* in the commonly accepted sense of the word. With the exception of this pathological case, an organization is controlled on the one hand by institutions and, in extension, by historicity and class relations, and on the other hand by exchanges with an environment over which it has no mastery, whether this environment be that of the markets or of any other type of demand and supply structure, outside of total planning, which is impossible.

The cardinal features of society

1. Moving from historicity to organizations, analysis descends towards open systems, in constant interaction with an environment.

2. But all forms of production also become turned back into reproduction. Alongside the organizations there appear *reproduction agencies* which aim to transfer social situations, cultural attitudes or forms of knowledge. Similarly, the reverse of the institutional system is the *rule*, the decree which imposes a norm and sanctions the deviations thereto. Ultimately, *order* becomes *repressive* when it disregards class conflicts.

3. Order severs social relations and creates a pathology of social life by replacing conflict with the opposition between adherence and exclusion. The product of an organization in *crisis* is dysfunction. At the level of institutions and of the decision-making system, *rigidity* eliminates and *prohibits* political forces, a process which may assume the form of enclosure. Finally, at the level of historicity, the rupture of class relations by power creates a form of *exclusion*, and oppositional behaviour becomes rupture behaviour. A crisis of historicity leads in the end to *decadence*.

4. All that is excluded, prohibited, repressed, is kept beyond and beneath the social order by a central power – that of the state. But the changes in the environment or the internal growth of society make it impossible to maintain this separation. A society must evolve; its *changes* may in particular occur at the level of its organization through a process of *modernization*. Political mechanisms may also emerge to reform society by adapting it to its environment. Or else these mechanisms may be more global, corresponding to a more voluntarist form of state intervention. Society is then controlled by an agent of *social liberation*.

Thus the field of sociology begins to take shape by being already aware of the relations between its four component parts: *action*, *order*, *crisis*, and *change*.

A sociological treatise should respect this interlocking of the major themes. Historicity becomes transformed into social organization, which presupposes the formation of a power to create *order* in a historical community. Order causes social relations directly or indirectly to disintegrate, and changes them into an opposition between inclusion and exclusion: whatever has been placed outside of society can become an agent of *change* if the state endeavours to meet the new demands of the environment by drawing upon its 'reserves'. It has been necessary to present this table of sociology in order to locate the study of social movements not only at the centre of a sociology of action but also in the whole field of sociology, which must be laid out on the basis of the sociology of action.

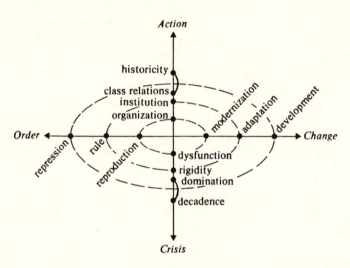

5

The social movements

A new idea

The social thinking that is furthest removed from the idea of class struggle still resorts to the idea of conflict. The liberals find evidence everywhere of competition and the struggle for survival; others attribute the greatest importance to the state, to international relations and war; and yet others stress the values of a community, setting them up in necessary opposition to whatever is foreign, whatever threatens them from without and within. But the essential choice entails situating the conflict either on the boundaries of society or else at its heart, by linking it to the most fundamental social relations. By contrast with this first orientation, I hold that the cultural field, the historicity of a society, represents the stakes in the most important conflicts. Society is conflictual production of itself.

The idea of social movement should therefore be preferred to that of conflict. The field of historicity is the ensemble formed by the class actors and by that which is at stake in their struggles, i.e. historicity itself. *The social movement is the organized collective behaviour of a class actor struggling against his class adversary for the social control of historicity in a concrete community.* Cultural orientations must never be separated from social conflict; in past societies this separation could never be avoided. The separation of social order from metasocial order has always resulted in the separation of conflict, occurring within social life, and a cultural field, situated above the conflicts. Practices were in the past recognized as being conflictual; values or tendencies could not be conflictual. And between the practices and the metasocial order, separating conflict and meaning, there ruled contradiction – whether one defines it as such or prefers to call it collapse.

The social thought and the revolutionary political action of the industrial era were still dominated by this separation, and as a result the social movements were unable to emerge as the principal actors of that society. For Lenin, for instance, the trade-union movement was defined as a pure economic actor subordinated to political action and political theory. My purpose here is to reorganize the entire body of sociological analysis around this new idea, that of social movement. These words may arouse astonishment. How can one claim that the idea of social movement was absent from industrial society, when our social history and social thought have for so long been dominated by the workers' movement, the theory of class struggle, and the experience of strikes, trade-unionism and revolutionary parties? But does anyone think that at the moment when I claimed the absence of the idea of social movement in the past I was disregarding these elementary facts? I even recognize that in the doctrines on the Labour movement the most direct preparation was to be found for the idea of social movement, and I hope that my own efforts will prolong the social thought of the last century while at the same time parting ways with it. But it is with these differences that we must begin.

The representation of social movements that we have inherited from industrial society is as follows: a dominator imposes laws, beliefs, and a political regime just as much as it imposes an economic system; the people submit to these impositions but revolt against them when their physical and cultural existence becomes threatened. This revolt is not only defensive, it is also a preparation for the future since it explodes the contradictions of the social order and destroys the barriers erected by individual interest and blocking the way for the general and natural progress of society. This vision conflicts with the idea of social movement as I have defined it over two vital issues. *Firstly*, it never introduces the image of a historical actor, i.e. one who is guided by normative orientations, by a *plan*, in fact, by a call to historicity. The popular actor is merely the expression of social contradictions or the conveyer of natural forces; he is not a social actor. This explains why the study of the workers' movement – beyond the historiographical descriptions – was illuminated particularly by the study of the capitalist system, right through from its cyclical fluctuations to its general contradictions and their tendency to worsen.

During the past few decades, this tendency has become even more strongly marked by the institutionalization of industrial disputes in the large capitalist countries and the extreme importance attributed to national struggles, revolutionary outbreaks and counter-revolutionary or repressive coups d'état in the dependent societies. In Latin America for instance social analysis has been dominated by the study of the world capitalist system, or, less sweepingly, by the study of unequal exchange, while the popular social actors within these societies have been represented as being broken down, crushed or alienated by this domination imposed from without. It is true that popular movement is not an armed hero charging at the head of his army onto a battlefield to engage a foe of almost equal armed strength; it is also true that domination undermines the capacity for action and organization of the dominated. But first of all one must recognize the existence of an oriented action, that of a class which is not merely dominated but which also belongs to a field of historicity, which is struggling to control this field and to win back for itself the knowledge, the investments and the cultural model that the ruling class have appropriated to their own interests.

Secondly, the collective behaviour recognized by social thought of the industrial era was defined historically or naturally. Its meaning is not to be found in the society of the present but in that of the future. The workers' movement is not only anti-capitalist, it is also preparing a socialist society that will follow on from capitalist society, and this socialist society is defined more by its reconciliation with the forces of production than as a social project. Not only is it history that must interpret the workers' struggle as the preparation for a socialist society, but it is also only a political agent that can bring into being this society which will accord better with the state of the forces of production. The separation of social practices from metasocial order, which shifts the meaning of the greatest struggles to a different level than that of their inherent action, has made it impossible to conceive of society in terms of social movements. Using this old form of social thought, it is particularly impossible to apply the same concepts in analysing the action of the dominators and that of the dominated. Speaking of the bourgeoisie brings us quickly back to analysing the laws and evolution of the capitalist system, while the study of the working class is by contrast one of material defence or global revolt. Thus, like all those who speak of social movement, I must in return shoulder the weighty responsibility of applying this idea simultaneously to the ruling classes and to the popular classes. This is a task that had already been undertaken by Weber, and later by Schumpeter and the historians of industrialization, but their efforts were often thwarted by the preference given to the study of the capitalist system over that of the industrializing and dominatory action of the ruling class. I shall admit here, at this early stage, that the focus of this book will be strictly on the study of popular movements, and that this imbalance is dangerous. The approach I am putting forward will never truly be able to be understood and judged until it is also applied to the ruling classes, i.e. when there has been a reinterpretation in terms of social action, and in particular class action, of what is generally presented as the logic of a system and which, in order to analyse the behaviour of the rulers, resorts only to the idea of a permanent and sovereign determination to maximize profit, a theory whose poverty strikes us as soon as we endeavour to understand economic policies or the logic of firms.

The disagreement between the conception of social movements presented here and the conception which has dominated the movements of Marxist inspiration breaks to the surface over three essential issues:

– Firstly – and this is the essential point – I define social movements as socially conflictual behaviours but also *culturally oriented* forms of behaviour, and not as the manifestation of the objective contradictions of a system of domination.

I do not conceive of the workers' movement solely as a proletarian uprising but just as much a counter-model of industrial society proffered by the workers, who are in possession of the work-force.

Secondly, the action of social movements is not fundamentally directed towards the state and cannot be identified with political action for the conquest of power. It is a *class* action, directed against a truly social adversary. There may be convergence or alliance, but never unification, between a social movement and an action for the transformation of state power.

Thirdly, a social movement is not the creator of a more modern or advanced society than the one against which it is fighting; within a given cultural and historical field, it is defending another society. The idea of superseding must be replaced by the search for an alternative, and this runs counter to the evolutionist ideas which governed the social thinking of the last century.

This first outline of social movements may appear to be restrictive. How can it be made to correspond to most of the protest movements, and anti-establishment actions and currents of opinion?

It is true that in a given society, and therefore in a certain system of historical action, there exist only a few main antagonistic social movements, but these social movements are present in a great deal of the more specific conflicts or those which are seemingly less closely bound up with economic activity. These movements must be sought out and separated from other forms of rupture, protest or hope, remembering all the while that in every society there is a field proper to social movements, i.e. that of class relations and historicity, and that conflict by rising up towards social movement draws closer to the principal stakes of society.

The stakes and the adversary

A social movement is not an affirmation, an intention; it is a double relation, directed at an adversary and at what is at stake. The perfect integration of these two components is never achieved, and most often, therefore, the movement reaches only a low *project level*, i.e. weak integration of its aim towards the cultural stakes, its conflict with the adversary and with that which links these two relations, in other words, its picture of the domination exercised by the adversary over the cultural stakes of the struggle. One should not accept too readily the diagram I have often used, which seems to be purely descriptive.

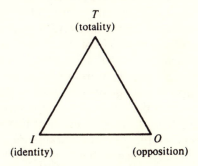

The social movement is presented here as the combination of a principle of *identity*, a principle of *opposition*, and a principle of *totality*. If one is to fight, however, should one not also know in whose name one is fighting, against whom, and on what grounds? Reduced to these simple ideas, the diagram can be applied to all forms of social behaviour since they all involve the actor in a relation and because there is no relation without a social field. What characterizes the social movement is primarily the fact that what is at stake is represented by historicity itself and not by institutional decisions or organizational norms, and that the actors are therefore the classes, the only actors to be defined by their conflictual relations with historicity. What next characterizes the social movement is the fact that the interdependence between stakes and actors – indicated by the triangular form of the diagram – is total, and it is never total in the other types of collective behaviour. In a political system, the actors can be defined independently of one another, at least to a certain extent, as different socioeconomic categories endeavouring to obtain financial support from a state or fiscal system which would be favourable to them, and the field of their struggles for influence is defined independently of them either by law or by the state. In an organization, the relations of authority work within the confines of general norms, which explains why one may be tempted at this level to separate the system and the actors, structure and power. But I cannot repeat often enough that, on the contrary, historicity and social classes cannot be conceived separately.

In the I–O–T diagram, therefore, one must recognize far more than merely a description that can be accepted by all without difficulty. *The relation of actor to adversary*, the conflictual dimension of the social movement, takes on a different meaning depending on whether it is linked to the relation between the actor and the stakes or instead to the relation between the stakes and the adversary . . . In the first instance, this relation gives rise to relations of production in the strictest sense of the term, relations between workers and the ruling class; in the second case, it is instead marked by relations of production. In other words, this relation is both that of the ruler and the rebel, and that of the dominator and the dominated. There is no need for the reader to seek unnecessary subtleties in this: these words, which seem so close to each other, actually cover very different forms of social behaviour, each of which occupies a vast position in history. Class relations have both a light face and a dark face. The light face reveals the clash between conflicting classes for the control of historicity, for example the struggle between employers and workers for the management of industrialization; the dark face is that of the people's defence against the dominant order. *The relation between the actor and the stakes* does not define the aim of action but rather the stakes of a relation. These stakes can be reconstructed by analysis, starting out from the adversaries' ideology, but they can also be located within the social movement itself as being that which is recognized as non-ideology, as being external to social action, and hence as the limit which ideology sets itself. Consequently, the workers' movement does not satisfy itself with setting a society of workers against a society of employers; it also aspires to serve progress and to encourage the development of the forces of production against the wastage and irrationality of private profiteering. Thus industrial progress does indeed represent what is at stake in class warfare, since the employers are also speaking in the name of progress and the development of the forces of production, and are attacking the forms of worker resistance to this progress – e.g. slow-downs – from which Taylor hoped to free the industrialists. There is therefore a double relation between the actor and the stakes. A ruling class identifies itself with historicity, but it also identifies historicity with its own interests. A popular social movement fights against a culture insofar as it is dominated by the adversary class, but it also recognizes the 'objectivity' of the stakes, for which it is struggling against the dominator. It does so, in particular, by calling upon the intellectuals of the historicity agencies. Industrial society acknowledged the role of scholars, the experimenters and interpreters of the laws of natural development. The workers' movement made constant appeals to them, but it did so in a double fashion.

At times, the aim was to defend a science that served the people, particularly a medicine in the service of the poor; at other times, however, the purpose was to defend the independence and stature of a science against the profit-oriented spirit and the brutality of profiteering.

And still today, pure science is lauded by many leftwingers over applied science, which is condemned for being in the service of the employers.

If the relation between the actor and the stakes is cut off from the relation between the stakes and the adversary, these stakes are no longer defined socially but in terms of modernization. A. Melucci* rightly criticized this notion, which strips the social struggles of all their vital importance. The struggle is waged in the name of progress against tradition, universalism against particularism, and, no matter whether it springs from the ruling class or the popular class, it becomes
· socially undetermined. But one should not, for the sake of this criticism, forget that the social struggles have most often been associated with battles for modernization, i.e. for the extension of social participation. The women's liberation movement is above all a modernizing one; the determination to win greater opportunities and more rights for women is in fact the central issue of this movement, branching off from which are certain tendencies that are closer to the ideology of the ruling class and others that are on the contrary more anti-establishment and more concerned with being linked to other social movements.

The relation between the adversary and the stakes is in itself external to the actor, but it does concern him too, since it is indicative of the domination to which he is submitted. A social movement reduced to this component would have to restrict itself to the denunciation of the dominant order, and this would force it to provide a non-social definition of the actor himself, a definition in terms of organic needs or moral principles, subsistence or liberty. In a more complete movement, it is at this point that whatever is *negative* – opposition or revolt – takes root; i.e. the rejection of order or of crisis, the desire for liberation, and, at the very top, the revolutionary movement. I call this negative because here the affirmation of a project is replaced by the struggle against the obstacle, which has become nonsensical rather than hostile, a privilege rather than a profit. No social movement exists without this negative dimension; nor does any movement exist which is reduced to this dimension. A pure force of the destruction of order cannot but open the way for a new ruling class or a new state power. Conversely, a movement without a negative force is swiftly reduced to institutionalized conflict, to a struggle for influence between different groups of interests within a system of political representation. Alberoni* speaks most appositely of this breach.

A social movement can never be defined by an objective or a principle. It is nothing but the ensemble made up of these three components, an unstable ensemble, never fully coherent and almost always mixed up with other forms of collective action.

This is what contrasts it with the violent *disorder* which Gary Marx* showed to be based neither on collective belief nor on practical objectives and which he felt to be better suited to a crisis of the mechanisms of social control and in particular of the forces of repression.

Riots and uprisings may enter into a social movement, but they should rather be placed in opposition to it, for the movement is always normatively oriented and inscribed in a real social relation.

It is more difficult to contrast social movement and revolution, but these notions have so long been confused that it is necessary to separate them. A social movement cannot be defined as an agent of change that has been blocked. It lies within a social system whose dominant forces and political or cultural bulwarks it threatens. It aims more at overthrow than change. As we shall see, social movements are in practice associated with struggles associated with forms of social change, but their definition derives from the analysis of the functioning of societies and not from the knowledge of their patterns of development.

The struggles

The more closely these three dimensions of social movements (I–O, O–T, I–T) are integrated, the more one tends to describe the *project level* of a movement as being raised. When the movement acts effectively according to the I–O–T formula, its capacity for historical action is extremely strong. If, on the other hand, the three components are separated as I, O, T, this capacity is weakened, though this does not mean that the movement is of little importance. It may, at a given moment, play a decisive role, but this role is likely to be limited by specific circumstantial constraints, and consequently the movement will be extremely heteronomous in relation to political or ideological agents, or else in relation to another social movement. An upper level movement is one which integrates organizational demands with institutional pressures, i.e. those which result from decision-making. It is also such a movement that leads to the victory of positive class action over the critical action of destroying an order in crisis.

A social movement, therefore, does not act alone, and is never completely separated from protest and pressure, from crisis and rupture, all of which give rise to different types of struggle. *I use the term struggle for all forms of organized conflictual action carried out by a collective actor against an adversary for control of a social field.* A social movement represents a particular form of struggle, but the most important one. A struggle cannot be recognized as such unless it matches up to four principal conditions. First of all, it must be waged in the name of a *committed* population. There are worker or peasant struggles, but there are also struggles by consumers or by the inhabitants of a district. No matter how important they may be, movements of opinion or of ideas, of religion or tolerance, cannot enter directly into consideration here. Secondly, these struggles must be organized and should not exist purely at the level of opinion, for an organization must exist in order for conflict to take shape and for the movement to attain a certain integration. Thirdly, it must fight against an adversary, which may be represented by a *social group* even if, as often occurs, it is defined in more abstract terms, as capitalism or the state. The absence of a specific adversary reduces the struggle to a modernizing or anti-modernizing current. The women's liberation movement, which has been strongly marked by its modernizing tendency and which is opposed to traditions and principles, has endeavoured to gain in depth by defining its adversary more specifically than merely by opposing women to non-women, i.e. to men. The success of this undertaking has assured its importance as a struggle and all the more as a social movement. Lastly, the conflict with the adversary should not be specific; it should be a social problem concerning the whole of society: it is this that separates an action struggle from a pressure group whose objectives are more restricted. There is no social category that can by nature indefinitely represent struggles or social movements. One of the richest veins of sociological research is the emergence of new actors springing from either currents of opinion, modernizing innovations, or more limited sectorial problems.

It is necessary for struggles to be classified in accordance with the principles of analysis already given. On the one hand, in accordance with the distinction drawn between the three principal systems of action – historicity, institutions, and organizations – and on the other hand in accordance with the opposition between positive struggles, which aim at extending the actor's sway over a particular field, and the crucial defence struggles against a form of domination that has not been legitimized by historicity and is therefore in crisis.

Positive struggles – the level of historicity: social movement

It is this type of struggle which lies at the centre of our preoccupations.

It is one which has already been analysed and can be represented as in the diagram below.

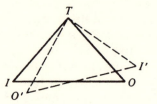

The two actors (*I* and *I'*) are both adversaries of the other two (*O* and *O'*), although the definition of the actor given by himself does not coincide with that given of him by his adversary. These actors have a common stake (*T*) in their conflict.

Positive struggles – institutional level: institutional or political pressures

The actor endeavours to increase his influence over decision-making within the limits defined by the cultural orientations of historicity and by class domination. This struggle takes place within institutions and within procedures that are considered as legitimate, but, like any strategy, it does not preclude recourse to force. The efforts of the trade-unions to obtain recognition, to participate in the discussions and in the decisions made in spheres affecting work conditions, derive from these struggles and form a type of trade-unionism that I have described as the trade-unionism of control. This in no way precludes recourse to strikes or to various forms of pressure in answer to those implemented by the firm's management – using considerably more powerful means – against the workers. This institutional pressure can be represented as follows: *I* is the actor, *O* his adversary. They are competing for influence in order to obtain an institutional decision.

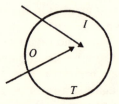

The fact that the arrows partly protrude from the institutional field is a reminder that the actors are not fully located within this field but that their action aims at modifying decisions taken there. Worker trade-unionism – after having been the social movement of industrial society

– tends in most industrial countries to be limited to this institutional pressure. This is particularly true in the social-democratic countries where trade-union participation in decision-making has long been organized. Mixed up with these institutionalized forms of conflict, however, there does also exist a class consciousness, which is powerfully rooted in industrial production and in other kinds of struggle. Institutional pressure, which gives precedence to an intermediary level of collective action and of the social system, is in fact constantly overburdened on the one hand by more immediate claims and on the other by class action.

Positive struggles – organizational level: claims and protests

Struggles to improve the relative position of the actor within a hierarchized organization; the battle against authority. Here the actors are located within the organization. They are fighting for better wages, less difficult working conditions, and a change in the forms of control. Let us recall once more that in a factory a concrete form of protest may be expressed through other forms of struggle than protest action. This therefore justifies both the role of the trade-unionists who drive their claims up to the level of institutional pressure and social movement, and the role of the sociologist attempting to separate the components of a historical event such as a strike. Protest is represented by the diagram below. This illustrates that every organization, here rep-

resented by the circle T, relies upon a system of authority, and that all claims or protests are aimed at modifying the relative position of the actor (I) on a hierarchical scale controlled by the managers (O). Those who put forward claims for the equality of rights, opportunities or remuneration for a category considered as under-privileged or as the victim of discrimination go no further than this level of protest, not even when they are defending their cause with the utmost vehemence. Conversely, no social movement can be solidly formed if its claims are not built upon a wide base to which it accords great autonomy while at the same time endeavouring to rise to a higher level of opposition.

The social movements

Critical struggles – organizational level: crisis behaviour

Although these struggles all remain at the same level as the protest claims, they are very different in nature. They no longer aim at improving the actor's relative position in an ensemble but at defending his position against a state of crisis, for instance against unemployment or against the changes that threaten the old forms of social and cultural organization, e.g. following the penetration of new forms of economic activity or new beliefs. Crisis behaviour can only be negative; it does not conceive of a new social organization, but attempts rather to reconstitute the organization that has been disrupted either in its economic activities, its social norms of functioning, or its beliefs and outlooks. It is the adversary, then, who separates the actor (*I*) from the organization (*T*); he is an obstacle (*O*) rather than an enemy. This position can be represented as in the diagram above.

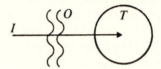

Critical struggles – the institutional level: pressures against obstacles

These struggles are the counterpart of institutional pressures. Often both are involved in the same struggle. A strike, and more generally the resorting to force, occurs because the actor cannot gain better access to decision-making in the framework of the existing institutions. The consequent mobilization – one must perforce use military expressions in order to stress that the action does not occur within a field of social action – is an appeal to what lies beyond the negotiable.

As in the previous instance, this critical action aims less at transforming a social system – here the political system – than at filling a void. In the dependent societies, the populist movements have to a large extent been pressure drives by or for the 'marginals', attempts to enable the outsiders to participate in the system of decision-making policy. This is a participation which is thus conceived as an end and not as a means serving, for instance, a class struggle. It is a purely political action which may be violent, like crisis conduct, and this violence sets it against the instrumental orientation of institutional pressures and organizational claims.

Charles Tilly* has offered a general analysis of political violence, which he explains in terms of the struggle of certain social groups to acquire, or not to lose, a place in the political system. In his analysis he stresses the link between violence and what I describe as institutional pressure. Violence, therefore, assumes limited forms in situations of simple rigidity, i.e. of the limited enclosure of the institutional system. If this system is entirely closed – as it is in an autocratic society – the struggles are forced to rise immediately to the highest level or else to disintegrate under the hammer-blows of repression. This type of struggle can be represented by the diagram below.

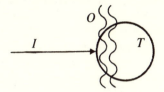

The actor (*I*) has no access to the decisional field (*T*), which is occupied by the adversary (*O*) who guards the gates. The actor is engaged in direct struggle with his adversary, but he still strives to make a forced entry into the institution, whose legitimacy he is therefore not challenging.

Critical struggles – the level of historicity: revolutionary action

I have often employed the term *critical action* to describe struggles waged against a form of deprivation, and the term *critical revolutionary actions* to describe struggles against a domination no longer associated with the controlling action of a ruling class which opposes historicity and destroys it. One is tempted to add here that this critical action is directed against the state, against despotism and autocracy, rather than against a ruling class. This is a shift of extreme historical importance and one which will be analysed in the following chapter, but it should not cause us to forget that revolutionary action involves the destruction of a class domination and not merely an assault against state power, even though it may easily be associated with the conquest of state power. Such revolutionary action exists only if it challenges class domination in the name of reappropriation by the community of all the forms of the self-production of society.

As in the two previous examples, therefore, this critical action aims at restoring a community, a process which is to be seen especially in colonized or dependent countries. Such countries are subject to a domination – even a double domination – since dependence on the foreign country maintains or reinforces the dominant national class, which hangs on to its archaic privileges. The principle aim of the struggle against this domination is independence, and liberation from the conditions of under-development and dependence, but it would be mistaken to attribute only a national content to this aim; it is an aim reinforced by the struggle of the dominated class against an oligarchy bound up with foreign interests. This struggle against a truly social domination, against oligarchy, prevents there being any complete separation between a social movement and revolutionary action, even though they are extremely different from each other. They represent the two sides of the class struggle, and it is the mixture of them alone that creates the great historical struggles. Entirely positive class consciousness is in great danger of degenerating into institutional pressure and organizational claims, as trade-union history has shown. By contrast, a pure revolutionary action tends to be nothing but a form of disturbance without any social plan, or even the stepping-stone for a new state or a new ruling class. The diagram below indicates that the

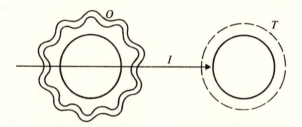

revolutionary action instigated by the actor (*I*) destroys a social order which is entirely enclosed by class domination (*O*) and aims at creating a new order (*T*) which is entirely oriented by its class action; this objective, therefore, no longer represents the common stakes for the adversaries: here we are moving completely away from a field of relations and social movements, and this is a movement clearly expressed by the theme of the dictatorship of the proletariat.

The breakdown of class relations and their replacement by the antinomy of order and exclusion, privilege and misery, leads to the clash of two totalities, the Manichean conflict between bourgeois society and proletarian society, which amounts to the same as the collision between bourgeois non-society reduced to the reproduction of privileges and proletarian non-society, empty and post-revolutionary, swiftly filled by an all-powerful agent of historical transformation, the State-Party, which retains the stamp of its revolutionary origin only in its doctrine. Social struggles, unlike political positions, cannot be aligned like colours on a spectrum moving, for instance, from left to right. To set up an opposition between the reformist attitude and the revolutionary attitude is more dangerous than useful; it is a transcription of social struggles in purely political terms. One must, instead, contrast protest and rupture, positive projects and critical action, as being two sides of the struggles and not as two degrees of radicality. The positive struggles combine cultural modernization and social conflict; they penetrate into all kinds of social relations and protect the subject's rights. Those who speak of democracy on a self-managing basis, those who insist on the independence of concrete social actors, and those who base their action on moral foundations are on the side of the positive movements. By contrast, those who fight primarily to liberate themselves from the unbearable, to put an end to the scandal, while at the same time striving to break down a power, are accepting that their action be taken in hand and controlled by political, even military, agents. The more they attack the powers that be and a state in its extreme form, the less they act at the level of culture and of the elementary forms of social relations – authority and influence. A positive project for change often tends to degenerate into re-patching or into readaptation of the power overthrown; a critical struggle, arising out of revolt and rupture, may avoid this watering-down process but it is in danger of helping towards the formation of a new power and widening the breach between the dominators and the dominated. In many situations the two orientations of social struggles become intertwined without ever being inextricably mixed up; the same holds for the three levels present in each of them. The discussions of the social democrats in Germany, Austria and Russia before 1914 were dominated by the polarity between parliamentary action and revolutionary struggle, and still more specifically by the opposition between the popular masses and the party. Even today in France, as in Italy or Spain, what some people have referred to as Eurocommunism is in fact the search for a compromise – always unstable – between on the one hand an organization and a form of revolutionary action, and on the other hand participation in a representative democratic regime. The series of agreements and splits between the left-wing parties which France witnessed from 1972 to 1977 testifies to the deep disparity between these two orders of struggle and the difficulty of firmly combining them in economic circumstances, which at the same time calls for modernization, transformation and rupture.

This classification of struggles aims more at separating types which rarely appear in their pure state than at casting fresh light on the conditions behind the formation of social movements, which involves an unstable synthesis of class action and revolutionary rupture, institutional pressure and revolt against crisis. Such an analysis may rub against the sensibilities of actors whose ideology forms a simple, highly integrated, image of the struggle they are waging; but sociology can find its own way only by distancing itself from ideologies.

One of the principal aims of the method of sociological intervention, described in the second part of this book, is to transcend this resistance by the actor.

A struggle is not weakened by the multiple directions it takes: a class action is never entirely located at its own level; it succeeds in becoming itself only by taking the claims and pressures in hand, and this presupposes that organized action, stemming from the rulers and from the ideologies, will intervene in order to bring out the general problems involved in specific demands. But this apparatus constantly tends to become a power, an anti-state mechanism, and to prepare an order already installed within the movement, which then becomes the party, the army, and finally terror.

This interdependence between the most strongly opposed forms of historical action explains why the consideration of *violence* maintains an ever central position in the analysis of social movements. There can be no greater opposition than that between the project of a movement and the violence inflicted by domination or caused by the contradictions of a social order. In the history of the workers' movement, trade-unionism, as a voluntary association, as a social and political project, was shaped and activated particularly by the skilled workers, producers and workers speaking out in the name of work and progress against capitalism, its irrational and at the same time unjust choices, and the states of crisis and unemployment by which it was nourished. But worker action was also carried on by the unemployed, by the manual labourers, who were proletarians rather than workers, exploited souls rather than fellow-workers. Although less able to organize themselves, they have nevertheless been a source of great strength to the trade unions of modern times; all the same, it has still never happened that a positive class action and a negative class action – directed more towards political intervention – have succeeded in becoming completely united. If the role of violence is great at the basis of the workers' movement, it is greater still in the movements battling against a despotic state or against outside domination. Revolutions are rarely made against ruling classes; their target is to do away with despotic state power, the barrier to change, or to free themselves from foreign military and economic domination. This form of violence becomes all the more manifest as class relations weaken, institutions become increasingly rigidified and social organization plunges deeper into crisis. It is not a simple reflection of such a crisis, but an outward sign of the deterioration of social movement which cannot manage to form itself in such conditions and in which the ultimate aim of the cultural stakes, of the project, is replaced by the desire to put an end to the absence of stakes and to the sealing off by the state of the field of social relations. This violence is ambiguous: it may be an appeal to a social movement, which it often assists in taking shape, but it may also become mere terrorism, an extreme form of crisis behaviour, the appearance of which is more likely when the actor does not occupy a clear-cut position in class relations and is defined instead by his opposition to the state. This is why terrorism, which has played a very limited role in the workers' movement, is so important in the national-ist movements, because whoever opposes a state – national or foreign – cannot go beyond the coup d'état and purely political violence because he is not situated within class relations. The form of violence which has the most positive public image is that which opposes a people to a state, because this is the violence most strongly associated with a real or potential social movement. It may be the revolutionary violence of the people invading the palaces and overthrowing the institutions that served the interests of the ruling class or the autocracy. It may be military violence, that of the soldiers of the year II and the Italian campaign, or of Trotsky's Red Army. Everyone knows that Bonaparte became Napoleon and that Trotsky was also in favour of crushing the rebels of Cronstadt: revolutionary violence is close to Jacobin terror or communist totalitarianism. But these facts, which nobody is inclined to forget, do not prevent the majority – of whom I am part – from being fascinated by the great turning-points of history, those moments when social history and revolutionary crisis are com-pounded before being reduced to ashes by an absolute power. Nothing is further removed from a social movement than war, and yet the greatest wars have contained their charge of social movement; and it was for this very reason that they were more extreme than the strategic manoeuvres of the eighteenth century.

I am writing in a country which has now ceased to be a great power after having been one of the central elements in the system of interna-tional relations: a country which is quickly forgetting the role that the state and wars played in its history and is being tempted – more than it is actually aware – by a purely civil picture of social movements, even though the communist party is inherently a force created for revolution and social war. It is important to remember here that both the light side and the dark, the project and the rupture, the expectations and the revolt, and war as much as freedom, are all the offspring of historicity. How inadequate these words are for grasping the terrible historical realities to which they refer! But what point is there in constructing down to the last detail a reference grid of the social and revolutionary movements? It is by relating to each of these movements, and first of all to those for which this book serves as an introductory study, that the concepts will be enriched and their usefulness assessed.

One society, one movement

The greater the diversity of struggles, the more each society is animated by *a single* social movement for each social class. Corresponding to a system of historical action there is a main class relation and consequently a pair of antagonistic social movements. The historical system of action represents the most immediate stakes in their conflict. Social movement and class struggle are synonymous expressions; only the former will be used here, because to speak of class struggle would seem to indicate that classes, objectively defined, enter the struggle to defend contradictory interests. To speak of social movement is to state, on the contrary, that *there exist no class relations separable from class action*, from its cultural orientations and from the social conflict in which the movement occurs.

I have often found myself speaking of social movements or – and it boils down to the same thing – the student movement, the Occitanist movement, or the women's liberation movement. It is indeed difficult to disregard such commonly used expressions; but these expressions are acceptable only if one does not forget in using them that they contain the hypothesis that the popular social movement of programmed societies is manifested through the struggles of students, Occitanians or women. For the complement to the unity of the social movement of each class is its fragmentation into differing struggles. We occasionally forget, in speaking of the workers' movement, that it has been present in the same way in trade unions, parties, co-operatives, benefit societies, municipalities and cultural associations. The unity of the workers' movement cannot be confused with the always unreal existence of an organization which would embrace all aspects of worker action. It remains for us to eliminate the two possible misinterpretations in the conception of social movements.

1. *A social movement is not a peripheral phenomenon* of deviation or outright conflict. It is true that, particularly at the beginning of its history, the social movement takes the form of ruptures and fundamental disputes. But nothing could be more mistaken than to reduce it to these forms of behaviour. Social movements are the fabric of social life and, when associated with the orientations of historicity, they produce social practices through institutions and through social and cultural organization. In industrial society, the workers' movement and that of the directors of firms, i.e. the actors in industrial conflict, provide the

historical actors in relation to which the whole of society must be understood. The research studies, of which this book is the first in a series, are designed to provide a reply to the question: *which social movement in post-industrial society will occupy the central role held by the workers' movement in industrial society and by the movement for civil freedom in the merchant society?*

Further research will have to engage as quickly as possible on the study of the technocratic movement which has taken over the place of the movement of the industrialists and which, like this movement, assumes very different forms depending on whether it occurs in a capitalist country, a communist country, or a nationalist regime.

If one stops looking at a society and instead considers a social formation, one can clearly discover several social movements within it, each corresponding to one of the systems of historical action, which in combination make up the social formation. It is also likely that only the social movement corresponding to the dominant system of historical action can be highly structured. The other movement(s) will be drawn away either towards institutionalization or, on the contrary, towards crisis behaviour or rigidity.

2. It would likewise be mistaken to believe that social movements are by very definition *agents of historical change*, forces for the transformation of the present and the construction of the future. This is an interpretation that is all the more tempting and dangerous in that it often seeks self-justification in appealing to the concept of historicity interpreted as the production of the future, perhaps even as a general programmation of social change. Such usage of the concepts of historicity and of social movement runs entirely counter to that which I have for many years been following, and which has not varied. I have placed increasing insistence on the need *to separate synchronic analysis from diachronic analysis*, the analysis of functioning from that of change, by abandoning all evolutionism. A society which has a very powerful capacity for acting upon itself should undoubtedly be defined in terms of movement rather than of order, but, like other types of historical society, it constitutes a particular system of historical action, and nothing permits us to claim that this sytem will not be replaced by another. A social movement fits into a field of historicity in which it is one of the main actors. It is born and dies with the society of which it is part. There is nothing more vain than the great evolutionist visions that have accompanied the advance of the workers – the vision of happiness or improvement in the standard of life – ever since the most remote times of antiquity. The social movements of different societies can be analysed using the same concepts, but their content is different.

The social movements

We find it hard to recognize this at the moment when a social movement, together with the type of society of which it is part, enters into decadence while still retaining a political importance far superior to that of the first – contradictory and unstable – forms of the new social movement.

Above and below the social movements

It is necessary to widen still further the scope of research into social movements and, more specifically, into social struggles. These struggles occur in different systems of action, fields of historicity, institutional systems and organizations, showing at one moment their light face, at another their dark face. But a social movement outstrips these limits. On the one hand, it soars upwards as far as the cultural orientations of the society, so high that it sometimes seems to detach itself from all social conflict; and, on the other hand, it plunges so deeply into crisis situations that it seems to disintegrate in them and become lost in marginality.

1. The social movement can penetrate to the heart of historicity, since it never escapes wholly from class conflicts and never glides above social relations. The social movement, therefore, seems to become compounded with a modernizing trend, a critique of traditions that have lost their raison d'être. What separates this movement, however, is that it fights against domination and is consequently always located in the field of social relations.

Such *cultural movements* herald the appearance of new social movements; they are not directly engaged in fighting a class adversary and they take care not to become merely a trial ground for other social movements. But in combating the archaic forms of social domination that have silted up in the collective awareness, they weaken the ruling class, which is never independent of a dominant bloc. An up-and-coming ruling class, however, also attacks the past in order to entrench its power more firmly, and likewise it relies on modernizing trends and on the intellectuals. Hence the ambiguity of these cultural movements. They are most often carried forward by the ruling elite, the aristocratic salons or intellectual circles, but they are also fed by popular protest against the double weight of class domination and the transference of a heritage of inequality and privilege. Cultural movements are unstable; they split quickly. On the one side, there is a modernizing strain which cannot elude the ruling elite except by seeking refuge in an intellectual critique of modest scope; on the other side, there is a trend of protest, which is revolutionary because it is battling at once against both the dead and the live elements of social domination. Opposed to these 'progressivist' cultural movements are those which, like all critical actions, struggle against crisis and seek to re-establish values. The cultural models of the past are left floating in our society, without ever finding direct social expression. They may be latched onto by nostalgic groups hoping to rediscover the core of a lost civilization, whether it be the idea of God or that of progress; these past cultural models are most often reinterpreted by the new social movements and particularly by critical actions desirous of rediscovering a principle to replace the void created by crisis. This is why crisis behaviour is reinterpreted in France, particularly among the middle classes, in *religious* terms, which gives rise to communitarian movements mixed up with a political commitment that is often closer to waiting for the Day of Judgement than to strategy and negotiation.

2. At the opposite extreme of the cultural movements, shreds of social movement descend even lower than organizational crisis, and there spread out in violence and defiance. The boundary-line is never clearly drawn between protest movements and behaviour of opposition or revolt by the sub-proletariat. It is still more difficult to pin down the transition point at which this opposition or *revolt* shifts over to the hyper-conformity of the 'marginal' who steals in order to acquire the consumer objects offered him by society, while at the same time refusing the means considered as legitimate for acquiring them. There is for instance the ambiguity of the revolts by prostitutes, hemmed in by scorn and repression, yet also fascinated by money. In this half-shade, one almost always notices – on the analytical side – those only who speak with a clear conscience of deviation or those who, in a manner that is more religious than social or political, see in downfall a sign of grace and holiness. Nothing would seem further removed from protest and from the determination to achieve social change than the behaviour stirred up by the breakdown of social relations, by rejection or abandonment. But in every social struggle there is also present an element of protest against society, an aggressiveness towards people and property, a longing – as a student we worked with in Amiens expressed it – to 'bust up the works'. It is only the reinterpretation and remodelling through social struggle – with the solidarity and responsibility this involves – of this destructive and self-destructive behaviour that can lead to the liberation of those who are trapped. Our present research programme does not yet dare to approach these difficult problems, but it will have to tackle them once the methods used have been strengthened and proven. For the analysis of social movements should enable one to cast a new look at the entire

range of social behaviour, from cultural innovation to madness and self-destruction.

Ideology

A movement produces an ideology, i.e. a representation of its social relations; it also produces a Utopia, by means of which it becomes identified with the stakes of the struggle and with historicity itself. But the movement cannot integrate this ideology and this Utopia, for this can be done only if one no longer adopts the outlook of the actor, but takes instead the point of view of social relations. Only the sociologist succeeds in doing so, though as yet only in his analysis. If he wishes to transform the ideology into directives, he becomes no better than a doctrinaire whose influence weakens the action.

One cannot be both judge and defendant at once. Ideology is opposed to sociology just as the actor's picture of the relation is opposed to the knowledge the actor derives from this relation.

A social movement cannot act entirely as its own analyst, since it is of necessity organized. By becoming a 'personage' it produces an ideology. When the organization is strong, when a movement is located entirely within a voluntary association, ideological resistance to analysis is very strong; it may be insurmountable. Conversely, when a struggle over-reaches all associations, which occurs in the most important cases and indicates the probable presence of a social movement, it is far more capable of carrying out its own analysis. But then, does not the struggle appear as such, but in a more broken down form, as a body of discussion? Analysis has no choice but to enter through the gap that separates a movement from its organization.

The Utopia of the working class is socialism, i.e. the society of the workers. The working class and progress form a unit and they destroy the irrational obstacles that profit and private privilege have erected along the way to collective progress. All of a sudden, the working class becomes less a social force than a natural force, a new Gargantua overflowing with life. Its *ideology*, by contrast, is the ideology of struggle, of the opposition of interests, which leads to social warfare, to the mobilization of the popular forces, and the organization of combat by the chief powers. As much as the Utopia is naturalist, so the ideology is political.

For the *ruling class*, the Utopia also identifies the actor with historicity. It sings the praises of the movement, the innovation and the enrichment which will triumph over the resistance set up by prejudice and routine. But it appeals less to nature than to reason, which provides social domination with its guarantee of objectivity. The same difference is to be observed in the ideology. The ideology of the ruling class does not exalt the struggle and its strategy but rather the rationality of order, and the laws of economics, balance or growth. Marx provided the classic critique of this ideological reduction by the bourgeoisie of social relations to the laws of political economics. Every ideology of the dominant class tends, therefore, to impose itself as a *dominant ideology* – to put it in global terms – while still wielding specific power. But its triumph is never complete. This is partly because it cannot acquire complete sway over historicity, since a cultural model or a form of knowledge are never purely ideological. Religion is never just the opium of the people. And partly because the resistance of the popular class is never annihilated, and the ruling class therefore cannot speak as representative of an entirely integrated society. It must always resort to *repression* and, at the same time, to justificatory language. The bourgeoisie is convinced by its progressivist role; this is its Utopia; but when it comes to speak of the rationalization of economic laws, it never forgets that these are arms against the workers' movement. The fact that the ruling class is no better able than the popular class fully to unite its Utopia and its ideology prevents us from accepting the reduction of social practices to the attitudes of a dominant ideology. The ruling class always interposes social struggles between the Utopia and the ideology of the ruling class. It is not all reproduction, because conflict and repression are always present.

In a comparable way, the ideology of the dominant class can never be identified with a metasocial guarantee of a social order. This guarantee is not produced and used by the ruling class in its own interests; it is the non-social basis which a society lays down for its action upon itself. This distance between social relations and metasocial guarantees explains why these guarantees have always been linked to the state – which is the principle of unity and therefore non-social – controlling social life. The further the field of society extends, at the same time as the metasocial guarantees grow weaker, the more directly the state produces the arguments which endeavour to provide a non-social basis for historicity and social relations, until the moment occurs when the totalitarian state disallows any appeal either to transcendence or to historicity, in order to set itself up, arbitrarily, as the sole basis for the functioning of society. Some people will use the term ideological to describe these non-social (metasocial or statistic) bases of social organization, but this is only admissible if all confusion between the ideology of the actor and the ideology of the system is eliminated. Such confusion, i.e. the confusion of the interests of the ruling class and of culture, and hence a set of symbolic systems, must be actively combated.

The life and death of the movements

Not all movements have the same history, but they are all born and they all die. Consequently, they all rise and fall according to a scale of project levels, and in maturing attain more powerful integration than they lose in ageing.

I have spoken of the natural history of social movements, in order to recall the fact that they do not live as the result of a constantly renewed creative act. The more class relations – and within them the relations of production (rather than reproduction) – hold a central position in social life, the more social movements attain a higher level. Once relations become institutionalized, social movements degenerate into political pressure. This is what happened to the workers' movement with the emergence of post-industrial society, even though this evolution may have been slower in France and Italy than in other capitalist countries. In moving from one type of society to another, one notices, therefore, social movements dropping in level, or, by contrast, protest struggles mounting and becoming transformed into social movements. In the market societies, social movements were urban movements; their base was the town or the district, and their main objective the freedom of the citizen – and hence of the inhabitant – and the commune against the lord, the prince, or the great merchants. In industrial societies, the urban movements were no more than forms of institutional pressure. Today, the urban problems are debated at the organizational level: on the one side are the problems of planning and adjusting, on the other the problems of segregation, exclusion and the reproduction of ine- qualities. In either case, one is as far away as possible from the centre of class relations, which shifted first towards the industrial firm then towards the opposition between the mechanisms of production and the social territories on which they imposed their power.

Conversely, at the time of the formation of a societal type, class conflicts are concealed by the alliances necessary for the breakdown of the old order. When the relations of reproduction weigh heavily upon the relations of production, social movements overlap to a great extent with modernizing movements. This is what has happened in our part of the world, where the appearance on the horizon of the workers' movement has been matched by the still confused formation of new movements, in symbiosis with the modernizing trends. It would be erroneous to blame an emergent – or withering – social movement for having a low project level, for this would mean forgetting that in every situation there is a maximum of *possible historical action*. If the organized action occurs below this maximum, it is filled out and overcome by wildcat movements. If it is situated above the maximum, it is threatened by excess Utopia.

6

Historical struggles and the state

Social movements need to be isolated from the more concrete social struggles which occur in various fields of social action or in a combination of several of these fields. These social struggles, however, cannot be immediately discerned, as they are set in a purely synchronic perspective which has had to be constructed by analysis. The historical events which bring collective conflicts to the fore are more complex: in them, the social struggles are mixed with other struggles which are associated with the mechanisms of change and which I have referred to as *historical struggles*. We have already mentioned on several occasions this necessary division between the problems and the forms of behaviour associated either with the functioning of the social system or with its change. We must now provide more direct justification for this separation and conclude what its consequences are for the study of collective action. First, therefore, I shall define the opposition I have established between mode of production and pattern of development; next, I shall show that this leads to a parallel opposition between the ruling class and the state; I shall then position myself at the point of intersection between these two axes – the central position of sociology – in order to define their inter-relations. And finally, I shall consider the forms of historical intervention by the state, which means I shall be making a parallel examination of the state's role as an agent of historical change and the historical struggles, i.e. the struggles carried out during the transition from one type of society to another.

Mode of production and pattern of development

Class relations and social movements occur in a system of historical action whose economic aspect may be described as a *mode of production*. A mode of production is governed by the economic dimension of historicity, i.e. by the level of economic life at which there is investment of the part of the consumable product which has been accumulated but not consumed. In simple agrarian societies, investment is used only in order to produce surplus without altering the methods of production, and particularly in order to guarantee the subsistence and ensure the continuation of the specific life-style of the priests and warriors. When investment occurs at the level of the distribution and exchange of goods and services it produces a merchant society; when it is used to change work organization and the division of labour it gives rise to an *industrial society*; and when it is used to change production itself, that is, to create the means of management and invent new products, it produces a *post-industrial* or *programmed* society. Each of these major societal types, therefore, is distinguished by a particular kind of class relation: *all* merchant societies, like *all* industrial societies, have the same class relations which are those between trader and producer (craftsman or farmer) in the former case, and that between organizer and worker in the latter. Some people have voiced their opposition to the idea of industrial society, because this was an idea which did not take class relations into consideration; most often, such criticism has proved grounded. My approach, however, is quite different. As a societal type, industrial society cannot be defined in technical terms; it can be defined only in terms of specific class relations. On the other hand, in order to situate the class relations I have not had to speak of *capitalism* or of *socialism*, which may cause some surprise. Let us therefore examine these terms which are such common currency that one no longer troubles to define them.

These two words would appear to designate opposing forms of class society, one of which is dominated by capitalists, the other by workers. But class relations in industrial society have nothing to do with ownership relations. The organization of labour produces a growth in productivity, and it is those who wield the organizational power who enjoy the resultant profit: they are the ruling class. It little matters whether the ruling group is a private owner, an incorporated company, a co-operative, a public-controlled firm, or the state itself. *From the point of view of class situation, there is no difference between American workers and Soviet workers.* Workers' class consciousness is by nature the same in all industrial countries, and nothing could be more similar to the slowdowns or other forms of resistance to the pressures of work organization or piece-work payment in a capitalist country than the comparable forms that have been described in socialist countries.

What, then, is the source of this difference between capitalist countries and communist or socialist countries, if it does not derive from class relations? It does not derive from a society's manner of functioning but from its *pattern of development* and change, and in particular from its mode of industrialization. *A capitalist society is one which has been industrialized by its national bourgeoisie.* There is absolutely no reason for differentiating between only two modes of industrialization. Even the most simplified typologies are unable to distinguish fewer than five or six types. Capitalist societies apart, I myself have differentiated *dependent* societies, economically controlled by a bourgeoisie – but a foreign bourgeoisie; *colonized* societies, more completely controlled by a foreign state apparatus; *nationalist* societies, whose development is governed by a national state; and *communist* societies governed by a state which is either born of a revolutionary upheaval or else lays claim to revolutionary origins.

The first formulation indicates that the problem we are considering here is that of the direction of change and not that of social domination. Market economy has no particular link with class relations. *Control of the economy* cannot be confused with the *social relations of production*. One has no more reason for always calling a society capitalist that one has for continually referring to it as industrial or for saying that it believes in progress. This language is part and parcel of bloc propaganda: the capitalist bloc and the socialist bloc – these are expressions which mean no more than the American empire and the Soviet empire.

In order to draw a clear division between the two principal axes in the analysis of a society – the *synchronic* axis, that of functioning, and the *diachronic* axis, that of change – I shall be speaking of the development not of a ruling class but of an *elite*, of a group which directs a historical change, nor of a popular class but of a *mass*, governed by the ruling elite. The contrasting of these two kinds of category is all the more important since it is not a general type of society that becomes transformed into another, but a concrete historical and geographical ensemble – a *country* – which undergoes transition from one type to another. The main actors in the change cannot therefore be defined directly by reference to a field of historicity, and in particular to class relations. The change occurs within a community or collectivity; it is primarily the work of an agent who imposes his own transformation on this community by interpreting outside pressures in order to overcome the resistance of the systems of reproduction. This agent, defined by his *sovereignty over a territorial block*, is *the state*.

The transition of a community from one type of society to another can no more be the work of the entire collectivity than can historicity be borne by a community. Identity cannot produce change. Since a society forms a system, the transition from one system to another presupposes the existence of a particular agent of historical transformation and of a logic of action which do not belong to society and which can be designated only by the state.

This separation between the two orders of analysis is recent. Prior to the sudden increase in societies' capacity for self-transformation, the principle of social evolution was confused with a metasocial guarantee of social order. The transcendental world held sway as well over a philosophy of history, both in the Christian philosophy of redemption and in the lay philosophy of progress.

In the nineteenth century, the idea of progress was based on the principle of the natural passage from the simple to the complex, on the pressure exerted by the increase in the forces of production or by the increase in demographic density. Prior to the industrial society, the market society tended rather to display confidence in the triumphal onslaught of a world-conquering reason which would open up new ways and cause orderly knowledge to penetrate into the shades of ignorance. On the contrary, however, the more society is explained by action itself, the more *history is shaped by organized initiations and becomes historicity, instead of it being society that lies within history*, conceived of as an evolution. Thus, the idea of a social system necessarily involves that of the *discontinuity* between the systems.

The more a society possesses a powerful historicity and a great capacity for acting upon itself, the more its change becomes separated from its functioning. Before industrialization, societies appeared to be defined in their very organization by their place within an evolution. After industrialization, they became defined simultaneously but separately by their functioning and by their relations with an environment made up of other societies and of the natural conditions of existence. The more powerful the historicity, the more one must seek beyond it for an explanation of change. A society's capacity for self-transformation – which defines a level of historicity – does not explain the transition from one level of historicity to another. We are still too strongly dominated by an evolutionist vision to be able to accept unhesitatingly this separation between functioning and change and to recognize the externality of the state with regard to social relations.

But, if we look around us, is it the progress of industry or the intensification of all kinds of communications which has triggered off historical changes of all kinds throughout the world? Is it not rather war, revolution, the overthrow of colonial domination, and the confrontation between empires? And is not the main actor in all these upheavals the state? Global historical change – which we refer to as development – can no longer be regarded as the result of growth. These two notions, which are so often confused, belong to different orders of analysis. Historical change does not take place without discontinuity: it is the transition from one system to another and not a process of moving up a ladder of modernization or productivity. This is why a community's capacity for historical change is associated with its fragility, with its vulnerability towards outside dangers and stimulations.

It is the external threat or the conquest, war or imperialism, competition and national defence, it is the world of inter-social relations which governs the transition from one society to another. It is here that the state, representing not social forces but a society, is to be found; the state as a political unit confronted by other units on the battlefield and in economic warfare. How can one disregard the state if one is to understand the emergence of a new type of society? Is it the capitalists who have created capitalism? But then, where do the actors come from who have preceded the system to which they belong? What one describes as history is in fact a chainwork of systems and alterations, of class relations and state interventions. *The state is the chief agent behind the pattern of development, just as the ruling class is the dominant figure in a society.*

For a long time, however, and in spite of the most blatant evidence, we have been prevented from recognizing this separation between functioning and change by the fact that we were fascinated first by the example of Great Britain, then by that of the United States, and by their exceptional success. These were or are capitalist societies 'par excellence', in which the ruling elite is the ruling class, and in which the state is in the hands of the bourgeoisie, at least within the national territory. Here we have a coincidence between the principal agent of the system and the principal agent of change which has never since been reproduced because it can exist only at the core of the capitalist system. It was already no longer true in the France of the nineteenth century, in which, as Marx observed, the bourgeoisie did not elect Louis-Napoleon, who was nevertheless to become the best agent for the development of capitalism. It was even less true in Germany, where it was not the bourgeoisie but Bismarck, the junkers and the bureaucracy who created the Empire and its economic power, or in Italy, united by the monarchist and aristocratic Piedmont, or in Japan, where the Emperor Meiji, with the support of the great 'daimyos', drove out the Shōgun and the foreign fleets. *Outside of the centre-point of capitalism, the state and the ruling class never correspond.* In the greater part of the world, it is the industrialist state which governs today, for the countries which used to be colonized are now involved in an industrialization which cannot be implemented by a weak or non-existent national bourgeoisie, but which is directed by a nationalist, post- or counter-revolutionary state. The liberal tradition, re-adopted in certain Marxist analyses, particular during the Second International, which identified the state with the ruling class, must be fought against. The state is not independent of classes: *it is located on a different axis.*

Occasionally – as in the case of hegemonistic capitalist countries – the state is at the service of a hegemonistic ruling class; most often, however, they are separated.

A pattern of development is defined, therefore, by the nature of *the ruling elite* which controls state power, or, more precisely, by the relations between the ruling class and the ruling elite. *The closer one is to the centre of the pattern of capitalist development, the more the state is dominated by the ruling class,* which causes it almost to be confused with the representative political institutions. Even so, this statement reflects only half the reality, for this state, so weak and so civil within the national boundaries, is a *conquering* military state outside its frontiers. The English state was reduced almost to parliamentary government, which was not much more than a board of directors of the bourgeoisie. But the Royal Navy was not a political institution; as part of the state military apparatus, the Navy enforced order on the seas and in the Empire. By contrast, whenever the state is most directly the main agent of development, the ruling class seems completely absorbed by the state apparatus. In the party-state of the *communist* countries it is not easy to distinguish a ruling group which could be called a ruling class. Conversely, this all-powerful state performs the same role both inside and outside its boundaries. All-powerful inside, and a dominator or negotiator outside, it operates in all areas as a pure state which is the agent of none other than itself.

Is it not strange that so many of those who daily follow up in the newspapers the action of state rulers – whether communist or not – continue to repeat a curious catechism which says that the state is the agent of the ruling class, or even only of its most important, most monopolistic fraction? For a quarter of a century in France we have seen our political life disrupted by the cold war, and the class struggles weakened by the opposition between the communists in solidarity with the Soviet empire and the socialists faithful to the American empire. And yet this brutal fact, which testifies to the powerful influence of the struggle between states and of international relations on social life, has had no effect on a great number of mortar-boarded scholars who have dismissed the objection by simply stating that the cold war was a class struggle at international level between the American bourgeoisie and the country of the workers. This is a statement whose arbitrariness is well suited to a theory so blatantly opposed to common sense. But today, when those who still dare give such a reply are rare, should one not abandon ideas which had a vestige of truth only at the time of the most extreme liberal capitalism? Those who will not face up to the evidence always resort to the same objection: if the state is not linked to the ruling class it must be because it is not linked to anything, because it is hanging 'in the air' – a naïve objection, but one which nevertheless deserves two replies.

The first is that the state always has links with the ruling class. In the hegemonic capitalist societies, the state is even dominated by this class, while in other societies – particularly Communist ones – the state instead incorporates the ruling class into its own apparatus. But, whatever may be their combination, the class which controls the functioning of society is associated with the agent who governs its change. The fact that in a completely liberal society the ruling class is *also* mistress of the state does not, first of all, allow us to disregard the other, far more numerous, situations and in particular does not justify the confusion of class domination and state power.

The second objection is that the state is by no means hanging 'in the air'. State power, not merely as a monopoly over legitimate violence, following the Weberian formula, but also as an agent of historical change, is just as real as the domination exercised by the controllers of the economy. The state is linked in many ways to civil society, but, before describing these links, we must recall the essential point: that the state is the *sovereign*. The state is not the one who represents the metasocial guarantees of social order – important though this function is – but rather the agent of a concrete historical collectivity, situated in relation to other communities and to its own transformation. A class is defined by economics and by society, a state by geography and history. No state exists which does not fulfil three essential functions: making war or peace with other states; causing order to be respected and inflicting penalties; and committing the community to its future by long-term decisions, i.e. by controlling a substantial part of the investment.

The state is the central agent of development because it is a concrete historical ensemble which is transferred from one societal type to another. One can speak of the functioning of industrial society, but one must speak of the development of Japan or China. One must abandon the illusion that all the social categories introduced into analysis belong to the same ensemble. It is absurd to believe that individuals and groups are located only by reference to their place in class relations, the result of which is that a considerable part of the population is conveniently pigeon-holed under all-purpose categories such as the middle class or the petty bourgeoisie. European history since the First World War has provided sufficient contrary proof to those who became closeted in analysis in purely class terms and in absolute confidence in class solidarity for one to be able to recognize at least the existence of two analytical axes, that of the social system – which is also that of class relations – and that of change – which is also that of the state. It is superficial to try to solve this crucial problem by making the state the unificatory principle of class society, for such an expression is meaningless. A society's unity derives from a culture as much as from a state: will it be said that language is part of the state ideological apparatus? Moreover, a state acting as the preserver of unity, order, and integration could dominate only a society completely cut off from all exchanges with the outside world; this is a picture which might be appropriate for the Tibet of the Dalai Lama, but not for industrial societies deeply involved in change.

The patterns of development

The state is considered here as the central agent of development. The form taken by its relations with the ruling class defines a pattern of development.

Development is not the upward progress of a society to a higher level of production or rationality, but the transition to a higher level of historicity and to a different system of historical action. This is why a theory of *development* or structural change lies at the opposite pole to a theory of *evolution*. A theory of development does not explain the direction of an advance but the mechanisms behind the *transition from one ensemble to another*. A society's development is its exit from a system *A* and its entry into a system *B*. If one restricts oneself to considering economic development, each of these systems can be defined in the simplest way as the relation between a capacity for economic initiative and a form of social participation, for there is no 'historical' society without the concentration of a society's capacity for self-production and in particular of the power to invest, nor – in a complementary and contrasted way – without the integration of a community around this historicity. This is a tension which in a simplified manner represents the conflict between the social classes. The passage from system *A* towards system *B* works therefore on the presupposition that first of all the constituent elements of system *B* will have been established: on the one hand, *investment* ((3) in the table below), and on the other hand new forms of *social participation* (4). As far as the system of exit is concerned, the conditions of development are negative rather than positive. At the social level, it is necessary for order and the mechanisms of reproduction to be in a state of *crisis* (2), to be shaken or challenged, and at the economic level that an outside *stimulus* (1) be felt, that an opening present itself.

Development is the combination of these four elements, but this combination does not occur spontaneously. Each of the elements may appear in isolation, giving rise to specific consequences which easily

109

become transformed into forces of social disintegration. Crisis can lead to decadence; outside stimulus to the draining off of capital and manpower towards new places; investment can become monopolization and participation may become involved in conflict with investment.

Hence the absolute need for a *central agent of development* whose existence is not bound to any element of the social system, but who ensures the unity of the system of change: *an agent of history and not of society.*

	Economic	Social
Old	stimulus (1)	crisis (2)
New	investment (3)	participation (4)

The diagram demonstrates that no *historical* change is purely endogenous, which is not true of an organizational change, and only partly true of an institutional change, and only partly true of an institutional change. The discontinuity between one field of historicity and another implies that there has been an exit from one system and an entry into another. It is the *state* that directs these operations, but the state's action may take place in very different areas. If the bourgeoisie is a conquering bourgeoisie, it is capable of developing and changing itself without running up against insurmountable resistance on the part of the former ruling classes. But this evolutionary continuity presupposes an extremely powerful driving force. The English bourgeoisie decided to plunge into industrialization and to protect agriculture no longer, because it was confident of being able to obtain food and primary materials from overseas, thanks to the strength of its fleet, and hence of the state. Whenever historical change seems to be reduced to continued modernization and to follow a liberal course, it is because an imperial state enables the capital to specialize in the most modern sectors or because the national state organizes the conquest of the national territory and the economic expansion. Conversely, *voluntarist* development is development in which the state must intervene directly in order to overcome resistance from the past, often even through a revolutionary upheaval. Finally, in what I have called *contractual* development it would seem to be the political system which ensures adaptation without breakdown to the internal and external changes. But this political system is actually associated with a state, which is far more an agent of change than of adaptation, and particularly an agent for the destruction of the old forms of social and cultural domination. This pattern of development corresponds to the countries whose ruling class is in need of state aid in order to succeed in transforming the economy.

Historical struggles and the state

We must now provide a more exact analysis of the patterns of development and of the transition from one societal type to another by applying the general scheme already outlined. A *liberal* development is one in which the elements are interlocked in the simplest way, requiring least intervention by the central agent of development – the state – i.e. it is a movement in which detachment from the past precedes the construction of the future and in which the economic components occupy central place. This development may be represented as follows:

crisis (2) stimulus (1) investment (3) participation (4)

The disintegration of the mechanisms of reproduction makes it possible for outside stimuli to exercise an effect; these stimuli, which are primarily economic (geographical discoveries, conquests, scientific and technical inventions, international conflicts, etc.) generate investments, and the new economic reality gives rise – more or less quickly – to new forms of social participation (transport, information, training, political influence).

Voluntarist development moves in the opposite direction: here, it is the social elements which occupy central place. An outside stimulus – for instance, the penetration of capital or of foreign soldiers – sparks off a crisis resulting in a movement of anti-establishment participation which, after its victory, becomes an agent of economic growth and investment. This is represented as:

stimulus (1)   crisis (2)   participation (4)   investment (3)

Finally, in *contractual* development it is neither the economic elements nor the social elements which play the central part, but the communication between them, i.e. the political institutions, which are then closely bound up with the state.

These types of change may be combined or juxtaposed. France is a country that has been nourished by revolutionary traditions. The political forces have often aspired to create a state here that would be capable of overthrowing the established order and privileges: the institutions are weak, and anti-parliamentarianism is well married to the Republican spirit. The workers' movement here has been closely associated with a communist party organized for the overthrow of the state. In France, then, historical change is conceived in a voluntarist fashion, and the intellectuals have almost always exhibited scorn for the institutionalization of conflicts or the gradual adaptation of organizations to the changes in their environment. But this country, which has lived through so many major political and social crises, is also one of the foremost capitalist countries and has likewise reinforced its institutional mechanisms for handling conflicts throughout the excep-

111

tional economic growth of the last twenty years. Here, one finds a mixture of liberal, contractual, and voluntarist traits.

Class relations and the state

Now that we have distinguished between functioning and change, i.e. between synchronic analysis and diachronic analysis, we must consider whether these two orders of reality and of analysis are entirely separate, whether the state and the ruling class are thoroughly distinct historical figures capable of allying themselves or of fighting each other, yet just as different as a local oligarchy and a foreign conqueror. This problem lies at the heart of sociology, so much so that one could best define a sociologist by questioning him on this issue. My answer here would be that the separation is not complete and that *in the final count it is in social relations that one must seek for the explanation of the state's role*. This is possible if one recalls the opposition – introduced into the analysis of social classes – between relations of production and relations of reproduction. A class is involved in relations of production to the extent that its action is directed towards historicity at the same time as it is engaged in combat with the adversary; this class is situated in the relations of reproduction when it is defending its position within an order and its ability to transmit its values, its customs, its rank or privileges. This reminder enables us to formulate an idea of great importance for historical studies:

The state's autonomy relative to class relations becomes all the greater as the relations of reproduction gain increasingly over the relations of production. A society in which the conflict between the ruling class and the anti-establishment class is far more active than the conflict between the dominant class and the dominated class is a society in which the state has least autonomy in relation to the ruling class. This is the society of liberal capitalism. On the other hand, the more a society finds itself in a state of crisis and rigidity, the more the possession of privilege gains over innovation and the quest for profit and power, and the greater the state's autonomy the more this state defines itself in terms of its role of reproduction and the maintenance of order. Thus the point at which state order interlocks with class order is to be found *in the maintenance of order*. Class relations are not simple but double: relations of production and relations of reproduction. The former never entirely overlap with the latter, and the distance by which they are separated is the space of the state. Which amounts to saying that *the more complex a social formation is the greater will be the role of the state therein*, while in industrial Great Britain, which came far closer to the industrial model than any other country, the state was dissolving – at least as far as internal policy was concerned – into the ruling class. And in France, the importance of the state's role is explained by the weakness of the French bourgeoisie, the reinforcement after the French revolution of the rural middle class, the acknowledged political and ideological influence of the new social classes, recognized by the great bourgeoisie after the Commune, and by the fear of the working class.

The illusory order

These analyses are pointedly opposed to the confusion between class domination and state power in the more global notion of *order*. All dominant social or political forces tend to impose an order and to conceal themselves behind categories of social practice which seem to be purely technical or administrative. The role of analysis has always been to shatter this appearance, to disassemble the categories of practice in order to discover the social relations and the class domination concealed behind them. We are thus induced to recognize also that *this social order has no unity of its own*. It contains a mixture of the most diverse elements, all belonging to different systems of action, to varying situations of class relations and political relations. Their unity derives only from the assumption of a state form which imposes a set shape upon them, rather as a scrap-metal press transforms metals of different kinds and shapes into a compact block.

Social order is never reduced to assuming the form of class domination; nor does it ever completely correspond to the will of a state. And nothing could be more erroneous than to reduce the organization of a society to the omnipotence of social and cultural control mechanisms governed by the state and placed at the service of the ruling class for the reproduction of its privileges. This is an idea which leads to an impoverishment not only of the heterogeneity of the dominant order but also of the reality of the conflicts, the breakdowns and the negotiations. It is up to the historian to separate the elements that have been mixed together, by relating each to its original field of social action. There is no justification for confusing state order with the order of social relations under the misapprehension that the construction of an order by the state could meet the interests of a particular class. It may happen that state order falls essentially within the domination of the ruling class; more often, however, this order is opposed to the action of a ruling class which is still too weak – for instance, because it is too much subjected to foreign influence – to become hegemonic, as is the case with most dependent societies. At all events, whether the order is conservative, reformatory or transformatory, its action and its rhetoric cannot be reduced to instruments of class domination, even when this domination is powerfully to be felt.

This refusal to accept the representation of society as an order more universal than state power or domination by the ruling class, both of which aspects are combined within it, is a protest against the temptation of anti-sociology, which is so powerful today. As a reaction against the outworn and often distorted ideology of the workers' movement, one no longer dares today to speak of society, of social movements and classes. The world seems to be directed solely by power, the state, conquest, crisis and war, and in opposition to these forces an appeal is made only to general principles or institutional guarantees, so great is our fear of once again becoming victims of the illusions which, when they were lost, caused us so much suffering. I can understand this reaction, at least when it occurs in countries where the entire society is effectively dominated and crushed by the state. But I still fight against this abandoning of the analysis of societies. Today, instead of dreaming only of breaking with the social thinking of the last century or of concerning ourselves only with the state, we must learn to see our society, which is not to be equated merely with the ideology of the state. We must recognize its new field of historicity, its new class relations and new social movements. This is why I claim *the primacy of synchronic analysis and the central role of class relations and social movements* in reality and in social analyses. I dissociate myself from the theoreticians of Marxism, but I also refuse to go along with the anti-Marxists who wish to speak only of power and of the state. In a transformed society and a changed culture, I wish to establish a post-Marxist analysis which would finally attribute to class relations and social movements – and hence to conflictual action for the social control of a cultural field – the central importance that these relations and movements were still unable to attain in Marxist thought and which is denied to them by those who no longer see any other enemy than the state. The primacy of truly sociological analysis over political thought should not lead us to consider the state as a mere servant of the ruling class, which is an image that has become impossible to defend in the world today. Instead, this analysis should open up the way towards the study of the historical struggles which are always directed towards the state but which are also social struggles; all the more so since the state, as an agent of historical transformation, is for this very reason also a social force and not a pure political instrument or an absolute power over and above social relations and systems of international domination.

Historical struggles and the state

A double fight

This analysis, all in all an optimistic one, should be completed and possibly corrected by a more disturbing view of the place held by social movements in our types of society. Does it expand – as I say – to keep pace with society as it gradually acquires a more powerful capacity for acting upon itself, or are we instead not perhaps witnessing the over-running of civil society by the state, the destruction – to borrow the words of J. Habermas* – of public opinion, of the *Oeffentlichkeit* created by the English and French bourgeoisie? Actually, these two orders of phenomena are not directly opposed. The domain of public opinion has not ceased to expand. Its bourgeois expression has enlarged the expression given to it by the scholars, and now the barriers which had been set up to impede the onslaught of plebian opinion have been overturned. We have now entered the era of social movements, which is also the era of counter-culture, just as that of public opinion was also that of parliamentary-type representation.

But this enlargement which has been achieved at the expense of absolute power and the metasocial guarantees of social order also opens the way for the enlargement of the state's role. The conquering state, closely associated with the power of a dominant class anxious to ensure the reproduction of its privileges, was first replaced by a mod-ernizing state which imposed economic regulations, then by an admi-nistrative state which Habermas calls the social state, and which inter-venes in social and cultural organization as much as it does in the economic order. In opposition to this state there are anti-statist, demo-cratic actions which, after first being carried out in the name of a community, were then performed in the name of rights and are now carried out in the name of self-determination. One may be either optimistic or pessimistic with regard to the outcome of the struggle between the state and democratic forces or with regard to the ability of social movements to resist the pressure of the ruling class. But social order and state order cannot be confused. I shall come back to this essential point. Social movements can be quashed by the administra-tive state: they do not have the state as an opponent and are not confused with the political democratic movements against the state, even when they strike up an alliance with these movements. Belief in the birth of new social movements and in the enlarging of their field of action can be accompanied by the fear of seeing society overrun by the state; but this belief is not condemned by the fear.

The social movements

Order and change

Social struggles are situated on the synchronic axis of social analysis. They have two branches, one of action and one of crisis. At the top of the former are to be found the social movements, opposed to which on the other branch are the critical revolutionary actions. This general analysis of popular movements can be completed by the parallel description of the struggles of the ruling classes. Let us now leave this axis in order to pass on to the diachronic axis. This moves from order to change, from the crystallization of a social domination to the transition from one societal type to another. Here the duality of the classes is replaced by that of the ruling elite and the masses, in other words, the state and the people. One should therefore consider successively four orders of action:

– The establishment and maintenance of order by the state;
– Popular behaviour in opposition to order;
– The role of the state in historical change, which is what I call here the mode of state intervention;
– The action of the social forces that respond to this intervention by the state.

As the sole aim of this book is to study collective action, I shall leave aside its opposite, i.e. the establishment and maintenance of order, which are themes on which a great part of sociological thinking in the past two decades has been centred. But before considering the positive aspects of change – the actions of historical transformation – we must describe the forms of behaviour in opposition to order, which could also be called *liberation* behaviour. These forms of behaviour set life in opposition to death, freedom of choice to prohibition, participation to exclusion. They are distinct from all other kinds of struggles in that they are not fighting against an identifiable adversary but against a social or cultural order defined primarily as an obstacle to a 'natural' development of exchanges and initiatives. Other struggles which are of the same nature, but opposite in orientation, are those directed against excess change which threatens what is no longer called order but equilibrium. The accelerated growth of recent decades has given growing importance to these movements of defiance against overcrowding, pollution, and the destruction of natural resources.

In *liberal* societies, these positive or negative forms of behaviour with regard to change are closely bound up with social struggles. While in the voluntarist societies the social struggles are indissolubly linked to historical struggles and even to the struggles of the state as a social agent of change, in the central capitalist societies social struggles are so closely bound up with cultural movements – which may be either favourable to the opening up of a society or, instead, hostile to excessive upheavals – that these cultural movements sometimes utterly dominate the social movements, with the result that all the character of social conflict is lost. What are at the outset reformist hopes, evidenced in educational progress or in women's protests, or else manifested by anxiety at the upsurge of anomy, have often been borne by social categories with no clear-cut position in class relations: intellectuals, in particular teachers and students, but also members of the elite rather than of the ruling class. We come across them constantly in our studies on the social struggles in contemporary France.

This is why – in order to avoid an ethnocentricity that has gravely distorted our representations of society – we need to consider here with greater attention the other pole of the diachronic axis, that of the state as an agent of historical transformation. This study concerns all societies but particularly those which are at a remove from the centre of the capitalist system in which state autonomy, in relation to the ruling class, is weakest.

The modes of state intervention

We must now turn to the *historical struggles*, which are defined as *social conflicts in a situation of historical change*, and more strictly as *social movements within a pattern of development*.

But before considering the social actors, we must recall the role of the state. In synchronic analysis, social classes and social movements confront each other; in diachronic analysis, all social categories are situated in relation to the state, the central agent of development. Furthermore – and this is essential here – this state is not only an apparatus or a power; as there is no complete separation between the order of the classes and the order of the state, the state also functions as a social agent, either of reaction or of change, of support for the dominant classes or, conversely, of support for a new ruling class or popular movement.

Consequently, even before considering historical struggles in the proper sense – actions carried out in relation to the state – one must recognize the state's role as a *social agent of historical change*. It is the combination, the connection or opposition of the modes of state intervention and of historical struggles which best explains the different social ways and forms of development.

One must isolate the instance of the central capitalist societies in which the state is most directly associated with the ruling class. Here, the mode of state intervention is weakly composed: it is reduced to

an aid to *modernization*. Social change seems almost completely endogenous, at least if one does not take into account the international
hegemony exercised by these societies and the economic advantages
they draw from it. Modernization is located at the level of organization
rather than at the higher levels: it is a combination of ideas and
calculations rather than of institutions and of power. More precisely, it
is situated at the extremities of the social system. On the one hand, it is
found in the organizations which have to meet new demands, expand
and modify their methods of production; and on the other hand it is
found in the historicity agencies and particularly in the intellectual
circles which invent new representations of culture and society. The
combination of new ideas and new techniques is the main mechanism
of modernization and it emerges best wherever class domination takes
the upper hand rather than where state power is preponderant.

In countries where the state is dominated less completely by a
weaker national ruling class, the mode of state intervention adopted is
that of *reform*. This reform takes place at institutional level and causes
the state to intervene more directly, but more as an agent of the
political system. The state assists towards the weakening of the relationships of reproduction in order to facilitate the institutionalization
of the conflicts that arise in the relationships of production. Advantages are offered to workers who have claims to make on the old
middle classes, for instance the landowners with private incomes and
the smallholders.

In these two instances, state intervention is very indirect: the state
encourages technical progress and new ideas or assists towards the
implementation of new institutions.

Let us now consider the most active modes of state intervention,
those which dominate the world *outside of the central capitalist countries*.
These modes of intervention confer a double role on the state: the
state, as agent of *change, is also empowered with social force*. Historical
struggles – if they bear an image of the state, in particular when a
national liberation movement is involved – are also related to a state
which is in itself a social force, at least insofar as it is not only an agent
of order, and hence the opponent of all social forces. This complementarity is everywhere to be encountered, e.g. in the populist
movements and in the national-popular state. The state takes over the
historical struggles, and these struggles likewise have an effect on the
state. This reminds us that the fusion of synchronic analysis and
diachronic analysis leads not only to the separation of two orders of
problem but also, and above all, to the recognition of the *mixed* character of historical behaviour. It is this admixture which justifies expressions such as the Socialist state or the Populist state, which at first sight

appear as shocking as those of the state bourgeoisie or of the state mode of production. The state is clearly not socialist or populist in itself, but it is empowered with socialist or populist forces. This is clear when one considers the world as a whole, but it is opposed to the image of the state as a simple agent of order, an image which is the one that most often prevails in France. In a great part of the world, it is impossible to deny that the state is a historical actor and not just an obstacle to a progress which would be ensured either by the bourgeoisie alone or by a popular drive, or even by the forces of the market and competition.

The modes of state intervention are thus defined by the combination of the role of the state and the nature of social forces. The state is either an agent of order – here described as despotic – or an agent of change, a liberating agent (which does not preclude the possibility of its being authoritarian). The social forces are situated either on the side of action or on the side of crisis. Thus a mode of state intervention is not defined in pure terms of change, as is a pattern of development – liberal, contractual, or voluntarist; it can be defined only in mixed terms, which are both social and statist. This is an admixture which governs the political experience of most of the world and which cannot be ignored by any research study on historical struggles.

The combination of these two axes brings out four main types of state intervention. In the figure, the two axes are not perpendicular; this illustrates graphically the idea that state autonomy depends on the

Forms of state intervention

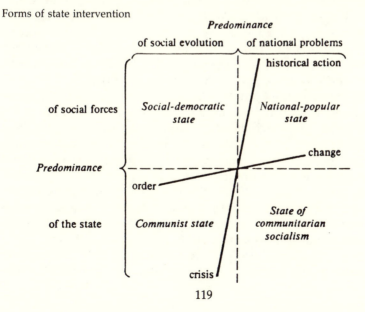

119

strength of the relationships of reproduction to the relationships of production. Whenever one has powerful relationships of production, and hence strong historical action, one is removed from a despotic state, one associated with the reproduction of privileges. A liberating state on the other hand reinforces the relationships of production at the same time as it strengthens economic development. The reasons for which the two axes are not perpendicular lead us to consider two of the four modes of state intervention as being the principal ones, and the two others as secondary. The principal types are more strongly structured, since they are compressed between the two axes, while the secondary types cover more varied situations.

1. I have used the term *national-popular state*, an expression borrowed from G. Germani,* to describe the mode of intervention that is most important from the point of view of an analysis of social movements, the mode in which the movements are most positively associated with state action since the social system is present in its positive aspect, the mode in which social movements, institutional pressures and organizational demands are entailed, while the state is battling against dependence on a colonizer instead of maintaining a despotic order, and is consequently more open to social movements or other types of positive struggle. This form of state intervention is familiar to a considerable part of the Third World, in particular Latin America, but also the Mediterranean countries and the Middle East. The most striking feature of this intervention is *nationalism*: it is not a peculiar feature, but it is one which is more central in this type of regime than in others. Outside domination leads to the *dismembering* of dependent societies. Since economic power lies in the hands of foreigners, the internal social and cultural life of these countries acquires extreme autonomy. Outside of the enclaves or zones governed by foreign capitalism there reigns a social domination which is more concerned with its own privileges than with its profits.

The modernized sector draws on manpower and capital from the rest of the country, which then finds itself increasingly excluded from economic growth, as for instance the peasant communities of the Andes, deprived of their lands and irresistibly dragged into decadence by the development of the great capitalist domains. In these dual societies, the state sets itself the principal task of reuniting the country and creating the conditions for its own existence. It is this that gives rise to its nationalism, which has been associated in the most diverse ways with populist movements. Here, nationalism is the creation of the state and of the middle class, created or aided by the state, rather than of the popular movements. The state may stir up demonstrations of nationalism as soon as it sets itself the aim of integrating the poorest classes or the immigrants into the nation.

2. I define the *communist state* as the statist mode of historical change which emerges as a solution for a society in crisis and for a despotic state, i.e. one which answers to a doubly negative situation which unleashes a *revolutionary upheaval* born of a critical action, but which also gives birth to a new state. Communist intervention is associated with the struggle for national liberation against foreign imperialism and against an autocracy whose weakness is both a cause of and party to foreign economic and military invasion. In Vietnam, the communist party demonstrated most impressively its ability to perform three roles: those of national liberation, economic modernization and class action. This act of triple liberation, which exerts such great worldwide influence, is far removed from the struggles for the defence and extension of the freedoms enjoyed in the central capitalist societies and even in the dependent societies. The call for *freedoms* makes itself heard when class movement or institutional pressure coincides with a desire for modernization, associated therefore with the positive side of the functioning society. The call for *liberation* is made by a state or by a counter-state against despotism and dependence with regard to foreign powers. Thus the two aspects of class relations – one of which is close to political institutions and the other to state power – lead, by using almost the same words, to two totally opposed political regimes. The liberation regimes are not softminded with regard to liberties, and those who must respect the liberties are also those who dominate the dependent or colonized countries.

3. The intervention which occurs in the zone which combines the positive aspects of the social system and a traditional state order can be described as *social-democratic*. Such regimes have in particular become installed on the periphery of the capitalist centre, where the ruling class runs up against cultural and political obstacles. The state intervenes here by combining the action of social movements with the modernizing and liberal struggle against archaism.

These countries are sufficiently close to the main centres of economic development for the class relations and conflicts to hold a central position there, but they also manifest either elements of archaism or else an external dependence which causes a central role to be assigned to a voluntarist state. The social-democrat state lies at the meeting-point between Labour pressure and a modernizing state. The further one is removed from modern class relations the more important becomes the role of the state in social-democracy, until the point is reached when it breaks its conflictual link with Labour trade-unionism and attaches itself to the social forces geared to the breakdown of a paralysing order: this is what marks the transition from the social-democrat state to the Communist state. Conversely, in the countries which have been more clearly industrialized by their national ruling class, the social-democrat state weakens, and becomes at best a welfare state, while trade-unionist independence gains in strength.

Modern France, like many European capitalist countries, has been exposed to a social-democrat current, but one which was never able to become united and make itself independent of other forms of organization of the political life. For it has been a peculiar feature of this country to be one of the pioneers of industrialization while still leaving the state an extremely important role.

4. Finally, the weakest mode of state intervention is the one which occurs in response to the combination of a society in crisis and a state liberating the country from its dependence. The more violently colonization has dismembered the national society the more deep-reaching is the social crisis. The state then cannot but be an all-powerful actor devoted to imposing a national unity which is far from actually existing. This *communitarian socialism* often leads ultimately to the hyper-development of the state and its doctrine and to a notable disparity between the actual social reality and the image of it furnished by the state.

These modes of state intervention can be regrouped according to the axes which have served to establish them. Wherever the state is dependent and is endeavouring to become liberating, the *national* – historicist – theme predominates; conversely, wherever the state is despotic from the outset, it is the evolutionist and *economic* theme which becomes over-riding. On the other hand, in a society in crisis, where the negative movements outweigh the positive movements, the *state* plays a role more central than that of the social forces, while in social-democrat and national-popular situations, where the relationships of production, the institutions and the organizations function positively, the *social forces* intervene more directly within the state and around it.

Two forms of the breakdown of state intervention

In state intervention, the association between social forces and state power is unstable. The state can either become a pure agent of power or, instead, change itself into an instrument for shaping a ruling class.

1. In the former instance, the state's main objective is no longer the

construction of a new society defined by investment and by new forms of social participation, but rather the development of its own *power*, the control of investment, and above all the control or prohibition of social movements. Here, the state becomes the agent of a *social counter-movement*. This movement is not the class opponent of a social movement, nor is it the social movement of the ruling class; it is the intervention of the state against social movements. The outcome of this counter-movement may be the creation of an authoritarian politi- cal movement, the avowed adversary of social movements of all kinds, acting in the name of national unity and integration, and hence in the interests of the state itself. These counter movements are *dictatorships*, backed up by integrist doctrines. It is, however, preferable not to label them all as fascist, since fascism is a term which would be appropriate for only some of them. The national-popular regimes lead towards a type of integrism which can be described as *nationalist dictatorship* if the dependent society has been forcibly split and dismembered, for the state then becomes extremely independent of the social struggles, which are likewise split.

In the regimes of *communitarian socialism*, the gap is even narrower between the regime itself and the patrimonial dictatorships which turn the head of state into the Father-provider and Father-chastiser of a whole people. These integrist dictatorships become more violent and have more tragic consequences whenever they are less nationalist and whenever the social movements preceding them have had greater importance and independence. In the *Communist* regimes, the connec- tion between the State-Party and the national and social liberation movement is replaced – when the connection breaks down – by the omnipotence of the State-Party, which then becomes the exclusive interpreter of a struggle which initially aimed only at destroying de- spotism and dependence, but which soon comes to repress the social movements and independent forms of political and cultural life. This *ideocratic dictatorship* establishes the most complete system of the domination of society by the state. Finally, the societies which have experienced powerful *social-democratic* intervention are those in which capitalist industrialization has been thwarted by social and cultural archaisms, which is the reason for the state's having acquired a central role. These societies, which in periods of prosperity develop towards the large-scale institutionalization of powerful and combative class movements and towards Labour-oriented democracy, can in periods of crisis veer towards *fascism*; when this happens, not only do the social conflicts become aggravated, but also the national existence imposed by the state seems to become dissolved. Here, unlike the example of the United States or Great Britain, the economic crisis becomes a national crisis. This state integrism, or extreme nationalist ideology, looks for support primarily to the middle classes in crisis and – without altering the class relations – bans popular movements, justifying this prohibition in the name of a national interest exalted to mythical heights and leading to the fight against foreigners or against the 'impure' and – as in Nazi Germany in particular – ending in their extermination. Whatever their differences may be, these dictatorships turn the state into an agent of power rather than an agent of development.

2. Socio-historical intervention by the state can also *break down and take the opposite direction*, by giving priority to the state's civil action, i.e. to the *ruling class* formed by the state or within it. The determining role of the state in the industrialization of Germany, Italy or Japan was most often placed at the service of the construction of a national capitalism, which, although marked by the conditions of its development, did form an integral part of the capitalist system. This tendency recurs in all the modes of state intervention. If the *national-popular regimes* may at times veer towards nationalist military dictatorships, they most often become transformed into regimes of *conservative modernization* – to borrow the expression of Barrington Moore Jr* – which may aid a national capitalism but most often develop an important public industrial sector, while at the same time aiding the multinational companies and giving important advantages to a national bourgeoisie, dependent on this sector, incapable of replacing the multinational companies, and therefore constituting more a class for backing up this *peripheral state capitalism*, in which Latin America, with Brazil and Mexico in the forefront, is uneasily balancing. Beginning with *communitarian socialism*, the development which is opposed to the reinforcement of the paternalistic dictatorship is the predominant penetration of foreign companies, often multinational companies, with which there is associated what may be called an *authoritarian neo-colonized state*. The *social democracy* which develops – as most often happens – towards the *social-capitalism* at present being experienced in the Federal Republic of Germany, is a social democracy that has replaced state intervention in order to eliminate the archaic forms of social domination by intervening in favour of better social and economic programming of the capitalist system. Finally, the *communist* regimes which have been attracted on the one hand towards ideocratic dictatorship, are on the other hand attracted by *state technocracy*, i.e. by the growing importance of the function of the ruling class within the state apparatus.

In all these instances, a transition is being effected from a pattern of development to a mode of production, without the former being however merely the road which might lead towards a Rome which would still remain the classic capitalist economy. One must deny any analytical privileges to the liberal pattern of development, while at the same time refusing to confine the patterns of development within the limits of their specificity. They give historical form to a mode of production.

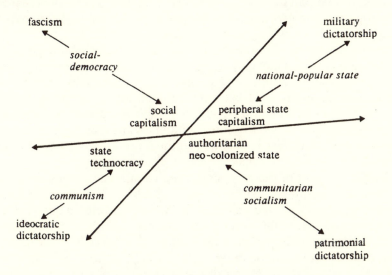

The diagram illustrates all the forms in the breakdown of state intervention. It shows the two opposing forms in the breakdown of each mode of state intervention. The outward directed arrow locates the 'pure' form of the state, which is marked by the diminution of the state's role as the agent of a ruling class. The inward moving arrow, on the other hand, is directed towards the accentuation of this class role of the state.

The types of historical struggle

This scheme of the modes of state intervention and their forms of breakdown leads us into the study of historical struggles. If the social movements occur within a type of society and if the modes of state intervention are a process of transition from one society to another, the historical struggles occur at the meeting of the twain, as the name indeed indicates. The epithet 'historical' reminds us that these struggles do not occur inside an analytical framework but within concrete historical ensembles, particularly in national societies, which are simultaneously social systems and communities in the process of becoming historical. The historical struggles are therefore realities closer to observable social practice than are the social movements. But here too one must recognize the *primacy of synchronic analysis*. The social struggles should be analysed as *modifications of social movements under the effect of a mode of state intervention*, as an expression of social struggles, but within a particular political regime.

It would be paradoxical – at the start of a programme of research bearing on French society – not to return here to the first comments made on historical struggles in the central capitalist societies. Their main orientation is to combine class action with democratic political action, a proletarian movement with popular pressure, which presupposes the use of institutional reform mechanisms and enables an alliance to be established between the working class and so-called elements of the middle classes, which are defined not so much in terms of class as by their access to political influence, and which are therefore hostile to the authoritarian state or to the sway exerted by the ruling class over the political system.

At the moment of the great crisis, the communist parties rejected this alliance, wishing to maintain a pure class line, a strictly proletarian action, which contributed – as Ernesto Laclau* has pointed out – to the middle classes being rejected from an alliance with the working class and to their being trapped in an ideological crisis which led to Fascism. The Popular Front, on the other hand, brought success to a historical struggle by allying the action of the working class with democratic political mobilization against a crisis of the economy and of the state and against the fascist threat. Today, the new social movements are striving primarily to entrench their position by rejecting any alliance with democratic political forces. This leftism cannot help leading again to the isolation of the middle categories, i.e. those whose class situation is not clear-cut and who therefore orient their behaviour towards the state in order to define the crisis in political or national terms and to give priority to the maintenance of order. The seeking or rejecting of an alliance between the new social movements and the democratic forces must become one of the main themes to be studied in sociological analysis.

Let us now return to the non-liberal modes of state intervention.

Here I shall give only a brief outline of these historical struggles, since they can be properly studied only by reference to concrete historical cases.

1. In *national-popular* regimes in which the state is a historical agent of development, the social movements preserve an extremely autonomous existence. Consequently, historical struggles have a class

dimension. The state, being either dependent or liberating, introduces from its side a *national* dimension into the struggles; furthermore, since a society is closer to the pole of innovation than to that of crisis, action against dependence is manifested by a *modernizing* orientation. This leads to the formation of the types of struggle I analysed in speaking of Latin America, struggles which *simultaneously incorporate a class orientation, a nationalist or anti-imperialist orientation, and a modernizing orientation*. I have mentioned elsewhere how these three elements can be variously combined in different situations. The diversity of the components of these struggles not only relegates them to a low level of integration, to a low project level, it also makes them particularly heteronomous, as is well demonstrated by the trade-union situation, which is often created by the state and almost always under strict state control. Historical struggles appear to be extremely powerful when they mobilize both social forces and the state together. But the source of their strength is also the cause of their weakness: their ability to withstand hostile state action is extremely weak. Hence the contradictory judgements pronounced on these movements: some see in them merely a form of political control of protest by an authoritarian state; others claim to discover in them the most important form of populism, generated by a nationalist middle class and bound to a state struggling against outside domination in the name of the dependent people. This latter interpretation best defines these struggles, but the former rightly reminds us of their fragility and hence of their poor capacity to instigate mass mobilization of the 'small' townfolk.

Populist and nationalist movements have *variants* corresponding to the forms of the *breakdown* of national-popular state intervention. If this intervention degenerates into nationalist dictatorship, thus losing its social charge in order to benefit its specifically statist role, the populist movement undergoes transformation, becoming reduced to violent combative state action, ostensibly in the interests of the people: this is a *revolutionary nationalism*, of which the Argentinian Montoneros offer the most important example, after the Uruguayan Tupamaros. Conversely, the reinforcement of the class dimension of this nationalist state causes the populist movements to evolve towards *truly revolutionary class themes*, as can be best observed in Brazil and Mexico.

2. In a *communitarian socialist state*, the state occupies the entire political scene, and the social movements are weakened by the absence of a direct link between the great mass of the population and the centres of economic decision-making. These movements tend to be split between *communitarian withdrawal* on the one hand and *participation in state power* on the other. Wherever urbanization and the penetration of market

and industrial economy are furthest advanced, it becomes possible for more consistent struggles to emerge, but these struggles always take the form of political movements, often controlled by the state. The underlying themes centre on defence of the community, involving appeals to a specific cultural or national quality against dependence or colonization, which are held to be responsible for the destruction of the social and cultural organization. The stakes in this struggle are represented by the construction of a national state. It is in this tension between the communitarian rejection of foreign domination and the support for the creation of a national state that the dynamics of the struggle reside. African messianic movements, or movements appealing either to pan-Arabism or to the defence of Islam are important examples of these forces which become involved in the construction of a modern state by means of state agents in the proper sense – most often military agents – following the Nasser model, or the Baathist, whether Iraqi or Syrian, or various other models in Africa south of the Sahara. Here too the breakdown of state intervention transforms the historical struggles. The more the state becomes a patrimonial dictatorship the more this popular movement becomes separated from it and reinforces its communitarian orientation, which is occasionally even an orientation of *ethnic defence*. By contrast, a more powerful link between this state and neo-colonialism produces an opposition movement which takes on a *class* orientation but which develops mainly within categories such as the *students*, who are more in contact with foreign domination.

3. In a *social-democrat* state, which is an agent of modernization but in the service of a national ruling class, the main actor in the historical struggles is *trade-unionism*, which is reinforced by mutual aid societies, cooperatives, popular education movements, etc. and which imposes more an institutional pressure of the Labour type than a class struggle. As for the state, it becomes largely identified with the political system owing to an extension of representative democracy, not only in purely political life and in working life, but also in numerous spheres of activity. These social forces and this state, both equally reformatory, become associated in a *moralistic* climate. Morals play the role here which the national state played in the situations earlier described, as though the absent social movement and the state, freed both of its role of reproduction and of its role of conquest, had been replaced by their opposites, by struggle and by willed historical transformation, i.e. the entrenching of a community of values rather than of traditions, of a modernizing rather than a traditionalist force. The breakdown of this form of state intervention modifies historical struggles in two very

different ways. If the social-democratic state is developing towards social-capitalism, the popular movement is fighting for *self-organization*, as is demonstrated by the importance of public committees in this type of society. Conversely, if the fascist state is substituted for social democracy, the opposition movement cannot but take charge again of the social dimension, and even the class dimension, disregarded by the state. *Anti-fascism* has not been the prerogative of movements of Marxist inspiration, but these movements have been the constant and resolute adversaries of Fascist states.

4. Finally, in a *communist regime* it is difficult to speak of historical struggles, and hence of social movements, even if they are immensely changed. The double struggle against crisis and against autocracy has created a new state, all the more powerful for having had to fight harder to triumph over attacks from outside, and all the more dominating for the increasing weakness of the class struggles in the old regime. The state engages actively in its task of historical transformation and mobilizes society in order to attain its aims. Communist intervention produces a popular movement. This movement, like the national-popular regimes, combines a modernizing dimension, a national dimension and a class dimension, but, instead of these three components being weakly linked to each other, as we have seen in the case of the popular movements of Latin America, they are here closely united within the militant action of a *party*. This party fights the foreigner, acts in the name of the worker or peasant class, and sees itself as the agent of industrialization. Nowhere else is this link between state intervention and popular movement as close as it is here, but it would be going too far to reduce the Communist movement in these regimes to an artificial mobilization. When the Communist regime develops either towards ideocratic dictatorship or towards state technocracy – and after the Stalinist period of the physical liquidation of all forms of opposition – opposition movements are able to form in spite of the intensity of the repression. One must now, therefore, distinguish between two types of opposition. The intellectuals appeal to *democratization* or at least call for a progressive opening up of the regime against an ideocratic dictatorship. This opposition becomes powerfully expressed when the political isolation and the violence of the repression begin to wane, which emphasizes the fact that this is opposition to the state rather than to a form of social domination.

The movements opposed to state technocracy, and hence to a ruling class, are however very different. Here the historical struggle changes into a social struggle in an elementary form of social movement. It is a struggle which is no longer waged by the liberal intellectuals but by dissidents, in the form of resistance to the crushing of society. It is a struggle waged in the name of a people, a culture, and straight survival in the face of a social domination closely associated with absolute political power and restrictive cultural domination. It is not yet a class struggle but a movement of *popular defence* quite different from the democratic liberalism for which the anti-authoritarian intellectuals fight. The strength of a man such as Solzhenitsyn is to have revealed – while also exposing the immense horror of the Gulag – the nature of this popular resistance to despotism. The content and the orientations of this movement may vary, but the resistance can never develop into a true social movement because the state completely crushes society.

Diagram of the historical struggles (outside of the central capitalist countries)

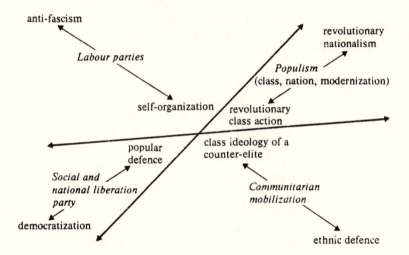

This diagram should be compared with the previous one. It indicates two types of historical struggle which correspond to a mode of state intervention, in the way that populism corresponds to the national-popular state, and it also marks the position of the two opposed forms of the transformation of these historical struggles corresponding either to the decline of dictatorial state intervention (the outward pointing arrow) or to its transformation into an agent for shaping a ruling class (inward pointing arrow).

These reflexions have been brief, all the more so since the research work to which this book is an introduction is at present limited to French society. But it is vital to understand what it is that separates a *historical struggle* from a *social movement* or a *mode of state intervention*, for the organized forms of collective behaviour on which we shall focus our attention will still have to be analysed from different angles. And it would be particularly unacceptable to claim to study facts observed in France by means of notions worked out in a strictly national context. It is most mistaken to portray national societies as a caravan, the train of which has to follow the route marked out by the preceding vehicles, so that the carriages in front can be studied without any concern for those at the rear.

There is no longer any substantiation for the pride of conquering nations. Western Europe has become the main zone of investment for the multinational firms, the great majority of which are American. These firms are able to establish peripheral – and therefore dependent – capitalism here, and this greatly reduces the distance which used to separate America from certain countries, in Latin America or else-where, on the way towards dependent industrialization. In order to understand the Occitanist movement, for instance, it is not impossible to use ideas borrowed from Latin America. Besides, have not the social and political movements of recent decades in Western Europe reacted more vigorously to the problems of the Third World than to those of their own countries?

Social movements and historical change

How far we are from social movements! The distance is immense that separates class struggles from the behaviour of historical change; it is even greater than this rapid analysis would suggest. For, the more our attention is focussed on change and on historical struggles, the more these struggles seem to govern social struggles and in particular social movements, and the more still these movements become broken down and even changed into something utterly different from what they were. The structural problems of society then become almost com-pletely overshadowed by those of its change. In the case of liberal societies, whose development is most directly controlled by the ruling class, social movement is initially reduced to the institutional level, which is true of trade-unionism in the majority of industrial countries – at least to a large extent; next, social movement is reduced to the organizational level, becoming an organ of straightforward protest, by which it may ultimately be led even to participating in the exercise of authority, as may be seen whenever a delegate of the personnel is sufficiently strong to oblige the staff controllers to come to agreement with him in order to have their instructions respected. The following step leads to the incorporation of the representatives of the old social movement in the decision-making system. And, finally, the repre-sentatives come round to defending the social system against that by

131

which it is threatened. How many trade unions and trade unionists have ended up not only as co-administrators but as full managers, often ardent defenders of the firm, of new technological methods and of the battle for production?

This developmental pattern can be illustrated as in the first figure below. In a voluntarist society, the pattern is different and the reversal of positions more drastic (see the second figure below).

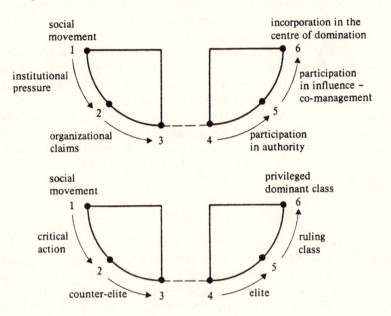

The social movement does not penetrate gradually into the organization and into the management system; it changes tack, becoming reversed into critical action, i.e. it attacks the state more than the ruling class, and forms around itself an avant-garde militant revolutionary organization which becomes the new state power after the revolutionary crisis. It is within this power structure that there develops a new ruling class which rapidly acquires the characteristics and the powers of a dominant class. This evolution occurs both in formerly dependent or colonized countries and in Communist regimes.

Class and nation

In concluding, we must return to the most general aspect of the relations between function and change, between the ruling class and the state in the domain of the social struggles. This aspect is the complementarity of *class movements and national movements*. No other problem has remained so constantly at the centre of thought on the social movements. It appeared in theoretical thinking largely thanks to Austro-Marxism. And it is a central problem in all parts of the world where social struggles collide with foreign domination, a despotic state, or a combination of the two. The national movement is a response to state domination, just as the workers' movement is a response to class domination. The national problems do not constitute a testing-ground for class struggles, any more than the class struggles disappear in the confrontation between the nation and the state, either national or foreign.

It is not possible to identify the national movement with the forma-tion of the bourgeois economy and to contrast it with a workers' internationalism as an answer to the internationalization of industrial capital. The history of central Europe has likewise revealed the futility of the Austro-Marxist compromise, recognizing the nation's cultural autonomy against imperial bureaucratic centralism, but placing over this autonomy the unifying force of a political life dominated by the clash between the workers' movement and capitalism. The Brünn programme was adopted by the social-democrat party in 1899, but in 1911 the socialist workers of Bohemia voted for the separatist, auton-omist wing of the Party, against its unitarian tendency. What we are in fact dealing with are not successive stages in history but rather two orders of problems which do not seem to have been confused except in countries, such as France and England, where early on there was formed a national state corresponding to a political system that became increasingly enlarged. By contrast, the Habsburg monarchy is the perfect example of a state that remained dynamic instead of becoming national. It was therefore on the territory of this state that for the first time national struggles intersected with social struggles. Since that period, there has been a constant resurgence of revolutionary national-ist parties bent on uniting national claims and social claims, but this endeavour has always met with failure, resulting in the tearing apart of revolutionary nationalism, as among the Basques or the Irish, or with the Latin-American guerrillas or the African socialist move-ments.

But one should not stop short after having defined these two orders of movement. The overall structure of this analysis requires that they also be combined, since the struggle against a state is also a battle against foreign class domination or against an obstacle in the way of economic development. A class movement cannot develop outside the centre of the capitalist system unless it takes national interests in hand, in the form of the economic progress and political independence of a community.

133

This is already true in France, where the appeal to the nation has caused the living community, its work and its struggles to be opposed to the archaism of the state, the agent of defence and of the handing on of privileges, and hence an obstacle to economic progress. This explains the *progressivist* character of the national theme among a great proportion of the left-wing and the connection made between the social theme and the national theme in the Paris Commune or in the thinking of Jean Jaurès. When one shifts much further away from the centre of the capitalist system, one has rather to wonder how it is that the national struggle concerns itself with class signification, instead of the reverse occurring. In despotic regimes, dominated by an autocratic state which is more a defender of privileges or beliefs than the agent of a still weak or foreign-dominated ruling class, the appeal to the nation is also a call to the popular classes, an appeal to their dominated side and no longer, as in the central countries, to whatever may belong to their anti-establishment side. This theme recurs in the most highly colonized societies, those in which social and cultural organization is destroyed by colonial administration. And in struggling against this domination how can one turn for support to anything but that which is most traditional, most deep-rooted, and hence least exposed to penetration from external forces? This is a thoroughgoing populism which may be dissipated in a purely negative cultural resistance, but which may also become allied to an action of political rupture. The struggle against the state is associated with leaning for support on the poor peasants or on the proletarized middle strata.

It is in the colonized societies that national action most clearly gains the upper hand, as occurs with guerrilla action directed against the state and against foreign domination. Fidel Castro and Che Guevara repeated often enough that the struggle in the Sierra was not at that stage revolutionary, and that it was only during a second phase that the defeaters of Batista undertook the revolutionary transformation of their society.

This was an extreme case because it was a response to an extreme denationalization of the state; but most decolonization struggles are comparable, and appeal still more to a national theme than to social themes which are introduced via the attack against the appropriation of national resources by foreign businesses. By contrast, in societies which are simply dependent, i.e. subject to economic domination but not to foreign sovereignty, class action and national action become combined rather than internally unified. This is what has occurred in the major Latin American countries and it is this that represents the chief difference between these countries and the Arab world reacting against a colonial situation. In the Arab countries, the integration of these two movements has never been firm, which explains why such importance was accorded to state intervention of the national-popular type, since the connection between the two currents occurred at state level and not within the popular movements.

Our conclusion is of general scope: *social struggles* and *national struggles* are not two branches of the same social movement. Nor are they entirely separated. And they are most closely linked wherever the capitalist domination is that of the international capitalist system and not that of a national bourgeoisie. But in this case – where one might be inclined to think that totally revolutionary movements would be formed – one finds that on the contrary the social forces and the national forces of opposition tear each other apart. This then runs counter to the simplicity of, on the one hand, a social movement invested with a national sense, and, on the other hand, struggles against the despotic state associated with foreign powers and controlled by an armed revolutionary party speaking in the name of the most dominated classes.

Conclusions

1. The first conclusion to be drawn from these reflections on social and historical struggles is that they preclude the hypothesis of there being a unique central principle which might explain both functioning and change, class domination and state power, social struggles and national struggles. Instead, these social struggles cause the social movements to jut out like a precipitous rock-face battered by opposing currents: on the one side, the current in which new powers and new states are formed, and on the other the stream which dreams of continued, pragmatic, liberal and libertarian change.

The interest of concrete research is to show, with respect to a particular case, how so many different and often conflicting forces come to be combined. Depending on the periods and the countries under consideration, the restitution of social movements to the central place in the analysis takes on many different meanings: at one time it is the neglected role of breakdown and violence that will be stressed; at another, it will be shown instead that the social movement has already become the opponent of the power born in its own bowels.

At the time and in the place where I am now writing I should like, by placing social movements at the centre of sociology, to react against the loss of history and perhaps even the *loss of historicity* by which we are threatened. Our society, which believes in the end of the great conflicts in the name of abundance or else, by contrast, in the name of the omnipresence of power, no longer sees itself as a conveyer of history.

In order to help our society not to accept decadence, I should like it to listen to the growing sound of new battles within it, I should like it to rediscover hope and anger, and to discover itself, not any longer as a material object or as the product of a dominant ideology, but as a field for social movements, social struggles and historical struggles.

2. By setting social movements and all the forms of collective action at the centre of the analysis of societies, I also wanted – at a more theoretical level – to refuse to subordinate social activity to a higher order which would also be the law of historical evolution. Any reference, direct or indirect, to a Spirit, whether it be called the World, God, Man or History, must be dismissed. This refusal entails another: the analysis of society is not that of its reproduction, of its functional demands, or of its submission to human nature; by suppressing transcendence we have also caused the idea of a nature of society to disappear.

3. But this double liberation, which comprehends both action and creation, also threatens our societies with subjugation and self-destruction. Though liberated from the Gods, they may still make themselves divine and submit themselves to laws which are all the more severe for being no longer based on absolute principles, which formerly served as a means of recourse as much as one of justification.

The state becomes the brute incarnation of reason. On the other hand, this society, which exalts its creative power and identifies it with an absolute power, suffocates itself by subjecting to its creative power a nature of increasing fragility, no matter whether one is concerned with natural resources or with the biological and psychological behaviour of human beings. This is a triumph of power and of the ruling class which ultimately leads to the proletarization of nature and to far more general crises than those which affected only the economy. The post-industrial societies, which I have proposed describing as *programmed*, cannot survive by transforming the Gods into the state and nature into primary matter. What may appear to some as an advance is no more than a pathology.

4. This means that one must place at the starting-point of the analysis two ideas which lend their meaning to the sociology of action and assist it in struggling against the dangers by which we are threatened. The first of these ideas is that a society's capacity for action on itself – its historicity – can never be confused with an order; it no longer derives from a metasocial world but it maintains a distance in relation to order and to the state, for it is at the same time creativity and social conflict.

Society, liberated from the Gods, must today fight against the power by which it is being devoured.

5. The second idea is that whatever resists to power and to its desire for order is not a moral principle or a natural force but a double appeal by social movements to historicity and to 'naturality'. The first challenges the power by which this historicity is appropriated; the second resists the ever-increasing sway of laws and rules. Neither can go without the other. If our society were reduced to its historicity, it would not be able to prevent this historicity from being confused with the absolute power of the state. And if our society wanted to return to a state of pure 'naturality', it would have to impose such violent constraints that it would suffocate in communities wholly bent on quashing historicity and its innovations. As ever, the ruling class seeks to identify the society with a historicity which it controls; the novelty lies in the fact that this effort now entails the reinforcement of state power and not, as during previous centuries in the West, its weakening. By contrast, the popular movements appeal to 'naturality', while in the past they derived support from traditional cultures; but they cannot undertake the reconquest and collective reappropriation of historicity unless they abandon communitarian utopias in order to push their protest up as far as class relations and the systems of historical action themselves.

6. Thus it is by studying social movements that one becomes able to construct a new image of society. The principal stakes in a sociology of action are: overthrow the old subjugation of social facts to a metasocial order, and in particular the submission to economic facts and to the supposed laws of evolution; battle against the reduction of liberated historicity to an absolute state power; prepare the popular counter-offensive which, beginning from a defensive withdrawal towards communitarian utopias, should reconquer the entire system of action in order to obtain the joint triumph of social conflict and cultural innovation.

7. I prefer not to end on this note of hope but rather with the expression of a disquieting thought which could rapidly become vertiginous. And this is that social movements appear to be fragile, and on the map of societies they appear as tiny as in the atlas the little cape of Asia where they were formed! In these societies which have been most recently and most peacefully industrialized themselves, are not social movements on their way to disappearing, crushed by mass society? Does not the opposition of social groups already belong to the past, while we are now experiencing the triumph of the forces of the unification and

domination of society? Confronted with this reign of the One and of the homogeneous, still masked beneath the enchanting features of equality, should one not be claiming the right to difference rather than the need for conflict? This is a disquieting thought that suffices to remind us that if social movements take place in the heart of society, society most often seems to disappear under the weight of the state. But since we have had the privilege of living several centuries in increasingly civil societies, is not our duty to seek the great alliance between the liberating struggle against the state and a social conflict to prevent this struggle from being waged only for the profit of the leaders of civil society? No study of social movements today can afford to ignore that its sphere does not comprehend all social reality; it is still more impossible to believe that the social struggle is naturally associated with the triumph of the state over the oligarchies, but one must defend the priority to be given in analysis to the conflicts and movements that animate a civil society, which, without them, would be unable to defend itself against the state.

PART TWO

SOCIOLOGICAL INTERVENTION

7

vvvvvvvvvvvvvvvvvvvvvvvvvvvvvvvvvvvvvvvvvvvvvvvvvvvvvvvvvvvvvvvv

The object and the method

In the first part of this book, I defined the main lines of a truly sociological analysis, or at least the core of this analysis. But of what good will it have been if this effort – so long pursued – fails to lead to the adoption of a new practice? We are a bit tired of learning what the sociologists think; we want to ask them what they are doing. And if a theoretical approach believes it can delineate the central areas of social life, it must put forward a specific method which would enable analysis to reach these areas.

Let us recall what was our starting-point: sociology studies social relations. Its main method should, therefore, make possible the direct observation and analysis of these relations. If one is to take as the object of study a situation, a trend or an opinion, one is already distancing oneself from the main field of sociology. This is why the old division of society into 'institutions' – the family, political power, the company, the town, etc. – has long been abandoned and replaced by new subdivisions which can all, directly or indirectly, be defined in terms of social relations: organizations and their relations of authority; political decisions and the influences leading to them; class relations and systems of order considered in their function of exclusion and elimination. But these social relations are not readily visible, indeed, they are more or less masked by order and domination. Sociology's chief problem is to bring these relations to the surface, so as no longer to be the dupe of the categories of social practice. This then presupposes the active *intervention* of the sociologist. His task is to bring out these social relations concealed behind a mesh of approved and organized practices. How is this to be managed? If one agrees that the relations are overlaid by order and domination, one must first turn to whatever is dominated and subjected to order, to whatever is

139

protesting and whatever is excluded. Not in order to give special emphasis to these forms of behaviour or the ideologies by which they are backed up, but in order to bring out the buried, hidden side of social relations and so discover them in their fullness. It is also necessary to discover the dominant actor behind the order and its technical, administrative, or moral categories, its social interests and its cultural orientations. Thus one arrives at a definition of *sociological intervention*: *it is the action of the sociologist, whose aim is to reveal social relations and make them the main object of analysis.* The first problem which sociology has to tackle is, naturally, that of social movements, because this is the most central problem. Moveover, the conflict between class actors for control of a cultural field is more difficult to disguise than the struggle of the outcasts against established order or the demands of members of an organization for an improved position within the organization. The disadvantage, as we shall see, is that the visibility of these great social relations is matched by the strength of the antagonistic ideologies. All too often, the history of social movements has contented itself with reproducing these ideologies and with lauding the grand exploits of the heroes of history. But we shall find a means of overcoming this difficulty. I should like the purpose of this methodological research to be clear: we are not concerned with outlining techniques or procedures but with inventing a method which will correspond to the sociological approach towards social movements and, more generally, to collective action.

A different approach

A method is not freely chosen. Each method presupposes a given idea of the nature of the facts under consideration. Anyone who wishes to follow up the development of a phenomenon must establish his series: and anyone who is interested in individual choice and in consumption – taken in the broadest sense – must establish a connection between statistical methods of preference, intentions, or real choices and categories of actors. By contrast, the study of a decision cannot be carried out in this way: it must re-establish all the actions which have exerted an influence. In this respect, both questionnaire investigation and historical research prove inadequate. Particularly historical research, since it recognizes only written documents or monuments produced by the social organization for clearly-defined aims, and because most often it is impossible to reconstruct the decision-making process purely from these documents, which do not allow one fully to grasp the relations between individuals, groups, or social forces. One must therefore reconstruct the field of decision-making by examining the actors, and occasionally by simulating the political process. The social movements are even more remote than the decisions belonging to the sphere of statistical investigation and to the domain of the historians. The historical documents relating to these movements are extremely inadequate, all the more so when a movement is weakly organized and engages few intellectuals. An abundance of historical documents may, on the other hand, prove to be quite the opposite of a wealth of material if these documents turn out to be no more than statements of belief, propagandist texts, or ideological tracts. A social movement is vigorously involved in conflict: the documents it produces are overtly ideological, and, the more agitated the conflict, the more difficult it is to gather observations which are not immediately declarations of a side taken. And, finally, the researcher himself, who approaches bodies of statistics without difficulty and who already experiences somewhat more trouble in discerning the underside of a decision, is most often kept at a distance from a social movement. How often have we not heard it said that our sociological studies could be of benefit only to the political and economic rulers, who are alone in being able to analyse and use the information gathered, although the popular movements were interested in receiving information on the situation to which they were being subjected and also on the organization or the intentions of their adversaries. The fear of being spied upon is just as great as the desire to be informed about the enemy. It would seem, then, that anything is easier to study than social movements. Questionnaires enable us to become informed about sets of statistics, while historical documents, traditions and texts provide us with information on what is most organized and standardized in a society: legal documents – like prison buildings – tell us much about the concepts of legality and of deviation from the law or criminality which a state or a ruling class endeavours to impose on society. But how is one to apprehend a conflictual collective action? How is one to comprehend this work of society upon itself, this drama in which a history is being invented, the text of which has not been pre-determined? And in what position is the analyst to be placed? If he becomes integrated into the movement, he is no more than an ideologist; if he remains neutral or removed, he is rejected; if he becomes the question-poser, his questions destroy the movement by soliciting individual opinions where collective action exists, or by requiring answers to a situation when it is the movement itself that is redefining the situation. Nonetheless, the ideas set out in the first part of this book oblige us to invent a method for the study of social movements, by abandoning the representation of society as a body of functions and rules, techniques and responses to environmental demands, and by replacing it with the image of a society working upon itself and building up its practices on the basis of its own historicity and its class conflicts.

Four principles

A social struggle – and still more a social movement – is a social conflict defined and limited by the cultural stakes which are common to the adversaries involved. Our objective, therefore, should be to create a research situation which would be able to represent the nature of the struggles. Either to restrict oneself to the self-awareness of the actors, or else to evade this awareness in order to locate and explain types of behaviour in terms of a situation and its evolution would be contradictory to the very object of our research. Consequently, we are induced to posit four demands and to translate them into research practice.

1. The first and most fundamental of these requirements is to enter into a relationship with the social movement itself. We cannot remain contented merely with studying actions or thoughts; we must come face to face with the social movement itself. It frequently happens that the actor becomes a recorder, historian, or sociologist; on the other hand, in sociological intervention, the actor remains an *actor*. The militants join in a movement because they consider their participation useful for the movement: thus, for instance, the militant students of Bordeaux caused a meeting of the Municipal committee of their organization to be postponed in order to allow them to participate at one of our working weekends. In the anti-nuclear movement an outright demand for intervention was formulated. Since our analysis concentrates on collective behaviour, it is directed towards groups of militants who are all aware of belonging to a movement, of representing a population which is involved but which lies beyond the more restricted circle of the militants. Thus the groups involved in sociological intervention are not merely opinion-groups, clubs of like-thinkers, for they reunite the participants in collective conflictual action.

These groups – constituted by the sociologist – know that their *'raison d'être'* lies in intervention, but they continually consider themselves as historical actors and as representatives of real or potential actors greater than themselves.

2. The second principle is to go beyond ideological language and to apprehend the group in its militant role. This is why almost from the start the group is confronted with interlocutors; the group's thinking about itself and its action can take shape only from these encounters, which are often more direct than they are during the course of conflict

142

itself. It is necessary that these confrontations take place, not only with opponents but also with representatives of other levels of action in the movement itself, either the leaders or the participants who enter from the bottom. Researchers are relatively little involved in these confrontations.

3. While it may be fairly easy to introduce in this way two of the three components of a social movement – the principle of identity (I) and the principle of opposition (O) – it is more difficult to bring in the *stakes* over which the opponents are fighting, i.e. the principle of totality (T). This principle can be represented only by the researchers themselves. Just as confrontation represents the I–O dimension of a social movement, so too the meeting with the *researchers* represents the I–T dimension, for the researcher causes the stakes of a conflict to emerge, and he cannot be identified with the actor and even less with his adversary. If the researcher becomes identified with the militants, he becomes reduced to being nothing but an ideologist or a doctrinaire, because he builds up a secondary ideological language on the basis of a first ideology. Instead, the researcher should be the person by whom the social movement is set in its context, the person who speaks both to the militants and to the opponents, and above all the person who endeavours to extract the social movement from the struggle and hence also to designate the social and cultural stakes of the conflict. At the outset, this T-presence is no more than indirect, and indicated by reference to research; as the intervention continues, however, it becomes more and more direct. The supreme moment of the intervention devoted to the students' movement was dominated by a lengthy discussion between the militants and the research leader who introduced with great vigour into the group the theme of knowledge and its social utilization, which, to his mind, represented the only stakes capable of elevating the student struggle to the level of a social movement.

4. When it has been thus constituted, the group can then function as representative of a struggle or a social movement: this it does by carrying out its own *self-analysis* and by replacing action by the analysis of the situation of action as reconstructed by sociological intervention. The analysis is turned into militant action and the researcher learns to become acquainted with the movement by participating in the group's analytical work. This analytical work is not to be confused, therefore, with the sociologist's interpretation, and the sociologist cannot become a member of the group on the same footing as the other members, because the group does not cease to be militant: the group's

categories of analysis remain linked to those of action, while the sociologist transcribes his observations into the categories of the theory of social action. The fact, however, that the researcher is an 'outsider' does not preclude his involvement in the movement: he is not a militant, but his independence is itself of service, for it helps to maintain the distance that is indispensable for the disengaging of a social movement from the fiercest protest struggles or revolts.

The method we have conceived, therefore, creates a very close association between a militant group's self-analysis and the sociologist's intervention carried out on the basis of his theoretical hypothesis. This intervention, then, is as far removed from an experimental approach as it is from an act of sympathy or merging with the movement. This duality can never become melted down through total integration, hence the researcher's two functions must be kept separate. The first of these, which I have called the *agitator*'s function, is the one which enables the researcher to assist with the self-analysis, to strengthen the group, to organize and conduct meetings with critics or opponents and to convey the group's viewpoints. The second, which I have called the *secretary*'s function, because in this case the researcher limits himself primarily to noting the substance of the meetings, consists in adopting an increasingly critical stance in examining the group, while also remaining as far as possible outside it. What matters is to distinguish between these functions, even though they may be combined in numerous different ways.*

The connection between *self-analysis* and *intervention* is fundamental: it is not a question here either of lending an ear to an ideology or of papering it over with interpretation. Through participating in the researcher's intervention groups, the actors begin to adopt a distance with regard to their practice, a distance made tangible by the fact that they themselves are becoming aware of the distance between their ideology, the image of them relayed back by their opponents or partners, and the diversity of their own public statements. They now attempt to understand the attitudes of their interlocutors and to integrate them into the analysis of their own actions. The history of intervention is that of an ascent towards analysis, setting out from historical experience, and of a descent towards interpretation of the intervention group itself. The group first sees various meanings of its own action unfolding; it then ascends by stages towards the central theoretical interpretation: what is there of a *social movement* in this

* Since we are now helped during the interventions by a secretary, I feel it would be useful to replace the terms agitator and secretary by *interpreter* and *analyst*. The interpreter helps the self-analysis to progress; the analyst leads the group from its struggle towards the social movement that is embedded within it.

action? The researcher then intervenes directly in this transition to analysis; finally, the researcher – then the group itself – *interprets* what took place during the intervention. The intervention, therefore, is far from being reduced to a technique; it is not a specific type of group-meeting. The method and its technical implementation are not separable from an analytical approach: they are the practice of a theory, without which they would not have been conceived. They are the action of a sociology which is itself a sociology of action.

Sociological intervention and other interventions

To speak of intervention and not of experimentation means that one is concerned both with practical and with intellectual aims.

A psychosociologist studies a group which agrees to analyse its professional roles or its way of controlling change with the idea in mind that his reflexions might increase the group's ability to intervene in a situation by which it is concerned. Training groups aim to remove certain obstacles barring their way to the acquisition of new knowledge; similarly, sociological intervention is aimed at the militants of social movements with the objective of raising their *capacity for historical action*, and hence increasing the strength and elevating the level of their struggles. We are not concerned here with defending applied sociology against pure sociology, by agreeing to the limits imposed by acceptance of the actor's interests, but rather with putting ourselves in a situation in which the object of sociology, social relations and collective action all emerge directly. I firmly believe that the main task of sociologists is to study as directly as possible the forms of collective behaviour in the widest variety of situations. Once one isolates individuals and their opinions one begins to distance oneself from the real object of sociology, which can never be justified except for practical reasons, such as the usefulness of having short-term decisions at hand or of knowing a market.

But the fact that there are common features in the approaches of the various types of intervention which all study a social problem through the behaviour of the group concerned should not conceal the other fact, which is that they do not have the same objectives, that they do not apply the same analysis and that they do not convey in themselves the same concept of society. Furthermore, within the very forms of sociological intervention one must also distinguish between those which tackle groups situated in systems of action – the only field I am considering here – and those which study reactions to an *order*, those which are concerned with *crisis* behaviour, and finally those preoccupied by the behaviour of *change*, which is a classification corresponding

145

to the four cardinal points of sociology as analysed in the first part of this book.

In the sphere of action, social relations are direct, they are relations of domination, influence or authority, depending on whether one is placed at the level of the field of historicity, that of institutions or that of organizations. The same does not hold, however, when one is involved in the sphere of *order*, of *agencies* of social control and socialization, whether they be repressive, integrational, or formative, for here the terms of the social relation are replaced by inclusion and exclusion. Action becomes withdrawal or revolt, the will to refuse or to overcome, attack and flight, to use the words of Bion.* The actor does not conceive himself as a collective body but rather as a mass or a desocialized *plebs*. Intervention, as described here, cannot be directly applied to this sphere: it must as quickly as possible be given a new form which would preserve the principles of the method while also adapting them to a new object. The same reasoning can be applied to *crisis* behaviour, the forms of which are the disintegrated and totally reversed forms of social struggle, and it can be applied even more to the behaviour of groups situated in relation to *change*. Here, we are very far from historicity, and sociological intervention must change itself by extending from action behaviour to forms of behaviour determined by order, and finally to those forms which are a reaction to crisis, before it moves on to consider the collective forms of the behaviour of change. In addition, certain forms of intervention occur at various levels of social reality, but do not attempt to comprehend social struggles or movements. And others aim at improving the functioning of an *organization* or of one of its components, e.g. by eliminating irrationality, routine, lack of co-ordination, by better defining the hierarchical roles and relations, and by detecting the infiltration of bureaucracy or the effects of authoritarianism. Then there is a second type of intervention which aims at improving a decision-making system, an *institution*, especially by permitting one group to adapt better to the internal and external changes affecting the institution. Lastly, there is a third type which aims at speeding up cultural *modernization* and hence eliminating outmoded cultural models and models of authority. These three types of intervention cannot help being different from the one presented here, even when it is searching for the presence of a social movement well away from its own territory, in struggles linked to crisis or to change. The further one descends towards the level of organizations and of modernization, the more one moves into psychological perspective and the more, too, one accepts being placed inside an ensemble which is nonetheless determined by the higher levels of social reality, those of institutions and of the field of historicity. This gives rise to the serious risk of becoming trapped in conservative logic. The only way of reducing this risk is to set oneself objectives defined in truly psychological terms. The intervention which occurs at the institutional level runs a more limited risk, which is that of preferring reformist behaviour and the behaviour of adaptation to change to the forms of behaviour which aim at a deeper transformation of the situation.

These risks should be a deterrent to the studying of institutional and organizational problems without due regard to their dependence in relation to the problems of historicity and class relations. Sociological intervention alone respects this hierarchy, and this is why it must not be confused with other types of intervention which, although they may be useful, always incur the danger of viewing society the wrong way round by giving priority to the very aspects which should be subordinated. I shall be returning to the deep differences in orientation separating sociological intervention – as presented here – from the adaptation groups devised by social psychology and the liberation groups inspired by psycho-analysis. Actually, the *only* feature all these methods have in common is that of working with restricted groups. Will such a choice – which is easy to justify for methodological reasons – give priority to a certain type of problem, will it reduce the great political and social problems to 'group dynamics'? One should be surprised at such a fear. By speaking of the *Comité de Salut Public* or the strike committee in a factory, is one reducing politics to group psychology? The action of social movements is most often directed by restricted groups: the cells, sections, groups, and the critics one attracts, are often made up of militants who themselves belong to groups of limited size. These very superficial criticisms in fact relate to quite a different idea: the authors of such criticism think that a social movement is less a voluntary action than a weak-point in history, a breakdown which occurs when domination enters a state of *crisis* and which acquires importance if popular protest finds its allies in the political system, and particularly if an organized avant-garde is able to profit from the circumstances.

Thus for them the social movement is not a normatively oriented action but rather the outer manifestation of economic mechanisms or else the expression of a desire or a need.

The same criticism has always been made to those who wish to listen to and magnify the voice of the dominated, for instance, Paulo Freire,* accused of subjectivity and reformism – and many of his replies, particularly in *Pédagogie des opprimés*, might be reproduced here. He criticizes the militant revolutionaries who at heart still cling to the myth of 'the natural inability of the popular masses', the result of which has been that they despise the people and adopt a propagandist attitude towards them which has swiftly led to the masses being reduced to nothing but the object of the revolution. Freire rightly dismisses the cut-and-dried opposition between the objective and the subjective. The most oppressed and exploited are not completely alienated: they maintain an awareness of their situation. As they are dependent in their daily life and limited in their capacity for initiative, they cannot think like those who conduct the great battles or grand manoeuvres in history, but then the latter, in turn, often yield to scientist illusions. Intervention, like teaching or group-work, and unlike activist propaganda, helps the actor to shake free of the constraints by which he is surrounded, to extent his field of analysis and become more capable of action. This leads us then from an apparently methodological problem to a choice that is far more profound. Yes, I do conceive of a social movement as an action rather than as a crisis, and I refuse to separate the resistance to domination from a positive counter-project for society. This is why I have distinguished between social movement and critical action. Those who speak unthinkingly of psychologism are the defenders of solely critical action and the denigrators of social movements which they see as being always marked by the stamp of reformism. This is a doctrinaire conception which carries within it the gravest dangers. Because it is bolstered up by mistrust towards social movements, it places absolute confidence in the political and ideological avant-gardes, which are led from this point towards establishing their own, no less absolute power.

Permanent sociology

The intervention group is not *centred on itself* and on its own functioning, but on a struggle and the movement this struggle represents. Those who participate in this struggle do not cease to belong to a movement, and once the intervention as such has been concluded, it has to be used by the actors themselves. The function of intervention is to establish as prolonged as possible an exchange between action and analysis: this is why I speak of *permanent sociology*. The connection between the actors' self-analysis and the sociologist's intervention in groups meeting regularly over several months would seem to be the chief form of this communication between action and analysis, but it must become increasingly completed by other forms of inter-relation, so that the initial results of analysis are strengthened by knowledge of the effects they will have had on the behaviour of the actors and on their struggle. It must be stated quite openly that the purpose of this research work is to *contribute to the development of social movements*. Nobody would be induced to believe that we dream of inventing or

148

fabricating social movements from a collection of bits and pieces – this would be absurd. Our real objective is to enable a society to live at the highest possible level of historical action instead of blindly passing through crises and conflicts. This is why the militants of a movement participate in an intervention: they realize that we want their movement to develop. Some people feel that history has passed through too many conflicts and ideologies. Unlike them, I feel that it has been dominated by wasted hopes, by thoughts inadequately adapted to situations, and by weakness of thought about social action. The economic actors are less unaware of the meaning of their actions than they were in the still recent past. Why then should social movements not profit from the progress of a sociological analysis capable of casting light upon their problems and their action? The most widely-accepted attitude at present is still that the sociologist should fill the role of expert, and advise the decision-makers as to the situation, in the same way as the weather bureau advises farmers or tourists. But here we are concerned with something quite different. Our attention is directed not towards the situation but towards the action, not towards intentions but towards social relations and fields of social action. In setting ourselves the objective of raising the level of historical action in a society, we also provide ourselves with the means of evaluating our own results and improving our research practices. This is why a permanent sociology – if it clearly defines its method from the outset – knows that its method will gain in depth just as the results obtained will set new problems. What finally counts is to accept a new object of research, calling for a new study method and entailing a change of relation between the researcher and the actors he studies. By settling on the more specific terrain of sociology, intervention reveals that between the objective and the subjective there exists the domain of social relations and social action, and that it will have need of an original research practice.

8

The group

Why a group?

A group is not the customary agent of a social movement, for a social movement operates through organizations or, more broadly, through collectives; moreover, it demands personal involvement. This is why some have proposed studying mass assemblies or demonstrations, while others – who are more numerous – turn quite simply towards the study of already formed groups, parties, associations, and trade unions. Yet if instead one were to hold a series of personal interviews with the militants, they might inform us as to their reasons for becoming involved in the movement.

Let us first set aside one illusion: a movement cannot be grasped as a concrete ensemble. What is the actual collective that represents the workers' movement or even a students' movement, or a strike gathering, or a general assembly? These dozens or hundreds of people cannot all be heard; their voices would have to be covered by those of a few leaders. And so we are brought back to reality. On the one hand we might listen to individuals, on the other to an organization, i.e. on the one hand we could hear the reasons for participating individually in a movement and on the other we could hear the political, strategic, and tactical form given to the movement. But between these two, the movement itself would be missing. It is precisely because our present history is so full of militants without movements and organizations which become substituted for movements that so many researchers want to app:oach a movement directly at the level of restricted groups, which may be little organized but which feel themselves to be actively engaged on behalf of far larger collectives. The danger of making such a choice is evident: it means according special status to sects and splinter-groups. This is a real danger if the splinter group forms a micro-party, as happens in many revolutionary sub-groups; it is not a real danger if the groups are weakly organized, if their projects outstrip their aims and their aims reach beyond their forms of action; the

150

danger is even less real if in this group one sees an initial gathering of ideas and practices, from which a new social movement is beginning to emerge. A social movement is an unstable balancing between the institutionalization of that movement and critical action against order, hence between a pressure group of interests on the one hand and a party or an armed force ready to take over power on the other hand. Far from being a stronghold, this movement is in fact a weak point, while the revolutionary parties or the reformatory trade unions are the strongholds of political life. As a central concept in sociological analysis, the social movement represents a border zone in social practice, and those who like to depict society on a large canvas give only scant attention to such movements, while remaining fascinated by institutions, organizations, and armies. The choice of restricted groups as the locus and agent of action in preference to social movements is a correct choice, since such groups of militants – even if they are formed by the researcher – represent the weakest imaginable form of the organization of collective action and hence the place from which one can advance closest to the social movement, well beyond institutional forces and well behind the deafening roar of war.

The intervention group

The intervention is carried out on a group of militants involved with the self-analysis of their movement based on their confrontation with opponents or partners. These militants are therefore both real actors and participants in an intervention devised and organized for the purposes of sociological analysis. Three major questions now arise: *how* are the group members *chosen* – by the researchers, or by the movement to which they belong? *Why* do they participate in the intervention? Might not *their two roles* be conflicting, since the sociologist's aims in compiling information and the militant's objectives for action are not always readily compatible?

1. The first of these questions brings out the danger of a possible confusion between the *movements* and the *associations* or *organizations* which represent the movements, even if all the members of the group are also members of the movement, for it would be dangerous to confuse a movement or even a struggle with its forms of organization. The group does not engage the responsibility of any association. It is formed as directly as possible from militants, and the researcher ensures that it should also be as diversified as possible and thus capable of holding discussions on the major issues which will inform him as to the nature and problems of the movement. The group must remain

limited in size in order to enable all members to participate in the discussion. One cannot, therefore, speak of it as being fully representative, but the researcher must avoid leaving out any important component of the struggle.

In carrying out our intervention with student groups, we were aware from the outset of the importance of the conflicts between the UNEF (The French National Students Organization), chiefly of Communist sympathy, and the other student organizations, and the clashes between these groups as a body and the non-organized groups. On the other hand, we did not possess any specific information on the differences in political outlook that may have existed between students in different study groups and research units. It was consequently our primary concern to ensure that each of the groups studied should include members of the UNEF, militants from other organizations, and students from the non-organized groups, while accepting that the participants should come only from the UERs (Study and research units), where the strike had been most active. Thus, in order to meet these same requirements, a study of the Occitanist movement had to form groups which would bring together cultural militants, political militants, and trade unionists or members of professional associations. Likewise, the study of the anti-nuclear movement had to be carried out through groups which would bring together scientists, workers in the nuclear industry, militants from local committees, and ecologists. This means that the responsibility for forming the group fell on the researchers.

2. What type of militants were we looking for? As far as possible, *rank and file militants* rather than leaders and organizers, who would hold too much sway over the rest of the group and would by their mere presence implicate their organization, for this would require them to act as spokesmen for their organization and therefore to adopt a stance of resistance towards open discussion and towards self-analysis itself. The militants chosen had to have taken part in conflict action. It would have been unwise to include in the groups either individuals whose active participation had gone no further than following a current of opinion or, conversely, those who had been involved in a struggle or confrontation but without feeling that they belonged to a movement. Neither the combat situation nor the mere presence of a current of opinion is sufficient indication of the presence of a social movement or even of a struggle. In the former instance, the presence of a cultural stake common to the opponents tends to be replaced by direct confrontation; in the latter, it is the opponent who may be missing or else too vaguely defined to be designated by the interlocutors.

These considerations would appear to impose restrictions on the sociologist's intervention. Restrictions do, certainly, exist but they are connected less with the method of intervention than with the object it enables to be studied. Sociological intervention is not well suited either to the study of an armed conflict – particularly an international one – or, conversely, to the study of a public opinion campaign in which there is no visible social conflict. But the researcher must be on his guard against giving preference to the representatives of trends who seem most willing to participate in the intervention, partly because they hope it will serve to establish a point of compromise or reunification. Similarly, he must avoid becoming enclosed in the world of the militants who are most active and most accustomed to holding the floor. The researcher should aim rather at forming groups of individuals who simply belong to *the population that feels most committed* to the students' struggle. Ideally, in order to study the workers' movement, one would form groups of workers, regardless of whether or not they were unionized or militant; and in order to study the anti-nuclear movement, one would simply install oneself in a region where a nuclear power-station had either already been established or was in the process of being established. One would do so, firstly, in order to avoid confusing the movement with an organization, and, secondly, in order to remain true to the idea expressed in the first part of this book – that there can be no role without role-consciousness, and, in particular, no class without class-consciousness. The groups would in fact be formed of those who, whether or not they were members of organizations, were sufficiently committed to an action to be ready to devote considerable time to thinking about a movement to which they felt they belonged. In what is to follow, we shall be speaking of actors rather than of militants whenever it is necessary to avoid confusion between participating in a movement and belonging to an organization.

What induces the actors to participate in the intervention, i.e. in reflecting about a movement outside of the organizations which lay claim to representing it, is their awareness of a *disharmony* between the movement and its forms of action and organization. A movement without organizational unity, particularly if it is a rising movement and is attempting to establish its importance beyond the limits of its material weakness, may expect sociological intervention to further strengthen the inherent opposition between what unites and what divides the movement. Conversely, if organizations – and even more so ideologists – speak in the name of a movement while actually having objectives different to those of the movement, it may happen that they resist research which might reveal the arbitrariness of their claim to represent the movement. Self-analysis, therefore, serves the role of offering an approach towards the movement which does not run counter to the organization but reaches beyond the limits and difficulties of the organization's practice. The actors do not turn towards an expert in order to ask him for an analysis of their situation in the way that a firm would approach a specialist to examine its financial viability. The actors instead work with a person who, being unaffiliated to any organization, reflects upon the movement and attempts to disengage it from whatever is mixed up with it and to strengthen its basic orientations. The group does not expect advice from the researcher, nor does it expect a cool diagnosis: it accepts its independence, but it also wishes to be assured that the researcher recognizes the existence and importance of the movement. The sociologist's intervention cannot be directed towards a group of disillusioned or embittered militants wishing to criticize an organization; there is also little likelihood of his intervention being requested or accepted by an organization which identifies itself with the movement as a whole. It is between these two poles that the intervention must occur. And it progresses all the more easily the more the organizational problems are subordinated to those of the movement's orientation and the militant participation of its members.

3. If the researcher has to combine his knowledge with his readiness to assist the social movement to develop, the participants in the intervention encounter parallel difficulties. As *actors*, they also become *analysts*. These *two roles* may conflict, and the more the movement is in crisis the more easily this opposition occurs: protracted examination overturns the slogans, undermines the convictions, and augments the conflicts and tensions. Furthermore, the person who places himself in the position of analyst adopts a critical distance towards himself, which may hamper his militant participation. Even if the group is formed of militants and confronted with real opponents of the movement, the intervention occurs in a climate which is not that of militant action with its solidarity, its splits, and its ideological mobilization. Can one remain a militant when one turns analyst? The answer is not only that one can; it is a response which should also confirm that this militant self-analysis strengthens participation in the movement itself, beyond the difficulties of the struggle. On condition that one adds immediately that sociological intervention does not occur on behalf of an organization and that it can consequently conclude as to the weakness or decline of a movement just as it can also reveal the importance of a movement despite the weakness of its organization. One does not undertake intervention without having good reasons for thinking that there is *some* social movement in the struggle under study, but we

wrongly conclude and state that the struggle, as it is organized, is largely or totally foreign to the social movement which is virtually present in it. Even more often, the conclusions will be still more complex, revealing tensions or misunderstandings between the element of social movement and whatever there is of a different nature within a struggle. If all interventions had to conclude in the panegyrics of an organized struggle, they would have but a small audience: the sociologist would be no more than the actor's historiographer. The actor cannot be unaware that the result of sociological intervention will be to confront him with an image of himself that is different to the one offered to him by his ideology, and also that he too will have been transformed by the intervention itself. Thus the strength of the organization risks making the intervention more difficult; but it can also make it more important. Wherever the struggle is little organized and weakly unified – as in the case of student action – the intervention is likely to have limited effect: what limits the pressure of organizations may also reduce the interest of the intervention, since it would have to be accompanied by a to-ing and fro-ing between analysis and action. The intervention would have to be flanked by two phases as important and as long as the intervention itself. The first of these phases would be that of the transition from action to analysis, hence of discussion with the militants in order to shape and define the request for intervention; the second would be that of the return to action. The results of the intervention would have to be discussed not only with the participants but also with the leaders or other militants. The participants, rather than the researchers, might conduct such a discussion in order to ensure the transfer of the analysis and the conclusions of the analysis to the heart of the organized struggle.

Organized movements and research

From the beginning of our first series of interventions we knew that militant associations or groups of leaders or of interpreters of movements would sometimes see a threat in sociological intervention. They would fear that the outside observers would misinterpret the spirit and the difficulties of a movement, that the distance created by analysis would serve only to cool militant ardour and to give priority to moderate, negotiatory, 'reasonable' orientations, or else, instead, that it would exaggerate the influence of the most extreme tendencies. There are two types of resistance offered by movements to intervention. Sometimes, an organization proclaims its identity with a movement, and fears an approach which looks for the identity of the movement beyond the struggle and the organization of the struggle. And the more the organization's material power exceeds its real charge of social movement, the more resistance it will offer. Thus it was that in a study, which was at the time still an enquiry into the workers' movement, I encountered the greatest obstacles from the most moderate of the trade-union confederations, the one which was also most involved in negotiations and the least militant. On the other hand, there may also develop a doctrinaire mistrust, coming from groups of intellectuals interpreting a poorly organized current of opinion. This resistance is all the stronger the more directly the protest is backed up by an identity, a collective being, and hence opposes the interior more directly to the exterior. During the great upsurge of Black Power in the United States it would have been difficult for white intellectuals to carry out intervention at Oakland, on the South Side of Chicago, or in Harlem.

These forms of resistance can be insurmountable and can cause the failure of an attempt at intervention. But if the failure is not due to incompetence, and if several attempts terminate with the same rejection, is not this a powerful indication that the social movement is missing from places so well protected and that it is above all this absence that the resistance conceals? Wherever critical action prepares the way only for the seizure of power by force, wherever – by contrast – the claim-making apparatus is no more than a market trade-unionism, and wherever persons of importance protect their own power by defending the specific quality or the independence of a territory or a social category about to lose its specificity or independence, intervention is feared because the reference made to a social movement risks being revealed as artificial. Modernist or anti-modernist counter-elites speak in the name of a people or of a category without the collective action of the latter being visible. Wherever we might encounter failure we would not go so far as saying that there is no social movement, but simply that it is invisible, which would cast serious doubt upon its real existence. The presence of a social movement must, on the contrary, be revealed through what is a factor favourable to intervention, through questioning the militants as to the purpose of their struggle and through seeking profound commitment beyond the specific conditions of a particular battle. For this reason, intervention is possible only if it is based on active participation by the militants, even outside of the group which participates directly in the intervention, and on real interaction – as constant as possible – between researchers and actors. If there is no interaction, the researchers may be led, whether they like it or not, towards a critical attitude simply by the resistance which militant mobilization offers to their effort to acquire knowledge, while the associations may seek to thrust aside intrusions and to maintain the monopoly over the interpretation of their domain of action.

The group

The interdependence between the researchers, the analysts and those involved in the movement, and the actors, who are both militants and analysts, is necessary for the study of the relations between a movement and a struggle and even more between a movement and the organization of this struggle. This is why intervention must be as close as possible to action and must have bearing on a *concrete historical practice* and not on an intention or merely on general ideas. The proximity of the action is all the more important the more powerfully institutionalized and organized the struggle is. Only reference to a collective practice can reveal the limits of the ideology and of the strategic *discours* of the organizations. It is desirable that intervention on workers' trade-unionism should be able to be carried out during a strike, or that militant feminists should be able to carry out their analysis at the time of an important trial. This simultaneity runs up against evident obstacles, which are at the outset material but are primarily psychological. In the heart of action, the militant is often seeking not the distance afforded by reflective withdrawal but rather the fullest possible participation in action. Nevertheless, this idea is better suited to a military struggle than to a social conflict, which will always be full of internal debates, hesitations, reflections, and efforts to convince or to encourage participation. The simplest solution is to bring in the intervention after the action, but it may be foreseen that certain of the interventions first prepared will occur before the events considered as highly probable or inevitable. It is most likely somewhat later that opportunities will occur to carry out analysis of the event in action. Furthermore, in this case, the preparatory period of entry into research must have already been initiated since otherwise the researchers would lose the advantages of being in readiness for the event if, by having to intervene unprepared, they were to find themselves ignorant of the struggle they were studying and left completely outside it. In practice, the formation of intervention groups should demonstrate co-operation between the researchers and the militants. If the responsibility for the intervention falls entirely upon the researchers, the leaders of associations in particular would have to be assured that the groups had not been determined from the outset by a particular bias and that there were no sizeable gaps in them, and especially that they were not dominated by a minority trend which the sociologist in his intervention strategy might use against the established leaders. It is necessary that the movement should as far as possible feel responsible for the proper conduct of the intervention. The researchers must also be protected against the tendency they may have to form groups close to their own interests or concerns, in which the intellectuals or the inhabitants of their own town or region would be accorded a place of excessive importance. It is so important to protect the researcher against his own appreciation of the situation – particularly when this situation is complex and tension-ridden – that any researcher who does not participate in the intervention should be asked as soon as possible to assist as a *consultant*.

It should not be easy, and it cannot be easy, to *attach* the intervention to the movement and to its self-analysis. This 'docking' of the intervention against the quayside of the movement gives the researchers the opportunity to find out about the nature of the movement and the struggle, and also induces them to criticize their own appreciation of the movement. This is particularly difficult to achieve in a situation such as that of research on the Occitanist movement, in which the researchers belong to the centre – Paris, for most of them – and even more closely to the Parisian intellectual milieu whose domination and remoteness is strongly resented by the intellectuals or leaders of the movement who are struggling against internal colonialism. The intervention on anti-nuclear movements was prepared under easier conditions, since one of the researchers had been for a long time closely associated with these movements. Nonetheless, the transition from the role of *participant* to that of *intervener* was far from easy. The researcher is in danger of being too closely allied to the group he has to study and of giving preference to group strengthening over the penetrating and often trying criticism of analysis. Nothing can help to avoid tension between the participant and the analyst; yet, in addition, it might be suggested that the researcher, who ought to have background knowledge of the movement and hence have participated in it to an extent, should as often as possible be associated with *partners* within the movement who are convinced of the usefulness of the intervention. Sociological intervention must meet a *demand*. Furthermore, it should be directed as the social movement itself. Intervention on femininist movements should not be undertaken at the request of a political party or of the government. It is not even desirable for the sociologist to intervene at the request and on behalf of an organization which identifies itself with a social movement. The request for intervention must come from the members of the groups themselves. A trade-union confederation may wish for the intervention to be carried out through trade-union channels; the researchers must then await a direct request from the trade unionists willing to participate in the group of their own accord, with the assurance that they will not be entering into conflict with their confederation and yet will not be acting upon its instructions or representing it. To identify from the outset a movement with an organization and with that organization's practices would be to run counter to the aim of intervention.

The group

Two or several groups

An extensive study, involving many individuals but dealing only with simple topics, and in particular separate subjects, such as occur in the questions of a questionnnaire or even an oral interview, is thus replaced here by an intensive study on a group of militants who carry out self-analysis of their movement and are confronted as often as possible by the researchers with the entire body of their statements and with their behaviour during the intervention. One of the inconveniences of this method is that it subordinates analysis to the particular characteristics of the intervention group. Who can assure us that the students' struggle is by nature the same in Paris as it is in Amiens, that to be a militant Occitanist has the same significance in the Languedoc, in Provence, and the Limousin region, or that the anti-nuclear movement is the same in regions where nuclear power-stations have been constructed as it is in Paris, where the intellectuals and particularly the scientists play a far more important role in demonstrations and associations? If a movement cannot be directly associated with an organization or linked any more closely to a particular dated and localized conflict, it is dangerous to study it through only one group. This is why sociological intervention attempts to defend itself against its own limitations by setting up two or several groups. Primarily, what must be done is to set aside the specifically local features and not confuse them with the general aspects of the movement, in order to devise an analysis which could be applied to several situations. But one must not restrict oneself to the surface features of each situation under the pretext of extracting the general features of a struggle. The analysis will be all the stronger the deeper the intervention goes and the larger and richer is the body of documents to be explained. Not only is there no contradiction between the particular features of each group and the internal coherence of the general theories, but the groups are also linked to each other.

The comparison of the groups should have a more constructive aim. Different, even opposing, aspects of the struggle should be represented in such a way that their comparison should bring out the characteristic discussions, tensions, or conflicts of the movement. This is why the two groups do not remain separate all the time. If one wishes them to work at the same time, they must have had lengthy contact immediately prior to the time when the researchers divulge their interpretations.

In our intervention among student groups, we had decided not to form groups in Amiens and Bordeaux for specific reasons; nevertheless, our impression that student problems were experienced

159

differently in a small university situated in a region strongly influenced by workers' action and in a large university town, which was also the capital of a region of relatively little industry, proved even more accurate than we had thought; and the comparison and the interaction between the students of Amiens and Bordeaux became rapidly revealed as a good means of learning about the students' movement. As far as the Occitanist movement was concerned, it was clear that it was defending a cultural identity and at the same time economic interests, most of all in the Languedoc vineyards; it could therefore be considered useful to compare and contrast a group situated in one of the main cities of Occitania with another formed in the vineyard regions. In studying the anti-nuclear movement, it was possible to compare groups formed in two regions directly affected by the nuclear-power policy, or, alternatively, a group from one of these regions and one from the Paris region. All these examples showed that the formation of two groups involves a choice – always relatively arbitrary – between several possible comparisons, thus limiting the scope of the intervention. Only concrete studies could demonstrate how far these limitations extend. I have no doubt that a third group, formed in Paris, would have enabled us to acquire a richer view of the student movement; at the same time, however, I observed that it was possible to integrate the body of information produced by these two groups into the analysis, and as a result the need for a third group was not established in this case. This need may emerge for more material reasons. Neither the students' movements nor the Occitanist movement appear to be strongly differentiated in spite of the diversity of the organizations of which they are composed. This is perhaps because their chief opponent is the State; it may also be because they are small-scale movements. By contrast, workers' trade-unionism – even if defined restrictively, by disregarding the professional categories that are not strictly speaking worker categories – forms a far larger and more diversified ensemble. In studying this movement can one content oneself with forming a group based on trade-union confederation? Must one define the object of research more narrowly, for instance by setting out from prior theories as to the nature and the central role of workers' trade-unionism, or instead by choosing recent zones of syndicalization?

The formation of groups must be associated with the definition of a field of research and must take into account the degree of internal differentiation of the struggle under study. One must begin with the movement itself, its themes of debate, its orientations and internal tensions, and seek for the localizations which will best bring them to light.

The group

The interlocutors

At the moment of its formation, the group is a *witness-group*. During the first encounters with the researchers, when the size of the group has not yet been sufficiently stabilized, the group proclaims its collective existence by referring back to its past action, particularly if it has experienced a great conflict. The researchers must keep it as close as possible to this real conflict in order to avoid the immobilizing expression of an ideology which would also perform the function of protecting the group against the researchers. Having thus become a *confrontation group*, it ceases freely to construct the direction of its action; it has to answer to interpretations that differ from its own, and to correct the image it formerly had of its opponents. In the initial stages of intervention on the students' movement, particularly in Amiens, the idea dominated that the reform of the *second cycle* (of higher education) had come in response to the direct desire and pressure of the industrialists (the employers); the students, who had requested to hear a representative of the regional industrialists, were astounded to hear him express very different viewpoints, just as they were also surprised to find teachers favourable to the reform expressing attitudes of professional and corporative defence which were scarcely supportive of the adaptation of studies to suit the business world, which they considered prejudicial to the traditional disciplines to which they often belonged. This was a double surprise, which gave rise to great discussion in the group and to a deepening of the self-analysis.

If a struggle is more ideological than practical – as has hitherto been the case with the ecological movement – the confrontation between opponents is likely to be less productive than in instances where the actor and the adversary refer to precisely the same events in order to offer different interpretations of them. But we have seen that the presence of interlocutors stimulates the group and leads it to discovering – beyond the facade of unanimity – the divergences or inner conflicts. This may serve to speed up self-analysis provided that the tensions are not reduced by an escape towards ideas that are too general, towards principles and feelings which do not allow for the provision of any particular practice.

Such confrontations may even seem inadequate: one can imagine a more complete study bearing on the conflict and not just on one of the actors. One could, for instance, form a group of worker trade unionists and a group of company directors; each group would be confronted by interlocutors and would perform its self-analysis before the two groups were set in front of each other, possibly even in the presence of

161

representatives of institutions for negotiation, intervention, or mediation, such as work inspectors, magistrates, lawyers, parliamentary
delegates, and other elected officials in the case imagined here. Such
an extension of the method of intervention would be in keeping with
the analysis on which the intervention is based and which has constantly reminded us that the proper concern of sociology is the social
relation. Once again, our practice, which is still in its early stages,
suggests the extension and development of a method which cannot be
reduced to the procedures used when it was first applied.

But the essential does not lie in the intervention procedures; it lies in
the idea that one must not become enclosed in opinions, that one must
instead place the actor in relation with his opponents or partners in
order to overcome his rationalizations and provide a realistic basis for
his work upon himself.

The confrontation between the actor and his social partners is therefore an essential approach and not merely a special technique which
might be replaced by another, for instance by the presentation of
documents. It is during these confrontations that the actor begins his
self-analysis. He is no longer a mere witness of his struggle, since he
agrees to be given an image thereof that differs from his own or even
contradicts it; thus he is obliged to emerge from his ideology and hence
to shift from the point of view of the actor to that of the relation and
even the social field of action.

This role of confrontation operates in particular for encounters with
opponents. It is different when the interlocutors are *allies* or *partners*,
for they reflect back to the actors a less external image of their action,
while also helping them to locate themselves on the social scene and
hence better define the nature of their action. There is, moreover, no
clear-cut boundary-line between these two categories of interlocutors,
and occasionally the group does not wish to decide from the outset
whether they are to be opponents or allies: the students had this same
ambiguous attitude with respect to the main teachers' union and even
towards the trade-union centres.

Finally, the interlocutors must also be other *participants* in the movement, situated at a different level and engaged in different activities
from those of the group members. Once the group, after having met
various opponents or allies, has begun to carry out its reflexion, it must
be able to match its thinking against other conceptions of the movement, including both those offered by the leaders and those deriving
from the base in whose name the movement is conducted, even if this
base does not participate in a militant and organized way in the
movement's activities.

The groups must be encouraged to answer their interlocutors by allowing themselves to be drawn freely into each confrontation without attempting to defend and elaborate upon a general policy. This is the phase of exploration, in which the group explores several directions, and reacts at different levels, thus providing itself with highly diversified and little integrated matter for reflexion. The researchers encourage this exploration by assisting the group to overcome the stereotyped image it often has of its opponent or partner, an activity which is rendered easier when the discussion is focussed on specific historical events rather than on general ideas. The interlocutor is occasionally too strong, occasionally too weak for the group. If he is too weak, two people need to be brought in instead of one; if he is too powerful, it is up to the researchers to defend the group and prevent it from becoming blocked by the arguments of an over-persuasive interlocutor. The purpose of the confrontations is not to provide the researchers with a complete picture of the group's opinions, but rather to expose the group itself to the diversity of its own reactions in order to enable it to get beyond the defensive repetition of a general ideology.

At present, the behaviour of the interlocutors and their statements are studied only indirectly, and hence very partially. Readers of *Lutte Etudiante* will find no direct analysis there of the policy of the teachers' unions, the State Ministry for University Education, or the Employers' Association. The intervention of these bodies will be seen only through the analysis of the student militants. As for the researchers, while offering the interlocutors every possible opportunity to express themselves, they should neverthless place themselves on the *group's side*, since the group is the bearer of the movement and because the researcher's main role is to speak to the group from the point of view of the movement. As the confrontations occur at the beginning of the intervention, the researchers – and in particular the 'agitator' – will also wish to strengthen the group by demonstrating solidarity with it before it tackles the major phase of its work – self-analysis. The interlocutors must be introduced into the group upon consideration of the group's needs and characteristics. Priority must be given to interlocutors who have been most directly and personally involved in real conflict with the movement, except in instances where the militants are in danger of finding themselves confronted by an adversary who might later take reprisals against them because of statements made during the intervention. An opponent who is too far distanced from the movement and whose presence and action can be fitted into a stereotype will be able to provoke only predictable behaviour and reactions from the group.

The presence of an interlocutor should prevent the group from becoming centred on itself and on its inner life; the main aim of introducing the interlocutor is to stimulate the group to act as the representative of a real struggle.

The interlocutor's emotional reaction must be subordinated to the discussion on the movement; but during the course of the discussion, relations are built up which are often different from those the actor had predicted and which bring out better the real nature of the struggle.

The *researcher* therefore has a limited role during the confrontation phase. The secretary intervenes as little as possible; the 'agitator' strengthens the group while at the same time assisting it to break free from its ideological defences and accept open discussion. If the researcher were to intervene more directly it could only be in order to overcome his own insecurity and, particularly, to be more readily accepted. These are psychological mechanisms with extremely negative consequences which run counter to the logic of research.

The researcher's role can be built up only from within the intervention; during this first phase, therefore, the researcher's role must remain discreet and restricted. Similarly, if the group is not a real historical group, a natural group, its responses may be governed by the desire to please or to displease either the researchers or the interlocutor. This is why, during this phase, the group should in every way be encouraged to behave as a historical actor responsible for the interests and the future of a movement. The researcher recalls past militant actions, reminding them of the importance of these actions for public opinion. He is in no sense a judge and he must avoid letting the group or the interlocutor address him in order to win him over. What he does instead is to organize the most direct possible face-to-face confrontations, in order to avoid having the group feel that it has been placed in an experimental situation. He helps the group to reaffirm its militant commitment and start upon its self-analysis, particularly by persuading it – once the interlocutor has left – to continue the session in order to analyse the encounter which has just taken place.

The main difficulty in this first phase of intervention is that the intervention must not only form or strengthen the group's identity but also melt down its protective *ideologies* in the heat of confrontation. These two aims are complementary, but they represent two poles between which there is always a certain tension that is indispensable to the success of the intervention. The group must be an actor, but not in its group capacity; it must be an actor insofar as it *represents* and bears in itself a struggle or a movement. The researcher is the one who establishes a relationship between the group and its opponents and partners, and who therefore transforms its ideology into action while at the same time offering assistance if the group seems in danger of losing its balance or its identity under the pressure of the opponent's blows.

The group

By the end of this first phase, the group will have received so much new information about its interlocutors, and particularly about itself, that it will feel the need to reflect, all the more so since not all the participants will have reacted in the same fashion to the different confrontations. The group senses the presence of latent discussions and debates within itself. These are confined by the presence of the interlocutors and develop only later during the *closed sessions* – without an interlocutor – which are arranged as rapidly as possible at the initiative of the researchers or of the participants themselves.

Length of the intervention

It is difficult to know when each confrontation and each series of confrontations should be brought to an end. At present, we envisage between twelve and fifteen sessions of two to four hours each for all the confrontations and closed sessions. Subsequent experience may lead to modification of this practice. One sole principle must be defended: the main aim of this phase is to prepare the ground for the actors' self-analysis, and the phase should end when the group expresses a powerful need to move on to self-analysis. With regard to the overall length of the intervention, it at present lasts some thirty sessions, half of which occur at weekends, and the entire duration is around three months. In addition to this, preparatory meetings are held with the groups, and, at the end of the intervention, personal meetings take place, followed later by discussion of the researchers' final report and, lastly, meetings between certain members of the group and representatives of the organizations to which they belong. The interventions also involve a fairly long phase of entry into the research. In the case of the study on the anti-nuclear movement, the researcher who played the main role in organizing the study had already been an active participant in the movement for over two years. As the intervention on the Occitanist movement has had to be postponed, the phase of preparation for the entry into research will have lasted for an equivalent length of time. It is preferable, too, that the post-intervention phase should develop over as long a period as possible. One can at present, therefore, describe intervention as consisting of a central, intensive, phase of about three months, flanked by a pre-intervention phase lasting from several months to two years, and a post-intervention phase of one year at least. The longer the total duration of the intervention, the firmer the link between analysis and action. It is not desirable to prolong the isolation of the intervention group; the moment at which its activity should end is the moment when the group's internal problems begin to outweigh the group's roles as image or analyst of a movement. The interpersonal relations may play an increasingly important role, and, in particular, the group may put an end to its very special relationship with the researchers, either by incorporating them or by rejecting them. In future, the main effort towards innovation will have to be concentrated less on the intervention itself – the methods of which should nevertheless not be considered intangible – and more on the pre- and post-intervention phases, particularly the latter. Intervention should give concrete shape to our objective of *permanent sociology*.

An intervention cannot be crammed into a very short period, for it would then degenerate into group interviews and would thus lose its essential specificity. One must instead aim at ensuring as far as possible a lasting intervention to accompany a movement which is not merely a particular conflict and which holds a central and durable position in the life of a society.

The field of study may be a particular, circumstantial struggle; but the object of study can be only the movement, which is revealed in this particular struggle as it is in many others.

9

Self-analysis

A group of actors, exposed to its own action through confrontation with interlocutors and through recalling its expressed opinions and its behaviour during intervention, undertakes self-analysis through the desire to advance its militant activity: this is the principle of self-analysis. The group's work consists in analysing its own internal discussions, for it should not confine itself to seeking consensus, to reducing the gap between its own perception of the situation and that of its opponents and partners, or to diminishing the distance that separates the ideology of the movement from the opinions and the analyses that emerge from the group during intervention and the distance that separates the militant group from the researcher, who is conjointly a relatively external observer and a spokesman for the point of view of the movement, i.e. for the struggle in its most elevated sense. The group should not reaffirm its identity and its ideology through complicity with the researcher; nor should it renounce its militancy and behave as a 'subject' group submitting itself to an experiment. It must work upon its own experience in order to resolve the tensions that have been imposed upon it.

The group's work is the work of the movement involved in a conflict situation. The militants perform their analysis as militants; they endeavour to understand the stakes of their struggle and the reasons for their success or failure. Self-analysis leads the group further and further from its past experience towards an understanding of the movement itself. All progress in this direction is described as *flexion*.

Flexion may also be defined as self-criticism of the group's ideological language, since a group reflecting on its own struggle starts out not so much from a historical experience as from interpretative and justificatory language. We have described as language of the left this initial view of the student militants, who interpreted everything that occurred in the university as an expression of the interests of capitalism. The anti-nuclear movement also sets out by describing society in a language which is that of Utopia, i.e. the 'natural' condemnation of an adversary identified both with irrationality and with inhumanity. The supporters of the Occitanist movement, like the militant femininists, also set out from interpretative language rather than from a conflict or an event. What may be true of the 'young' movements is considerably less true of the 'mature' movements, which become increasingly reduced to a more or less institutionalized conflict. It is just as difficult to cut across this language as it is to reach beyond the categories of the dominant order: both alike transform social relations into natural categories and moral principles. Sociological intervention must reveal the relationships concealed by this language. And this is more difficult than one might imagine, since the youngest movements are those which least well define their opponent and which are most inclined to confuse the definitions of the actor, the opponent, and the stakes of the conflict by merging them in a global, Utopian image of society. The intervention programme is linked to the transition from the language to the practices of the struggle and hence to the internal differentiation of the group, which first emerges as the unanimous transmitter of a particular language, and then gradually reveals itself as a centre for discussion and political choice.

Flexions

During these confrontations with the interlocutors, the group is already defined by its participation in the intervention, and hence by its self-analysis. Even though it may act as a witness to a historical event or a social problem, it is no longer a real historical actor. It cannot negotiate with its opponent in the conference hall; it does not make its decisions publicly known; and outside the sessions, group members maintain a discreet silence as regards their work. This, then, is the first of the flexions which are to mark off the stages of self-analysis.

From the moment when the group goes back to discussing its statements and former experiences, it is performing a second flexion, that of reflexivity. The witness-group, which was also a confrontation group, now becomes an image-group: its internal life is a figuration of the problems of the movement represented by the group. The discussions between the various trends within the group are representative of the debates held within the movement itself. The group's capacity to adopt a position with regard to certain problems or, conversely, its tendency to evade others, is an indication of the movement's orientations or its capacity for action. A new flexion – the most important of all – known as *conversion* (a term which has no religious connotation) transforms the image-group into an analyst-group. The group is no longer merely reliving the general problems of a real historical struggle;

it is now moving over towards analysis of the social movement; like the researcher – and with him – it is reflecting upon the nature of its action and on the presence of a social movement in the struggle. Thus at times the group rises as high as the struggle itself, occasionally even higher. It no longer analyses the past; it explores the possibility of a social movement and, more concretely, the possibility of overcoming crisis or of attaining a higher level of action and mobilization. Finally, one last flexion leads from the analyst group to the *mixed group of self-interpretation*, based on the communication to the group of the researcher's interpretations and on the subsequent joint reflexion. The group, which now includes the researchers – whose interpretations are also relevant to their own role – analyses both the movement and its own activity, i.e. the history of the intervention.

Self-analysis is thus the process by which the actor is transformed into analyst without abandoning his participation in the movement and by maintaining a relation with the researchers in the intervention group. The increasing distance from past experience that is introduced by self-analysis may be created by the group itself. This occurs as soon as the group discusses a confrontation once the interlocutor has left; it happens in an even more pronounced way when the group decides or agrees to hold closed sessions in order to devote itself to a problem, a conflict, or a discussion that may have arisen during the preceding meetings.

The anti-nuclear militants, in particular, demanded far more such closed sessions than had been initially envisaged, thus demonstrating their readiness and ability to engage swiftly in self-analysis. This occurs in particular whenever the group meets for one or two weekends in an isolated place. The group becomes more and more freely installed in a time and space of its own, which it organizes. But this distance is also created by the researchers, in two main ways. The first, known as *reminding*, involves setting before the group all the information it has produced so that it is obliged to provide coherent responses to the entire body of problems with which it has been faced. Full tape-recordings are made of these sessions so that the group may, on request, return to a particular point and hear it again; the typed records of the meetings are forwarded to the group as rapidly as possible. During some sessions, the main topics of previous discussions, or important statements by certain participants, are noted on loose sheets, which sometimes completely cover the walls of the conference room; these sheets may be drawn up either by the participants or by the researchers. Finally, the use of video-tape would seem to be highly recommendable since it recaptures a past moment in the discussion far more effectively than recording tape.

This reminding work is by no means easy; the group prefers to carry on discussions fairly similar to those its members are accustomed to holding in their militant action rather than be confronted with their own statements and have to set them in order. They are well aware that in undertaking this task they are exposing their own internal divisions or the conflicting themes intermingled in their action and their ideology. The great interest aroused by video-tape – once one has overcome the narcissism of those who merely want to see themselves again – helps the participants to acquire a group memory and to view their own statements from a distance. This flexion, which is known as reflexivity, must be followed through as completely as possible; it is the agitator who takes the initiative, for, by being integrated in the group, he can help it to examine and analyse its earlier statements through listening again to them.

The second form of intervention by the researchers can be the joint act of two researchers. Once the agitator has enabled the group to form itself and has thus become associated with it in encounters with the interlocutors and in the subsequent reflexion on these encounters, the other researcher can emerge from his silence, leaving aside his task of recording the sessions, and take a more active part as a speaker in order to stimulate the group to conduct its own analysis, to adopt a distance towards its own experience, and to assume the point of view of the social movement, i.e. a principle of analysis, which is no longer simply the point of view of the struggle and of the historical event. In other instances, it is the agitator who plays the main role in the *conversion* which transforms the image-group into an analyst-group. Although reflexivity is assisted by the technical instruments of reminding, conversion cannot be achieved without the direct involvement of the researcher, an involvement which is manifested through his efforts to descry the movement within the struggle, i.e. to discern the meaning of this struggle at its highest point.

The researcher's intervention is indispensable in order to enable the group to advance beyond stereotype formulations and also to prevent it from closing in upon itself and becoming dominated by its interpersonal problems. The intervention group must break free from the *group illusion* so well analysed by D. Anzieu.* This illusion is important because it is not a simple group defence mechanism against an intervener or an outside authority; it makes its appearance when the group gives up its search for liberation, its rejection of established authority in order to indulge in its freedom, its power, or simply its removal from the constraints of social action thanks to an experimental situation. The group's defence of its collective identity or of a maternal image against a paternal type of authority may lead it to become

170

trapped in an illusion of freedom. Intervention guards against this group illusion by putting the group back in a situation of social conflict and thus establishing a close link between cultural liberation and social conflict, instead of dissolving the latter through a socially indeterminate image of the former.

During the intervention, the group, while not ceasing to be militant, and even moving further and further towards the point of view of the social movement in question, embarks upon an analysis of its former experience and of the intervention itself, right up till the final phase, when it becomes a mixed, self-interpreting group reflecting on its own history, a process which leads it very far from the witness-group it formed at the beginning. It is this self-analysis that the researcher studies: sociological intervention is *an analysis of self-analysis*. The study of a social struggle will therefore be published in the form of an analysis of the history of the intervention.

The intervention – through its history, its content, its discussions, and its internal events – enables us to reconstruct the analysis of the struggle, its nature, its orientations, its internal conflicts, and its transformations. Materially, this self-analysis is carried out essentially over a short, intense period. The longer the confrontation phase has to be – in order to avoid giving the group the opportunity of meeting a succession of interlocutors with artificially coherent and constant arguments, which would prevent it from using material sufficiently rich to enable it to carry out its own self-analysis – the greater are the chances of prolonged work leading to a successful transition to the crucial moment of conversion, which permits the figurehead-group to evolve into the analyst-group. This is why, after a protracted series of meetings, the interventions are concentrated on two or three working weekends. The conversion could take place during the first weekend, the second being devoted to meetings between the groups, and the third, and last, to the researchers' report and their interpretations. The procedures may vary, but it is important – at least at the present stage – to ensure that all interventions are given the same general form, which is that of a series of flexions which get the group working on increasingly internal data and thus give central importance to the conversion as a result of which the militant group ceases to be the actor in a struggle to become the analyst of the social movement in which it is itself involved. It should be clear, therefore, that the researcher does not intervene here as an expert, nor does the group function as a headquarters for devising a strategy or a tactic or answering the question: what is to be done? That the group cannot expect the researcher to provide an answer to its problems should be stated explicitly to all from the very outset.

Sociological intervention

The researcher's role is to develop hypotheses as to the nature of the struggle and to introduce to the group the most fitting hypothesis, i.e. the one which sees in the struggle the manifestation of a social movement of central importance. The researcher intervenes in the name of a 'favourable prejudice', which involves the danger of proffering too positive an interpretation and one which will be too easily accepted by a group flattered by the importance accorded to it. Thus, outside the group and inside the research team, the researcher must formulate very different and far more critical hypotheses. During the intervention, one of the two researchers – the one who does not take the initiative in the conversion – must introduce these other hypotheses, not as criticism of the struggle but as a representation of the base, i.e. of a little differentiated action in which withdrawal, protest, rupture, pressure and social movement are commingled in the experience of the militants and of the population in whose name they are acting. All flexion therefore requires good co-ordination between the two members of the research team: one must be drawing the group forward while the other is resisting this traction and at the same time protecting the group's homogeneity and hence its capacity to create a collective history.

The image-group

At the beginning, the group becomes formed – particularly vis-à-vis the researchers – around historical memories and an ideology. What the members of the group have in common is that they have taken part, directly or indirectly, in conflicts; also, in spite of the diversity of their positions, they have in common an interpretation of these conflicts, an ideology which defines the actors and the stakes of these conflicts. This community of ideas and feelings is all the stronger at the beginning of the group's life the more the group expects to be confronted by opponents and the more generally it wishes to strengthen its collective identity at the moment when it is to undergo critical examination and questioning, and to be exposed to internal debates which cannot but be seen as a threat or at least as a test. At this moment, it is the researcher who seems most dangerous to the group and appears to be the weakest of its partners. The group therefore takes up a self-affirming stance against him, occasionally in an aggressive manner, sometimes by closing up in distrustful silence. This is a dangerous situation, and one which can cause the intervention to fail from the very outset. The group must therefore be able to form itself in other ways than by relation to the researcher or even to future interlocutors. It must make its first flexion succeed, by recognizing its own

172

existence and its autonomy in relation to the practice of the struggles. It is difficult to imagine a different starting-point for the intervention than the awareness of a distance between the objectives and the means of the struggle, the movement and the conflict. The case of the students was clear: they had just held the longest strike in the history of French universities, and had given it an organizational coherence that had never been attained in previous strikes. Many of the students, however, had the feeling of having been defeated, and particularly of having been betrayed. Others, by contrast, criticized the irresponsibility of the diehards who had dragged the movement into its final phase of disintegration. Each of the militants personally lived through this clash between the strength of a mobilized movement, the failure of a strategy and the evidence of a defeat. In 1977, the Occitanist movement likewise felt itself torn between the powerful affirmation of its cultural identity and its partial and unstable incorporation in a powerfully progressing national left. At this same date, the anti-nuclear movement was marked both by the events of Malville and the death of a militant ecologist and by the tensions between a mainly cultural current of opinion and direct participation in the elections, which was all the more tempting since it had already resulted in considerable success. Faced with their own problems, the actors saw the intervention as providing an appropriate context for reflecting on the problems and dealing with them. There was a danger of the movement being weakened by public discussions. Through intervention, however, it was possible to put the cards on the table and discuss openly in order to strike a new balance and continue the action in the best conditions. The confrontations, particularly with the opponents, disrupted the unity of their ideological speech and transformed already lived experience into a field for debate and divergent or conflicting interpretations. The witness-group became an *image-group*. During the sessions, the contours of the group, i.e. the distribution of attitudes and positions among the members, began to become more and more clearly outlined for each major topic. First of all, there were the already recognized conflicts which emerge particularly when the group includes militants from different organizations. One should not be surprised, in a group of trade-unionists, to rediscover the issues which separate the CGT (*Confedération générale du travail*) from the CFDT (*Conféderation française et démocratique du travail*) and the FO (*Force ouvrière*). The documents consulted before the intervention enabled one even to foresee – in the case of the students – the tensions which would arise between members of the UNEF (*Union nationale des étudiants de France*) and militants of other organizations on the one hand, and between the organized and non-organized groups on the other.

But the work of the image-group swiftly moves beyond ideologies to the discovery of other rifts than those which separate and oppose different organizations.

The researchers' role is to descry the real configuration of the relations within the group concerning all the major topics. The researchers fill out this configuration by encouraging the group to take up the same topics several times from different angles in order to ensure the stability of the respective positions and by requiring the group, and particularly the individuals concerned, to review certain of their earlier statements, particularly when they seem to represent a development or even a reversal. This reintroduction of earlier declarations enables the researchers to keep the group constantly under the pressure of its historical role, its conflict with its adversaries, and the events in which the movement has been involved. The general problems are repeatedly introduced so that the group is not given the opportunity to become locked in by its inter-personal problems. The researchers intervene by introducing facts and ideas that are external to the group, such as written or visual material, quotations, reminders of past events, political or economic data, historical or international comparisons, etc. Their objective is to fix firmly the configuration of the positions and relations which are taking shape before them and which they are helping to bring out. All information that produces a clear and stable interaction between the members of the group is a *pertinent* element for the construction of the movement. The researchers also ask the group to follow through their discussion of a topic until it has been exhausted, and they endeavour to make the group return to the topic and take it up again until no further information emerges and the same positions are adopted again by the same actors in spite of the changes that have occurred in the group's life and in the way these themes are introduced.

The presence of interlocutors is better than any other initiative as a means of bringing about the formation of the image-group. The livelier a confrontation has been, the more it generates discussion within the group. Thus, for instance, the students at Amiens, immediately after their violent confrontation with the chief leader of the right-wing students at their university, spontaneously engaged in a dramatic discussion in which members of the UNEF were set in opposition against the other participants. Hence the importance of the closed sessions, the exact place of which cannot be entirely foreseen since they are often rendered necessary as the outcome of confrontations.

This work by the group upon itself and the emergence of pertinent traits of the struggle and of the inner life of the movement produce important *tensions* which may result in the disintegration of the group or in the departure of certain members of the group, who are more or less clearly expelled by the others. During the intervention on the student movement, both at Bordeaux and at Amiens, the representatives of the UNEF, on being attacked by the other participants, were ready to break off the discussions, and decided to remain only because the researchers helped them regain their self-assurance, and even more because they were convinced that the success of their group would mark an important step forward in the direction desired by the UNEF itself. At Amiens, the only student to have introduced in his group the topic of cultural revolt, asking each person to declare his personal reasons for being militant, and according the greatest importance to the struggle of the women at the university, was attacked by the most active members of the group; after which, having participated in silence at several sessions, he disappeared towards the end of the intervention. It was not until a year later that he reappeared, at a session for discussing the researchers' report – and he still remained different from the rest of the group. Another student at Amiens, the only one to have defended the absolute priority of political action over union action in the student context, was attacked repeatedly and so violently that for a while he stopped participating in the research, and, during the joint meeting of the groups from Amiens and Bordeaux, went to sit in the midst of the Bordeaux students. One year later, his position had radically changed; according to him, this change was largely a result of the intervention. Thus there is formed a *research-history*, which is that of self-analysis; it cannot be reduced to the inner life of a group defined only by its present; nor is it the mere repetition of past events and historical discussions. It is the *image* of the problems of the struggle.

The group works because it has to resolve the tensions existing between its experience and its ideology, between its own view of the situation and that of its interlocutors, between the objectives of the struggle and the direction of the movement, between itself and the researchers, and even between the agitator and the secretary, since he too experiences this tension. In addition to these, there is a further tension, which is actually no more than a different formulation of the main tension between the struggle and the movement. On the one hand, the movement must project itself into Utopia in order to escape from the constraints of the domination which encloses it in a defensive position; on the other hand, it cannot define itself outside of its opponents and beyond their field of conflict, hence outside a strategy of struggle. A. Willener* has stressed the importance of the imaginary and of Utopia as a locus of social movement. This idea can be applied not only to a movement such as that of May '68 in France, which was as important because of what it imagined as because of what it achieved. This is why during self-analysis the group can be called upon to react to words, events, and topics which are sufficiently charged with symbolic value to appeal to the group's imaginary power.

But we should beware of giving priority to whatever is nascent and little structured and of being caught in the trap of making a superficial counter-distinction between spontaneous action and the organization of action, which is always considered as bureaucratic. A movement is important only if it fights against a real enemy in a domain that is central to social life. Its imaginary power should not distance it from the historical conditions in which it acts, but should rather raise it from a particular struggle towards a more general conflict. An action which was pure movement, hovering above concrete conflicts, might easily in spite of its possibly revolutionary appearance be merely a moderniz-ing current capable of overturning the customs and ideas of the past, yet still without being a social movement, i.e. not challenging any of the vital social relations. This remark holds in particular for what some people have described as the youth revolution, particularly in the United States. Where some people see a revolutionary uprising, I see the impatience of a cultural modernization movement, which is very different from the challenging of technocracy by American, German, or French students, in which the social movements of the future have already revealed themselves, even if confusedly. It is important there-fore to be precise in situating the struggle between these two poles, that of Utopia, which lies above the struggles but may also become a simple modernizing model, and that of strategy, which may be simple pressure or protest and which also stands for confrontation with an opponent and the definition of a conflict.

The analyst-group

The *conversion*, i.e. the transition from the image-group to the analyst-group, is the key point of the intervention, since at this moment the group ceases to operate at the level of the concrete struggle and of its ideology, to revive the event or debate the choices to be made as they arise in practice, and now turns to examining its action from the point of view of the *movement* itself, i.e. that of the very particular and very superior type of struggle which, according to the joint hypothesis of the actors and the researchers, is present in the struggle. The reference to past experience is replaced by examination of the possibility, the conditions and forms of a social movement in the field under consid-eration. The analysis of the real struggle has by then made it possible to distinguish between the components and has also revealed that the various members of the group attributed different meanings to the struggle. What must now be done is to adopt the point of view of only one of these meanings – that of the social movement – and to examine whether and to what extent it can govern action.

This transition from image-group to analyst-group would seem highly improbable in any other context than that of intervention. In intervention, the passage from one form to the other may occur spontaneously or it may instead be engineered by the researchers; it may be clear-cut or it may be confused, with the stages we have distinguished partly overlapping. But whatever the modalities of this transition may be, it must be the work of the group; at the same time, it demands active participation from the researcher, since his main role is to create – and get the group to recognize – a distance between the struggle and the social movement borne within it. The group manages its conversion more easily if it is not too strongly identified with a particular historical event and also if it feels responsible towards itself and independent with regard to the researchers. The first point would seem to have been proved by the contrast between the Amiens group and the Bordeaux group in the intervention on the student movement. The Amiens group was very close to the strike committee formed during the great struggle of 1976; this group proved to be more active than the Bordeaux group in confrontations with its opponents and showed itself capable of analysing its own action with much force and originality. But the very intensity of this group's involvement made it more difficult for the group to withdraw in order to take a more abstract view of the possible movement. By contrast, the Bordeaux group, which had played a less vital role in the strike and whose confrontations had consequently been less lively, succeeded in performing their conversion over a weekend at Toignan, while the group from Amiens, in spite of their extremely rich discussions, did not manage to achieve the conversion which they had nevertheless felt to be necessary. Each participant stuck to his guns; earlier statements were taken up again, which gave rise to new and often violent confrontations, but prevented the group from questioning the general nature of the students' movement, and from examining its objectives and the conditions for its success.

With regard to the second point, would not too positive and too powerful a link with the researcher incur the risk of either revealing or creating resistance towards going beyond the experience and hence the concrete life of the group?

The group should not expect reassurance, guidance, or protection from the researcher; conversely, however, too great a distance or too much tension between the group and the researcher can prevent the group from carrying out its conversion, for it sees conversion as sub-ordination to the researcher and to his point of view.

This conversion inevitably marks a break in the group's life. Its behaviour alters. The group becomes distanced from its specific ex-perience, particularly when it is directly defined by its involvement in a conflict, when its members are 'grass-roots' militants or even simply members of the population concerned, for there is then a very great distance between particular experience and general questioning.

The researcher intervenes in the research through the group from the historical field of action in which the movement occurs. What is the nature of the actor involved, and in what way is he a class actor? What is the character of his opponent? Finally – and above all – what are the cultural stakes of the conflict? Here it is that ideological resistance is greatest, for the actor must now no longer recognize what it is that sets him against his opponent, but what it is he has in common with him, i.e. the cultural field in which they are meeting and fighting. The researcher, therefore, is no longer a group 'animator' attempting to consolidate the group in the face of its adversaries or its internal divisions. He maintains a certain distance vis-à-vis the group; he raises questions, clarifies obscurities, and cuts down the silences, but he also puts forward proposals, mentions examples, and enters into the dis-cussion. The analyst-group aims primarily at working out the different meanings of its struggle. It does so by direct reflexion, aided by the researcher, and particularly by examining the situations in which it finds itself placed during the heat of the intervention. The group defines its relations towards its opponents and towards its own action: is this protest action, political pressure, opposition to exclusion, or a social movement? The researcher must ask the group to persist with its analysis until the sociological interpretation of this analysis seems clear and stable. If the researcher has the impression that the first results are not mutually coherent, for instance that the relation towards an oppo-nent may at times be fixed at the level of class relations and at other times merely at the level of protest, he confronts the group with the problem until they are no longer able to alter or reject their position.

Thus the group, by carrying out its own self-analysis, does not become a substitute for the researcher, even though the efforts of both are to bring two modes of analysis as close as possible together, for the group always remains militant, and therefore ideological, and adopts the viewpoint of its own action, i.e. the combination of the various meanings of its struggle in a given context of events, while the re-searcher, whose approach is less synthetic and more analytic, en-deavours to distinguish between the various meanings of the action. The actor, by becoming an *analyst* does not cease to be an *actor*; he progresses towards self-analysis, examines his action from a point of view which is not that of immediate action, but he cannot completely become an analyst and question his own fact-finding work, for this would cut him off from action. This is why the self-analysis group and the researcher's intervention are the two complementary agents of the work upon the movement. It is through the interaction between the group and the researcher that the action is analysed. Whether the researcher identifies himself with the group and expects it to provide him with a revelation of the truth, or whether instead he wishes to conduct the analysis entirely by using the group, failure is inevitable. The further the intervention advances, the more crucial becomes the dialogue between the group and the researcher, between the action being analysed and the analysis which aims at making the movement appear.

The researcher who plays the main role in the conversion finds himself in a difficult situation. Firstly, because he must distance himself from the group, resist its group-language and its solidarity. He speaks the language of the analysis and of the history to which the experience of the group and of each of its members offers resistance. Secondly – and perhaps even more so – because the distance between the group and the movement is evidenced during the conversion by the distance that grows up between the researcher and the group. No conversion is directly and entirely successful. Certain members of the group *rise* more swiftly than others; some, on the other hand, reject the conversion or do not accomplish it successfully. The group straggles out like a column of cyclists riding up a slope. The members of the group who resist conversion readily accuse the researcher of 'breaking up' the group or of placing the members themselves in a false position. Yet the researcher feels a sense of solidarity with the group, while at the same time becoming the interpreter of a possible movement. He suffers from the tensions which he himself provokes and at the centre of which he is placed. It is even to be feared that a researcher who identifies himself too strongly with the group does not dare to enter wholeheartedly into the conversion for fear of setting up a distance between the group and himself, which is probably what occurred in one of the study groups on the anti-nuclear militants. In the other group, which was from the outset extremely heterogeneous, a conversion carried out in a highly voluntarist manner ultimately led to the creation of a very great distance between the members of the group, as a result of which several members were driven temporarily to withdraw, while four or five participants were driven to the opposite extreme by this urgent intervention and went somewhat further than they should have, so that in the last part of the weekend certain among

179

them were obliged to retract their behaviour, which created an extremely uncomfortable situation for the researcher. These contrasting examples remind us that the researcher is not an observer in the conversion but an actor. Hence the need for a properly functioning research team. Whichever of the researchers is directly engaged in the conversion will need the support of the other, who must endeavour to maintain the unity of the group by alleviating the effects of his colleague's over-powerful intervention.

From analysis to interpretation

After its conversion, the group passes through three stages: the analysis it carries out with the researcher; its meeting with the other group or groups; the transition to a mixed group of self-interpretation based on the communication by the researchers of their interpretation of the research and the movement itself.

1. During the actual *self-analysis* of the movement, the relations between the members of the group undergo transformation: they no longer form a pattern representing the tendencies and choices of the movement; they are governed by the transition to an analysis which not all want to make or succeed in making. Self-analysis imposes upon the group members a certain interpretation of the event and, more generally, a concept of ultimate action. Consequently, one sees the positions earlier held being transformed into attitudes towards the social movement itself. Analysis of the differences in attitude is followed by analysis of the levels of the project and the struggle: institutional pressure, protest claims, crisis behaviour, or social movement. The main danger here is of becoming too far removed from real collective practice and of imagining a social movement without being able to convert general ideas into objectives and means of action.

2. The *group encounters* do not acquire their full importance unless the groups are already engaged upon their self-analysis. If they have assumed a position that is directed more towards the research than towards the movement, the encounter is likely to be dominated by the collision between two groups which have been formed both around a particular past experience and around a different relationship towards the researchers who use the same words but do not attribute quite the same meaning to them. By contrast, a group that is well advanced in its self-analysis seeks to apply its conclusions to the other group, and hence to consider it from the point of view of the movement. In the intervention on the students, the encounter between the two groups

was difficult because only the Bordeaux group had advanced with its self-analysis and thus, in its relationship with the research leader, dominated the main part of the work in common, while the group from Amiens, which had come to the meeting as a militant group firmly intending to impose its strength upon the Bordeaux group, revealed the fragility of its positions, reacted strongly against the opposing group, and then withdrew into distrustful silence. This imbalance revealed in particular the student movement's inability to connect analysis with action and to reconstruct practices from interpretations. The group encounters, therefore, already marked a return towards action, the transformation of an analysis into orientations that might be accepted and implemented by other actors.

3. The *communication of the researchers' interpretations*, on the other hand, leads us inwards to the analysis. The researchers communicate two sets of interpretation to the group. Firstly, interpretation of the struggle itself: is it a social movement or not? What other directions does it take? What are its main problems, its most important conflicts and choices? How can its evolution be defined? Secondly, interpretation of the intervention itself. The first set of interpretations goes beyond the work that has been carried out by the group as a self-analyst. It is presented in the language of sociology – not that of action or ideology – in such a way as to reveal to the actors all the implications of their own analytical approach. The group's reactions also help the researchers to adopt a critical attitude towards their own interpretations, which cannot be completely dissociated from the experience they have just emerged from or from their relations with the group and with the other researchers. This communication is therefore followed by a discussion which should lead to precise proposals concerning the transformation or reformulation of the researchers' ideas.

What is even more interesting is the presentation of the theories on the research: these must be precise. They bear upon the group's history, the inter-personal relations, the incidents that have occurred, the drift of certain discussions, and the interpretation of the relations between the two groups – both during their encounter and throughout the intervention – and also the interpretation of the relations between the researchers and the group. The researchers adopt a distance with regard to themselves, and, in so doing, become incorporated as participants in the intervention on the group under study, which puts an end to their position as outsiders and hence to the relation upon which the intervention is based. The researchers must say how they analyse the behaviour, the position within the group, and the personal development of each of the actors; this explanation will then elicit other interpretations from the group, particularly concerning the role of the participants, their relations with the researchers and the development of their attitudes. The importance of the interpretations of individual behaviour is such that, after the collective work has been finished, individual meetings are held during which the participants give a more complete account of their impressions of the intervention, of how they experienced it and how it altered their relation to the movement. The researcher profits from these meetings by collecting information on the participants which they consider it would be useful for him to know.

It is therefore during this final phase that the group, having become a mixed self-interpretation group, is able to analyse the *personal behaviour* of its members. During the greater part of its work, the group has not been centred upon itself, and still less upon the personal problems of its members. But as from the moment when, with the aid of the researchers, it becomes an analyst-group and defines the nature of its action, it must revert to its own experience and give an account thereof. Initially, it interprets its own history as a group; but it may go further, to explore the question of whether the behaviour of its members can be fully explained in terms of the movement's problems, or whether the reasons for their being militant do not perhaps extend to situations other than those of which the militants present speak most readily. In the intervention on the students, the desire expressed by some to have the reasons for being militant analysed right from the start of the research was rejected by the groups. This was a foreseeable attitude, and one which had to be respected, for the group's task is to move towards collective not personal exploration. At the end of the intervention, however, the group members must ask themselves why they are militant, how a problem or an action affects, interests, or moves them, and also what their participation in the group has meant for them. This may lead to a critical examination of earlier interpretations which did not take into account this level of examination. Considered in this way, the problems of personal participation do not lead to a psychological interpretation, but remain instead linked to the problems of the movement and of its objectives.

The post-intervention phase, i.e. the participants' return to action, is more difficult to conceive and organize than the intervention itself, since it does not depend on the researchers alone, but far more on the actual organizations behind the struggle, from which the participants should not isolate themselves during the intervention.

It is not sufficient for the researchers alone to communicate their results to the militant circles, nor even for them to incorporate their analysis of the militants' reactions into their final report; it is far preferable that the group members themselves should handle the communication of the results so as to ensure that these results become incorporated into the action and ideology of the movement. This should then allow for subsequent two-way traffic between analysis and action. In action, the former members of the group are able to match the conclusions of the intervention against their new experiences, on the basis of which they then return to re-examining the issues with the researchers. On the one hand, they will be proposing ways of completing or altering the hypotheses, and on the other hand they will be turning to the researchers for interpretation of the situations and the problems. Thus there should be born this *permanent sociology* which would enable analysis to progress unceasingly and the movements to act on the basis of an increasingly clear image of themselves, their opponents and their field of conflict.

I have several times heard militants express the fear that the intervention might lead to a therapeutic attitude, to a conciliatory quest for solutions or compromises. Such misgivings deserve attention, particularly when one is dealing with poorly organized struggles, for which strong institutionalizatio.1 would represent an advance rather than a retrograde step. But to yield to this tendency would at all events run counter to the very method of intervention, which presupposes the constant maintenance of a distance between action and analysis. Intervention does not propose solutions, nor does it seek to obtain agreement between opponents; it informs the actor as to the nature of his situation and his action; it should help him to reach towards the maximum action possible; and it enables him to understand his personal development or his internal problems. In short, it increases his capacity for action, and this may – depending on the situations – either cause deeper conflicts to break out or prepare the way for settling those which are less central than one had realized. In no circumstances, therefore, should the researcher accept the status of expert or intermediary in connection with his intervention. He is neither working on behalf of an organization nor acting as a defender in principle of the social peace; nor is he bound up with state arbitration. He has no power at his disposal; yet he must, in return, be assured of his independence. The results of his research are published entirely upon his own responsibility.

Return to history

After the end of the intervention, the researcher endeavours to strengthen his analysis by showing that it allows for better understanding of the documents and the events. This step is quite natural when one is dealing with the most important category of documents of this order:

ideological writings, statements and declarations, and reports of discussions. What is required is explanation of the actor's speech through sociological analysis of the social movement. Thus a social history may be developed which will be neither an appendix to economic history nor a moralizing epic recounting the liberation of the just or the misdeeds of the all-powerful oppressor.

One must nevertheless mark the limits of this rereading of history and of the strengthening it gives to the hypotheses worked out in and through the intervention. First of all, because the historical documents are often far poorer than those produced by and in the intervention itself, and hence they contribute scarcely anything new; next, because the intervention was undertaken with the aim of arriving at an analysis, at separating out the various significations of a struggle, while the historical document shows how they become intermingled at a given moment and in a particular place. One cannot require the sociologist to account wholly for the movement; this is why I prefer to speak of the strengthening rather than the verification or validation of the hypotheses.

Will it be possible to go further and reinterpret the documents of our past or of another society on the basis of information gathered from a set of interventions? How can one possibly renounce this hope? History has been ceaselessly enriched and transformed by recourse to the human sciences – initially economic analysis, and more recently anthropology. Sociological intervention is so closely linked to a sociology of action that it should provide social history with the analytical instruments it needs. It is my heartfelt wish that historians in their research might use ideas developed through sociological intervention, firstly in areas close to those where sociology is at present engaged, but later on for periods or societies more distantly removed from our own.

Group history and the meaning and direction of movements

For the historian, however, the usefulness of sociological intervention should not be confused with the usefulness of investigation or of participant observation, which furnish only documents. The aim of intervention is not to provide the researchers with information concerning a social struggle, information which may be more complete or more vital than could have been obtained through the consultation of historical documents or by holding individual or collective meetings. It is not a particular procedure for gathering data. All the less so since, if one were to regard it in this light, its advantages would not be unaccompanied by disadvantages.

If a research team is able to devote around four hundred hours (one hundred per researcher) to gathering information, why should this time not be used to discover the point of view of some hundred actors distributed over a far greater number of places and belonging to a great diversity of tendencies? Would not this be the best way of coming closer to the understanding of a population, since the concentration of research onto two groups of a dozen members each tends to reduce a movement to the organizations and currents of opinion which represent it only partially? Instead of working with Occitanist militants only in Montpellier and Carcassonne, or with student strikers only in Bordeaux and Amiens, why should one not cover all the regions of France in the latter case and all parts of Occitania in the former, contacting a wide variety of actors, some of them militants in organizations, others simply sympathizers, some opposed to the movement under study, others merely indifferent? These objections rightly remind us that the method of intervention, if considered as a means of gathering information, has more disadvantages than advantages since it concentrates attention on too small a number of cases and distorts the declarations by exposing them to prolonged action by a group in conditions very different from those of historical action. But the aim of intervention is different: it is to understand the meaning of a struggle by analysing the life and history of the intervention groups. And this is done by conforming to three principles which, in concluding, we must now recall: the analysis bears on the life of the groups; these groups are involved in analysing and interpreting both the movement they represent and their own activity as an intervention group; the researcher intervenes actively and studies the responses to his intervention.

1. *The group's life* makes it possible to reconstruct the movement's discussions, and hence the field of its political behaviour and, beyond this, the nature of its orientations.

At the conclusion of the first phase of research and particularly of confrontation, the ideological shell of the movement has been cracked or even destroyed; it becomes replaced by a great diversity of opinions and attitudes.

No actor any longer holds the monopoly over a meaning for the movement which the sociologist, like the other participants, is endeavouring to reconstitute, though without being able at this moment to go beyond simple hypotheses.

2. During the central phase of research, these hypotheses are matched against *the work of the group upon itself*, first as representative of a real historical struggle, then increasingly as an analyst.

The self-analysis reveals a struggle in the process of recognizing its various meanings and directions and ordering them in terms of whatever features of social movement emerge from the struggle. The further the self-analysis progresses, the more the group – in the histori- cal practice to which it refers – distinguishes between the various fields of action corresponding to the main types of struggle described in the first part of this book, or to their combination. This results in con- siderable revision of many of the opinions expressed at the beginning of intervention. The students, for instance, had set out by defining teachers as the ideological agents of the bourgeoisie. Self-analysis led them to adopt a very different position. On one of the loose sheets – which we nicknamed 'dazibaos' – we had written the question: are teachers chiefly ideologists in the service of the bourgeoisie and the dominant order, or are they rather mandarins protecting their corpo- rate privileges? By the end of the intervention, there could be no doubt as to the answer – it was the second that had been chosen; and this was further complemented by the students' increasingly clear recognition of the interest they brought to their studies. Instead of seeing them- selves as allies of the workers or as young intellectual workers fighting against bourgeois ideology, the students recognized themselves as being attached to the University and to their studies but rejected by a teaching-staff body wrapped up in its own language, its own interests and privileges. Their mixture of general social criticism of capitalism and attacks against the University gave way to the attempt to distin- guish two orders of problems – internal and external, university and general. This separation of the problems swiftly emerged as the central rift of the student movement.

The group may venture far with its self-analysis, yet it never gives itself over completely to it, for it never stops being a group of militants, and hence an ideologist. The researcher, then, observes the tension between the self-analysis and the ideology, and the difficult task for the group of working upon itself; the content and the limits of the mean- ing thus attributed by the group to its own action cause the researcher to penetrate far more deeply into the problems of the movement than he could by simply gathering opinions which are neither inter- connected nor exposed to the influence of other opinions.

3. *The researcher* must help the group engaged in this work of self- analysis, not only by asking it to explain its approach but also by offering his own theories both on the presence of social movement in the struggle and on the history of the group. This questioning should be addressed directly to the group, as this forces the researcher to enter as directly as possible into the discussion; his role being, after all, to ensure that whatever element of social movement, and hence of histor-

ical action at the highest level, is present in the struggle should be brought out and recognized.

Thus, by the end of the intervention, the researcher finds himself facing a powerful battery of arguments, debates and conflicts. It would be absurd to break down what had been thus constructed in order to draw out mutually isolated facts or to illustrate a historical account. Instead, one must propose a set of hypotheses which would account for this rich battery of statements and of behaviour. Intervention is more constraining than other methods. An opinion poll is a historical document, as Paul Lazarsfeld rightly remarked, and it therefore imposes only slight constraints on the researcher, who may interpret its historical significance fairly freely. On the other hand, it yields only opinions and judgements on a situation described directly in terms of social practice. By contrast, the results of intervention, through their mass and their interdependence, resist such freedom of interpretation. Our method increases still further the frailty of the ideas – no matter how perspicacious and imaginative they may be – expressed by the observers, who satisfy themselves with selecting a certain number of facts without saying or without knowing that these facts form part of a whole from which one has no right to extract and isolate them.

This is why the *history of the group* better defines the object upon which the researcher's work is focussed. Intervention is a fairly long process, and its purpose is sufficiently important in the eyes of those who participate for it to become a personal history for each of them, a history marked by changes of attitude, of friendship, and of plan. During the intervention on the students we witnessed friendships breaking down, militants abandoning their organization, others taking up new commitments, and some – by contrast – holding out in the same position against the force of wind and tide. Some reproached us with having created such crises and thus weakened the movement, a reproach which was truly unjust since in the case of the students these crises were not an indication of the effect of intervention on the individuals but rather of the fact that they had come to grips with the serious difficulties of the student struggle. Research will certainly not give a reassuring, hagiographic, picture of the movement which it is studying and it cannot guarantee to protect any participant against painful recantation of his commitments and declarations. It simply brings participants closer to the real situation in which they find themselves, which cannot but increase their capacity for collective action. All the same, all social struggles, in proceeding to self-criticism and self-revision, become torn apart by internal battles and debates. Are the most important movements those which give rise merely to a general but vague concensus among the participants?

Sociological intervention

Group work

The essence of the sociological method of intervention is that a group of actors, both in their group interaction and in interaction with the researchers, should be able to experience the problems of the movement and the choices it affords.

The intervention group is not just an observer or the representative of a movement: it is the movement. In an extremely particular situation, the group's life is analogous to that of the movement. The research carried out on the students gave precise expression to this general idea.

The students, or certain among them, were prepared to recognize that the social use of knowledge represented the stakes of the social movement which might be present in their struggle. But this realization became important only insofar as the group really undertook to reacquire the knowledge of the movement that had been introduced by the sociologists. The group feared being subjected to the appraisal of an expert; it wanted to have charge over its own knowledge of itself, which inevitably involved joint work with the researchers. In the same way, the students' struggle was unable to become a social movement without criticizing the way in which knowledge is produced and used, which involved the support of scientists and not the rejection of scientific knowledge. The group had to experience internally its own thoughts about the struggle. With regard to the relationship between the group and the researchers, one may generalize from the observation made of the students: for the femininists, the Occitanists, the worker trade-unionists and even the ecologists, the researcher – particularly if he is a man, a Parisian, and a member of the middle class, and a rationalist – is regarded as a threat to the group's past experience. The research situation itself is a threat to action. The militants must overcome this mistrustful opposition and declare their independence while continuing to use the knowledge contributed by the researchers, so that the existence of a social movement should be practically demonstrated.

Whatever occurs between the group and the researcher is one of the indications of the nature of the movement. The other indication is to be found in what occurs between the members of the group themselves. If the group behaves as a community concerned with maintaining its unity, particularly vis-à-vis the researcher, it means that the movement is unable to separate and to hierarchize its various significations. Every intervention group chooses between this top-heavy hierarchization of conflicts which are internal to it and a global attitude of ideological negation or utopian affirmation demonstrated by the priority given to

188

the group and to its collective identity with regard to its partners, researchers, or interlocutors. What matters most, then, does not lie in the opinions which the group expresses and which the researcher could reconstitute coherently in order to extract the principles of a movement, while also revealing the diversity of its members and their reasons for being militant; it lies, rather, in the group work, in the social relations between group members or between them and the interlocutors and researchers.

From the very start of the intervention, the researchers must avoid being considered as people who must be informed by the group in order that they may later be able to give as fair as possible a picture of the struggle. This is why the experience of the intervention group may lead some of the participants to abandon a struggle which could not be defined under controlled conditions, or else to modify or step up their militant participation as an outcome of the group results. These are two opposed effects of intervention which we encountered from our very first application of the method.

Self-analysis and interpretation

We must, for once and for all, be on our guard against the illusion of a merging between the researcher and the group. The group carries out its own self-analysis; the researcher suggests an interpretation and causes it to be discussed: do these two processes come naturally together in such a way that the researcher's interpretation becomes the culmination of a self-analysis that finds its recognition therein? Is this recognition the test of the truth of the interpretation; must the intervention end with the members of the group telling the researcher that he has understood them well? This idea is unacceptable. How is one to be protected against the influence of the researcher, who has been turned into a well-loved leader and who has managed to win the approval of the group which, in turn, wishes to be loved by him? The researcher must undertake alone the responsibility for his interpretation; the analyst-group is not a sociologist-group.

The group cannot completely analyse its own behaviour since the actors cannot unburden themselves of all their ideology without ceasing to be militants. This is why the group cannot be held responsible for the researcher's interpretations. But the researcher must be able to account for the group's reactions to his interpretations and likewise for the group's behaviour as a whole. The mixed self-interpretation group provides particularly important documents which are, however, not fundamentally different in nature from the documents produced during the other phases of intervention. It would be dangerous to allow the group to run away with the impression that it is to draw conclusions from the intervention and that the researcher is no more than its spokesman. It is this relative independence which enables the group to assess the consequences its work will have upon its own action and to maintain constant two-way contact with the researchers.

The gap which lies between the group members' analysis and the researchers' analysis is the gap which separates class awareness from the awareness of class relations. The worker subjected to labour organization is aware of being dominated or exploited, but he cannot be both judge and defendant; he is only defendant. He identifies himself with rationality and refuses to consider his opponent as an agent of this rationality and of progress. The sociologist, on the other hand, analyses not the actor's awareness but – beyond this awareness – the social relation between the actor and his opponent and the stakes of the conflict. Hence, it is normal that the researcher and the group, or certain members of the group, should not arrive at the same conclusions.

This divergence of opinion is even desirable, since it forces the researchers to explain the ins and outs of their reasoning and to base their conclusions as exclusively as possible on information derived from the intervention, and to be ready to present separately certain more general or more historical interpretations.

It is useful for the group to criticize and interpret the researchers' interpretation. The researchers must endeavour, together with the group and other representatives of the movement, to hold as long as possible a discussion on their interpretation in order to free themselves from the judgements imposed upon them by their situation and by their own opinions.

Pattern of an intervention

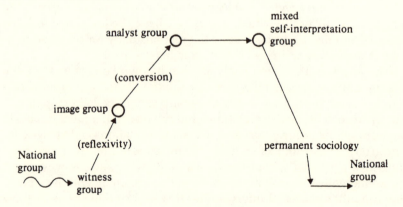

190

10

The researchers

The researcher's role is determined by his research objective. If one is concerned with observing the functioning of groups and their efforts to transform themselves, one can place an analyst-group before the group being analysed, in order to avoid the danger of a researcher emerging as a leader whose presence would diminish the group's autonomy and prevent it from liberating itself. If the objective is to study the conditions of adaptation of a group or organization to its environment, the researcher must be an experimenter, observing the group from outside.

In sociological intervention, it is up to the group to analyse a historical action, i.e. to distinguish between the different significations and extract the element of social movement in the struggle. The researcher is therefore in solidarity with the movement, since it is on the basis of the movement that he examines the group, but independently of the organization of the struggle. He intervenes in the self-analysis in order to emphasize the distance between a past experience and its sociological significance.

The researcher and the group

The researchers' role in the intervention has already been described, since it cannot be defined outside the interaction between the group and the researchers. But now we must adopt the point of view of the researchers themselves, the difficulties they encounter in their work and the conditions for the success of their intervention. One problem emerges from the outset: what should be the position of the researcher with respect to the movement he is studying and how can he combine his role as analyst with his involvement in the movement he is studying.

Let us recall again the principle of the method: the researcher looks at the struggle from the point of view of the movement which may be present in it. He does not, therefore, lie outside the field in which he intervenes; yet, on the other hand, he does not identify himself with the group on which he is working. He describes the movement through the group. At the beginning of the intervention, in confrontation with the interlocutors and particularly with the opponents of the group, he takes a stance of solidarity with the group, since it is he who must assist it to form itself into a representative of the movement. When the interlocutors are also other participants in the movement – at levels other than the militant level – the researcher begins to assume greater autonomy, since from now on he can adopt the point of view of the movement while still remaining as close to the interlocutors as he is to the group. In confrontation with the *image-group*, he is the one who questions but who still remains very close to the group and who – like the group itself – is placed inside the experience of the collective struggle. It is at the moment of *conversion* that the distance between the group and the movement is recognized by the group itself, and hence the researcher becomes the person who analyses the group in the name of the movement. His main aim is to bring out the link existing between the group and the movement, between the concrete struggle and a type of historical action. Finally, in communicating his interpretation to the group, he adopts a position which is – at least in appearance – one of externality, but it is a position which must be compensated by the initiative of the group, which also puts forward its own interpretation, with the result that a *mixed self-interpretation group* becomes formed, in which the group and the researcher are fused in an indentical relation towards the movement and in their mutual analysis of the intervention which they have just experienced together. Next, the researcher and the group move away from each other; the researcher develops his analysis and the group members transfer into the movement whatever has been gained from the intervention. Later, their interaction will take on new forms.

Agitator and secretary*

The researcher is simultaneously both the instigator of self-analysis and the actor of an intervention.

Let us mention again the combination of these two roles as defined at the beginning of this research programme. The agitator is the person who organizes the group, prepares the confrontations, conducts the sessions, and above all helps the group in its work by 'agitating' it, i.e. by pressing it to define its positions clearly, by pushing it to the limit in

* In recent 'interventions' we have used one researcher as a secretary, so that the remaining researchers can participate fully in the whole research process. We now call the 'agitator' the interpreter, and the 'secretary' – as described here – the analyst.

its discussions, and by reintroducing certain of the group's earlier statements or reactions.

But this definition is liable to prove inadequate. The agitator is better able to serve the group in its self-analysis if he accepts and experiences the re-questioning of certain of the group's attitudes under the effect of the movement in which it participates. He does not himself become incorporated in the action, but strives to enter into its cultural and social orientations. For how could he ask the militants to act as militants in the group if he himself did not behave as someone exposed to militant action, an action which might stimulate adherence or rejection, but not merely chilly attentiveness on the part of the experimenter?

Throughout the first stage of the intervention, the role of agitator is far more viable than that of secretary. The secretary takes notes, looks after the recording, prepares the transcription of the report of the sessions, and provides the documents the group requests; he may make observations, offer information in his personal capacity, or ask for clarification – but his role must remain secondary. It is not always necessary for such a distance to exist between the agitator and the secretary, but it is at all events preferable to a confusion of roles. This distance should not appear to be the result of hierarchization; generally, these roles should be relatively little formalized, and the actors should in no way be placed in a situation reminiscent of a laboratory experiment.

From the moment when self-analysis – and particularly conversion – develops, the secretary must be able to participate more actively in the group's work. At this stage, therefore, we ask another researcher to assume the secretary's role during the session.

This assistance may be offered to the secretary right from the start in order to enable him better to observe the group: the two researchers should not intervene simultaneously. The agitator's role is to help the group discern the presence of social movement within its struggle; the secretary's role is to criticize the struggle, i.e. to 'draw' it towards the social movement that may be present within it.

By intervening directly, the researcher – agitator or secretary – participates directly in the group's work.

Does he then become a group member like the others, expressing his personal ideas, taking part in the discussions, and supporting one side or the other? No. He is neither an observer nor an actor: he is a witness of the movement. In his relation to the group, he maintains a distance which is the distance separating the movement from the struggle; he questions the group less concerning real action than concerning possible action. But whoever observes the crucial moment of intervention will be particularly struck by the researcher's behaviour and by the strength of his intervention, so surprising for those accustomed to the non-directive approach of other group leaders and *animateurs*.

The researcher does not merely divulge his ideas, he endeavours to 'deliver' the group of the movement it 'bears'. At this moment, the group must be completely de-centred in relation to itself, motivated by the quest for the movement and by the historical role it may play.

If the struggle is close to a social movement, the secretary's intervention may remain limited, simply following alongside the group as it progresses. On the other hand, the further the struggle is from being a social movement, the more enclosed it is in its own limited protests and demands, and particularly in its rejection of order or in crisis behaviour, the more important the secretary's role becomes. In these marginal forms of struggle, the actor loses his capacity for action: he sees society as a rigid or a non-coherent order, as impersonal regulations or malign intentions, as something upon which he has no grip, something against which he pits his own subjectivity, his desire for freedom, self-expression, and attachment. The awareness of the presence of an objective obstacle and the inner pressure of a subjective need are two opposing forces which are mutually destructive and which drive the actor into alienation and contradiction. The researcher's role is to draw the group towards potential action, to give it the hope and strength of desire of a movement.

When the secretary assumes such a role, the agitator will be particularly concerned with maintaining the existence of the group threatened by the contradictions of the struggle itself. By contrast, wherever the movement is directly present in the struggle, the secretary has the more crucial role of separating the secondary significations of the struggle from its primary meaning, while the agitator intervenes little or even defines himself as the person who, through his participation in the group, draws closer to the movement, helps the group to understand it better and to become more powerfully attached to it. Thus each researcher's role cannot be defined independently of the nature of the struggle they are studying together.

One must break clearly away from the image of the researcher–listener. A psychological intervention, aimed at drawing closer to the problems of personality, at going right back to their formation by overcoming resistances and by decoding the unconscious, must be conducted patiently and silently. But here we are at the opposite extreme – that of history, not that of the individual. Confusion, doubt, and resistance must be dispelled so that one can come closer to the fire of society. The researcher realizes, humbly, that he is not an actor; but at the crucial moment of intervention he is a *prophet*. He does not call upon the group to move towards him but to go towards what he has proclaimed and yet does not possess – towards the movement, of which he will never be the guide. At this point, the relation between the group and the researcher is dramatic, and the researcher is drained by it. He is even in danger of becoming too personally engaged and of mixing his prophetic role with his personal situation and his reactions to the group. His co-researcher must therefore protect the group against over-intervention on his part and ensure that the group maintains control over its own self-analysis. When the time comes for communicating their theories, the researchers once again withdraw to a distance. The agitator is the one who puts forward the general ideas of the interpretation; the secretary follows by helping the group in turn to interpret both its own history and that of the intervention. The individual meetings and the sessions at which the researchers' reports are discussed are conducted mainly under the agitator's responsibility.

This distribution of tasks may be modified in consideration of the group's characteristics; what is essential is to avoid role confusion. In order to be effective, the method presupposes the combination of a highly structured situation together with the freest possible group initiative. The distance between the agitator and the secretary matches that between the struggle and the movement, and between analysis and action. This distance is therefore an essential element in the method. I cannot imagine an intervention group led by only one researcher assisted by a secretary entrusted only with writing up a report of the session and with controlling the recording. It might be suggested that the researchers should take turns in handling the intervention group in order to give greater opportunity for group initiative and to reduce the researcher's role in the analysis. But this procedure, which has been used by Gérard Mendel,* does not accord with the method of intervention in which one unites self-analysis with the researchers' intervention instead of attempting to separate them and, quite simply, to weaken the role of the agitator, who must constantly bring the past into the present.

The implication of intervention

The researcher does not endeavour to please the group, but he feels himself to be responsible towards the movement, as constructed both by analysis and by the militants' ideology. It is not up to the researcher to judge the group in the name of a movement with which he has no right to identify himself, and he should still less define his role within the group by his relations with the other members, without reference to a higher level of analysis and action. Lastly, the sociologist can

195

completely destroy all the conditions of intervention by abolishing the triangular relation of group–movement–researcher for the benefit of the group as an immediate collective experience or for his own sake as a manipulator or an exhibitionist.

The researcher who wishes to reduce his role in order to create a space of freedom and initiative within a group would be exposing himself to a curious contradiction, for the more he protected the liberty and spontaneity of the group the more he would isolate it from its own action, from its opponents and from the conditions of its initiative. Instead of extracting the movement from other forms of behaviour, instead of bringing out whatever was most creative and most challenging in the group, he would involve it in a total confusion of meanings, with the result that the group's truly internal problems and its role as representative of a more general movement would no longer be separable. The general meaning and direction of an action would then degenerate into the particular history of a network of interpersonal relations. This partly corresponds to the situation of militant groups wishing to break free from all organizational and institutional mediation for the sake of revolutionary spontaneity, or even of restricted communities which establish themselves outside the general network of social roles and which are privileged spheres of domination for minor leaders. Such groups rapidly become dominated by individual and collective forms of behaviour opposed to their ideology. In this kind of situation, the researcher's role is likely to be highly limited. What will most probably occur is that he will be driven out at the initiative of a leader who is disturbed by the intruding eye of an outsider even though he may be assured of the outsider's connivance.

This is why the researcher is far more tempted to reduce the relations of the group, the movement, and his own position to the mere demonstration of his power and his pleasure, playing upon the acceptance or rejection he inspires. Any effort to acquire knowledge of the movement disappears, therefore, particularly if such a researcher, once he has returned to his office, reconstructs the past experience by identifying his pleasure with social creativity and by contrasting it with the dead world of organization and order, while in reality he has found his pleasure only in destroying the actor.

Once these forms of behaviour – which are detrimental to all knowledge – have been thrust aside, one must consider those which merely deform the researcher's role as it has been defined but which are still more or less present in an intervention. The first of these is identification with the group, the second is the doctrinaire position which considers only the movement and which turns aside from the real group.

The researchers

The group's self-identification becomes strong when the researcher allows himself to be dominated by his own reinterpretation of the group's action; this self-identification becomes all the easier when the movement is sufficiently little organized and institutionalized for a particular group to be able to put itself forward as representative of the main direction of the movement. It may also be strengthened by other factors, related in particular to the actual functioning of the research team. A researcher may identify himself with the group in order to establish his status in the research team or to ensure the advancement of his team-leader or one of the other members. Quite simply, he feels himself to be insecure, and fears either that the group may reject him or that he may become its scapegoat. On the other hand, at the beginning of the intervention, he cannot indicate his attachment to the movement except by identifying himself with the group. This identification by the researcher strengthens the group in the first phase of its existence, particularly if its confrontation with opponents is occasionally difficult. The researcher's identification may even help the group to expand into an image-group and to carry out the first part of its self-analysis; but at the moment of *conversion* this identification becomes an obstacle, because conversion requires a change in point of view, with the researcher having to play an important role in shifting the group upwards from the level of the struggle to that of the movement.

No researcher, in fact, can maintain perfect balance between analysis and participation. Should one of the researchers, the agitator, identify himself strongly with the group the effect will be bad if the other, the secretary, is prevented from leading the group towards its conversion – or is unable to do so – or if a conflict emerges between the two researchers. On the other hand, this strong identification on the part of the researcher may be beneficial if from the outset the group is in danger of becoming unbalanced, or, alternatively, in situations when the agitator's support assists it in accepting the secretary's intervention at the time of conversion.

The reverse danger is that of the researcher adopting a *doctrinaire* attitude, confronting the group with an ideal image of the movement of which it is supposed to be the chosen interpreter. Such an attitude generates either a rejection or an acceptance, both of which destroy the interest of the intervention, which is then reduced to a grand lecture by the researcher.

Reference to the movement and to the general conditions for its realization should not occur until the moment of self-analysis, and particularly that of conversion. During the long phase of confrontation, such reference should not be made or should be made only very discreetly. The danger of doctrinaire intervention is great if the researcher finds himself in too powerful a situation vis-à-vis the group, particularly if he appears as the spokesman of the leaders or of the most influential group in the movement. To sum up: instead of defining the ideal image of the researcher one should rather stress the complementarity of his two roles, which are to strengthen the group's capacity for self-analysis and to assist it in achieving successful conversion away from the point of view of the struggle towards that of the movement.

Observation and commitment

It is this readiness to forge a vital link between militant action and analysis and this conscious use of the tension between the two roles as an instrument of research which contrasts this method to an approach which locates the analysis within the action, whether it be the weak formula described as participant observation or committed research (*engagée, comprometida*), which is more demanding.

Participant observation can provide only superficial information. If, for instance, an observer in industry produces as a result of his participant observation no more than an account of the workers' life, this document will be less interesting than the accounts of workers fully committed to and involved in the worker's condition. On the other hand, if the researcher resorts to participation in order to study the behaviour of workers and employers in specific work relationships, particularly in the implementation of pay systems or the work pace in a factory, his role will be considerable for he will cause what has been concealed to be revealed – slow-down tactics on the one side, and concrete methods for dominating the workers on the other. Anyone who observes the way – so difficult to perceive – in which workers in a work-shop under certain conditions establish their own collective production norms by resisting the incentives introduced by the management, will be enriching our knowledge of the workers' life and of the social relations of production. Other more classical methods may cast light upon these problems, but participant observation completes the picture in a most useful way. This method is important in such a case because the workers are responding defensively to an external pressure without having to question themselves as to the meaning of this defensive action. What one is dealing with, then, is a form of workers' action which, like absenteeism or staff rotation, may be described without the struggle that it represents being defined. If the group moves on to the counter-offensive and defines its objectives, the participant observation becomes less important. It is important only insofar as behaviour remains governed by a rejection of the adversary's logic.

Participant observation is a useful method for understanding the resistance of a dominated group, but it does not possess the means for separating the various significations of a more positive collective action.

Committed research no longer links the researcher to a concrete social group, subject to external constraints, but instead to an organized struggle whose objectives he accepts. For instance, he may participate in a unionization campaign, a drive for political organization, or a protest movement. It was Orlando Fals Borda,* in Colombia, who, in theory and in practice, most powerfully developed this concept of research. It has the merit of reminding us that knowledge of society is possible only in as much as popular movements shatter the categories of order and thus cause both the social relations and the mechanisms of domination to emerge. Sociologists must recognize their solidarity with the collective actions, without which it would ultimately be impossible for them to grasp the object of their research. But the sociologist is not obliged by this principle to take up a position within a political or trade-union organization, for such a body will have aims other than the attainment of knowledge, it will inevitably produce an ideology, and will be subject to tactical or strategic demands on account of which the requirements of knowledge and research will be relegated to the background. Nearly always, those who run complex and heterogeneous organizations are disturbed by research. If the movement is strongly organized, a sociologist who were to serve it would be placed in the same situation as the sociologist of a firm, i.e. limited by the conditions for the application of knowledge and doing no more than providing methods and information to serve aims which are not derived from knowledge. Orlando Fals Borda appreciates these difficulties all the more in that he has encountered them himself, particularly in connection with the journal *Alternativa*, the objectives of which were directly political. The organizations wished to retain or regain close control over his works and publications, all the more so since some of the committed researchers seemed to them to prefer the most spontaneous and least organized forms of action. Does not this prove that it is impossible for knowledge to be confused with action? A movement or a party cannot accept research which would presuppose a certain political line unless it has the assurance that this line is its own. Research into social movements is possible only if the movements themselves see an inherent advantage; but are they not more likely to find this advantage in the dissemination of topics and ideas than in direct participation by the researchers in political action?

Committed sociology can develop most freely wherever weakly organized movements are limited in their action – even when this action is powerful – by repression on the one hand and by cultural and social obstacles on the other.

This is a situation that frequently occurs in dependent societies. The sociologist is then not the agent of an organization but an agitator whose work can remove obstructions and prepare the ground for militant action without becoming confused with this action. This is then an intermediate situation between participant observation and intervention. As in the first instance, sociology intervenes where there is not so much struggle and movement as a situation of domination and potential action. It plays the role of mediator between defensive rejection and active participation in an organized struggle. But in such a situation why not submit as completely as possible to the demands of intervention? In assuming the point of view of the social movement, the researcher is actually seeking the meaning and direction of a struggle and is thus acting in the interests of knowledge rather than identifying himself with an organization and with a policy.

The method of intervention is above all a *theoretical* undertaking. I do not exclude the possibility of intervention being prepared by participant observation, particularly in the cases mentioned above; nor do I dismiss the idea that intervention might be associated with an action drive by a union, a party, or an association, provided that the researcher is left free in his approach and particularly in the publication of his results, which is a basic condition for belonging to the world of research. The more active and organized a movement is, the more the researcher must require to be accepted as a researcher and not as a participant.

Before and after intervention

The problems of the researcher's involvement in the struggle under study also arise – and even more directly – during the pre- and post-intervention periods.

1. At the *pre-intervention stage*, should the researcher be a militant of the movement he plans to study? One cannot lay down a general rule that researchers must be militants: in many cases, adherence to a movement presupposes a social status that the researcher does not have. The professional sociologist cannot at the same time be a militant worker; if he is a man, he cannot be a militant femininist; if he is French and is studying the black American movement or the Guatemalan guerrilla movement, he cannot be a militant of the movements he is studying. To claim that one can study and understand only situations in which one participates is tantamount to denying bluntly the possi-

bility of any historical or anthropological knowledge – which is a self-damning exaggeration. If the researcher is militant, it is indispensable that he should not be identified with an organization and with its apparatus, that he should have no authoritarian capacity or decision-making function, and that he should not hold a position of charge; it is also necessary that he should be associated with another researcher, external to the organization, and that he should allow him to assume the main role in conducting the analysis, since he would himself be too integrated into the group to help it achieve its conversion.

Practically, one may conclude that the researcher's belonging to the movement he is studying is positive in cases where the movement outstrips the organizations, and that it tends to be negative if the organization identifies itself with the movement and might therefore involve the researcher in a role conflict he would find difficult to bear.

2. In the *post-intervention* stage it may happen that the researcher, if his results have had direct influence on the orientations of the struggle, will be attracted by the struggle or even invited to join it as a militant. Such a case has already occurred, following research into the French family-planning movement, which was, in advance, a first experiment at intervention. As the result of an internal crisis in the organization, the researcher in charge of the project, Dominique Wolton, was called upon to participate in running the organization by militants who had been involved in the research and had become leaders of the movement. But the researcher who has become a militant can no longer play the role of researcher in the coming-and-going that must be set up between analysis and action; on the other hand, he can facilitate this two-way circulation and participate in it from the side of the movement. The researcher who is directly involved in the organization of a struggle no longer has the independence necessary to carry out the analysis of the struggle. If the intervention leads to modification or extension of an organization's action, the organization takes a favourable view of the research and will be disposed to continue with it under another form. If, on the other hand, the main outcome of the intervention is to reveal a very great distance between the potential movement and its real organization, the associations concerned may turn against the researcher and accuse him of errors, misinterpretations, or prejudices. An intervention, therefore, should never become the evaluation of a self-formed association, group, union, or other body, and the researcher cannot be directly involved in an organization, even less an expert engaged by it. As an independent person, who is nonetheless involved in the field he is studying, what is the researcher's material position? During the first attempts at interven-

tion, the question may be disregarded. The researcher's financial independence is assured by public funds. But the day will come when the problem of financing will have to be considered, for one cannot expect this type of research to be wholly and indefinitely financed by public research funds. I dismiss the idea that the researchers might enter into market bargaining relations with their 'clients'. The acceptable solutions will be those which ensure the researcher's independence. The aim of intervention is to increase the collective actors' capacity for action and not to increase their economic efficiency, which is the reason why companies pay the experts they engage. Some people will undoubtedly attempt to depict sociological intervention as another form of manipulating attitudes in the interests of firms or decision-making centres. Such an accusation is clearly based on a complete misunderstanding of the method and objectives of intervention. It is, therefore, worth recalling the spirit of this method in stating that those who carry out intervention will never use this method in order to acquire gains which would lead to personal privileges. The section of society which we are attempting to understand best is not the part of society which controls the money.

The fragility of the researcher's position

The researcher must maintain his independence, but his independence is not all that easily recognized. In the case of the students, the actors received the researchers – or at least those of them who were lecturers – with a certain amount of mistrust. On the one hand, they accused teachers in general of being ideologists of the dominant order or of accepting this order; on the other hand, they were hostile to the 'mandarins', even when they claimed to belong to the left and to be supporters of the students. The researcher–lecturer is seen by the militant student as an adversary or at least as an incursor from enemy territory. This mistrustfulness proved still stronger during the pre-intervention stage of the study on the Occitanist movement.

The resistance came not from the wine-growers or from the workers or employees, but from certain intellectuals who feared they might be deprived of their role as interpreters and controllers of the content and direction of the movement. Finally, the presence of male researchers – even in the position of secretary and not of agitator – in groups of militant femininists is likely to provoke reactions of mistrust or withdrawal. On each occasion, the researchers were seen – if not because of their behaviour, at least because of their affiliations – as representatives of the opponent and dominator. As a militant Occitanist put it: 'We don't want to be ethnologized', and his mistrust was proof against attempts to persuade him that intervention – more than any other form of research – involves self-analysis.

The researcher must, in fact, fight against a dominatory part of himself. He must, therefore, be exposed to the group's criticism; he must come out of himself in order to be able to speak from the point of view of the movement. The tension between the group and the researcher is an important element in the group's life, without which analysis would be far more difficult, perhaps even impossible. The researcher must be prepared for this group criticism by a preliminary self-criticism and by what I shall describe in a more general term as his fragility. A group can engage in the intervention only if it feels itself to be fragile, if it does not identify completely with the objectives and the ideology of the organization, and if it suffers from the divisions and splits, the hesitations and failures that have marked its struggle; similarly, the researcher must be sensitive to his own contradictions, i.e. that the fact of his being sympathetic towards protest movements is matched or countered by his belonging to a central and relatively privileged world, that of the University and of research. I myself have often experienced this fragility. Although I had sided with the May movement and defended its position at the University Council in Nanterre, and later in the streets and at the barricades, I nevertheless remained far removed from the verbal excitement at the Sorbonne or the Odéon, and I was attacked by some of those who participated in the action. Likewise, I fully supported the Chile of the Popular Front, but was in turn criticized by French leftists for my pro-Allende position. How is one to get beyond these tensions experienced unless it be by resorting to analysis? Would we undertake analysis if we did not feel ourselves to be internally divided, contradictory and fragile? Those who are all of one piece may become epic poets and ideologists; they have no need of analysis, which by clarifying what practice confuses, gives them the impression of being distanced from life. While the fragile analyst, through his work, reconstructs what seems to him to have been broken apart and deformed by historical practice.

The same idea always comes to the fore: research is not illumination, or the provision of proof or identification; the group and the researcher work together to reduce the tensions, dilemmas or contradictions they encounter in their action and their thought. But from the moment when they define themselves only by an identity or an affiliation, they become incapable of working on past experience, and the spirit of the intervention is broken. The researcher must therefore accept his distance in relation to the group at the same time as strengthening his sympathy towards the movement. Because it recognizes this sympathy, the group can accept that the researcher should help it to bring out the movement hidden at the heart of the struggle.

The research can go on only as long as the group sees the distance separating a struggle from a movement and an action from an analysis, and hence the researcher from the members of the group in which he is participating. All these distances, all these tensions, necessitate work aimed at reducing them. Once this work has been accomplished, the mixed group made up of actors and researchers is no longer either an analyst or an actor, but rather a countenance contemplating its own reflection in the mirror. It is no longer in the process of searching, it has dissolved in the research or in the enjoyment of its own identity.

The need for establishing this distance justifies the call to researchers outside of the movement. The intellectuals within the movement are worst placed to adopt a distance with regard to a particular practice; they seek to fill a central position vis-à-vis the practice, to become the expression of the movement, instead of adopting a critical distance towards it.

In the same way, the researcher who becomes identified with the group no longer helps it to work; he founders in the vain effort to suppress another side of himself which he cannot rid himself of, and he plays a negative role by cutting off the group from the movement which it represents by absorbing it into his observation of the group's relations with the researcher. The researcher should not identify himself with the group but rather with the theory that a social movement is present in the struggle under study. He must be capable of analysing the distance between himself and the group, or between the group and the various significations of its struggle. It can be easily understood that he may have difficulty in assuming this role and that he will be drawn towards his own incorporation into the group, but he cannot renounce his own work in favour of his own pleasure. This is the price that must be paid for intervention to be possible; the intervention is not carried out for the benefit of the group or of the researcher, but rather in the interests of the movement and of knowledge.

It will not be easy to gain admission for this point of view. If a struggle is highly organized, what will be required of the researcher is adherence to an organization, party or union; if it is weakly organized, what will be required is the researcher's integration with a group or circle, both of which are far more sensitive than a large organization to the clash between the internal and the external, between us and the others.

The researcher and those who participate in the intervention must recognize that there is a certain distance between them. The advantage for the participants is that they are assured that the researcher will not give preference to one tendency or attempt to influence the action of the movement; the advantage for the researcher lies in his acceptance of the aim to acquire knowledge. This contrast between the actors and the researchers must be revealed by having all documents produced by the intervention made available to all participants, with the proviso that the source of the documents should be indicated, that the researcher should not be held responsible for a publication produced by the actors and that it should always be the group as a whole – and not certain of its members – that decides to divulge its analysis of the documents or of the results of the intervention.

The researcher as theoretician

The researcher views struggles or conflicts from the point of view of the social movement they convey. He draws his support, therefore, from theoretical hypotheses which are not only general but also applied to a particular object of research. He cannot do otherwise. The choice of a field of intervention already presupposes that one expects to discover a social movement in it. But should one not go further? How can one be sure that these hypotheses do not govern the entire intervention in such a way that it effectively leads merely to clarifying or reformulating ideas that have essentially been developed in advance?

This is a superficial objection. Firstly, because there is a great distance between theoretical hypotheses and the analysis of historically situated behaviour; secondly – and above all – because the ideas regarding social movements, to which we may have access outside of our own analysis, are extremely poor. And the effort that has gone into bringing out the concept of *social movement* is also an effort which ultimately results in proposing the method of sociological intervention. It is through this same movement that we create the representation of society in which our hypotheses are rooted and the method by which these theories may be implemented.

Intervention is not a special means of gathering information, a form prepared by theoretical reflexion and completed by a historical type of interpretation. The exact hypotheses concerning the nature of the struggle take shape essentially during the research itself, and the researcher puts these theories to the test in discussion with the group. Theoretical analysis lies at the heart of intervention: it is only on this condition that the conversion of the image-group into the analyst-group is possible, and, yet more clearly, that the analyst-group can become a mixed self-interpretation group, since this group becomes organized in response to the researchers' communication of their theories concerning the group. This is exactly what happened during the first intervention performed. In 1968, I had developed the hypothesis that the conflict for the social appropriation of knowledge was the factor that could raise the students' struggle to the level of a social movement, but it remained to be seen whether the students' struggle of 1976 had in fact taken this direction. This was a problem to which we were tempted to reply negatively at the beginning of the intervention, since the students delivered increasingly numerous statements which reduced knowledge to ideology and exhibited great hostility towards teachers. Anyone who might have reduced the intervention to a series of group interviews would doubtless have concluded that the theme of knowledge, and of the social conditions of its production and use was missing from the student movement, except perhaps in its communist sector, where the rather different theme of the scientific and technical revolution was understood. It was during the conversion of the Bordeaux group, at Toignan, that the theme of knowledge appeared for the first time. And it was at Marly that I introduced it, obstinately, in order to derive from the group a reply which, after many hours of fiery discussion, proved in the long run to be partly positive, which thus enabled us in the post-intervention period to state that an appeal to knowledge as a cultural stake might set the student movement on the level of a social movement.

During intervention, the researcher puts his theories to the test. He observes whether the group is capable of organizing itself in a coherent and stable manner around a particular theme or whether, instead, it rejects this theme or reacts to it in an unstable or contradictory fashion. The general hypothesis introduced by the researcher, particularly at the moment of conversion, may have been developed before the research, but the interpretation of the group's history which he communicates to the group is the product of intervention itself.

Could one conceive of interventions of the type such as I have described but which would be conducted on the basis of quite different theoretical hypotheses and representations of society? I do not dare state that it is impossible; I accept the challenge with interest for the satisfaction of then seeing the idea of social movement, which has been excluded by most sociological theories, take its place in several of them, while also thinking that such a plurality of interpretations is impossible and should be settled by the triumph of one theoretical approach over the other or by a deepening of the approach on a particular issue. But it is too early to know if intervention can be used by a variety of schools or whether, as I believe, it is associated solely with a sociological approach. I should be glad to have to defend myself on this point a few years hence.

The researchers

The research team

The intervention is guided by hypotheses, but its results depend to a great extent on the functioning of a research team. What are the psycho-social problems that can arise in the team, and what are their effects on the research? What are the effects of the researchers' behaviour on the result of the group? How is the interpretation of the results worked out by the team and what happens if divergence occurs between team members?

1. The first problem is the most embarrassing because it seems most alien to the content of the struggle under study and because it comes as a surprise to the researchers, who become both the observers and the observed and do not know how to express their team's problems without aggravating them. During intervention on the student movement, the research team's internal problems interfered considerably with the work of the intervention group, particularly at the moment of the encounter between the two groups. One incident had serious consequences. During the first meeting between the two groups, a student from Bordeaux declared that one of the researchers had described the students from Amiens as *'des petits cons'* (little shits). The researcher in question affirmed this statement, which was taken as an insult by the Amiens students and no less by the research agitator from Amiens who, during the whole evening, regarded the behaviour of the two researchers from the other group as aggressive. During the weekend spent at Marly, the effects of this aggressivity were strongly felt not only between the two groups but also between the researchers, whose team-spirit before the intervention had been very close. This effect was heightened by the fact that the Bordeaux team differed little from each other in their approach – the two researchers being constantly on the reserve and fearing to intervene too much in their group – while in Amiens the agitator had become strongly identified with his group, leaving the secretary to intervene most actively during the first weekend.

2. The mention of this crisis enables us to tackle the second problem and to attain an understanding of the effects the researchers' behaviour may have on the results of the intervention. If the Amiens group, which had started off better than the Bordeaux group, later became exhausted and, in spite of its own efforts, did not succeed in its conversion while the Bordeaux group did, was this not on account of the researchers' behaviour – the over-powerful attachment of the Amiens agitator to the group or the over-active interventions by the

secretary during the weekends? It will not be possible to answer these questions precisely until we have at our disposal a large number of interventions from which instructive comparisons may be drawn. But one must beware of speaking too generally of the researchers' influence on the groups. A distinction must be made between three order of phenomena:
* the group exerts an influence on the researchers' behaviour;
* the respect or non-respect for the principles of the method of intervention has predictable consequences as regards the results obtained;
* lastly, the researchers and the relations between them exert an influence on the behaviour of the groups.

The first point is important. If the Amiens group was an excellent witness-group and a very active image-group but did not succeed in becoming an analyst-group, it was not only because – more than the Bordeaux group – it was a real historical group, a natural group, but also because it was dominated by two extremely firm, doctrinaire opinions, that of the LCR, of Trotskyist inspiration, and that of the UEC, the Communist students, while between the two there was the disintegrating MAS, the new student union, close at the time to the CFDT. These characteristics of the group are so important and so well explain its behaviour that it is difficult to establish the researchers' influence upon the group.

Speaking more generally, is it not dangerous to explain behaviour and statements that are strongly linked to problems and experiences external to the group by inter-personal relations within the group? Intervention constantly maintains, as powerfully as possible, the representative character of the group. This is not sufficient to suppress the psychosocial mechanisms present in all the groups; but it is enough to distinguish the phenomena which are explained by the nature of the movement and of the behaviour which occurs only within the group itself. The researchers' behaviour may certainly have a beneficial or detrimental effect on the results or it may give a certain tone to the group's life, but the analysis is not brought to bear on the group's life; what it bears on is the way in which the group handles the problems of the movement it represents. In a movement, the role of the leaders is decisive for explaining events, the outcome of action; it is not decisive for analysing a situation, problems, and discussions.

The same goes for the researchers' role in a situation which is not that of experimental groups formed in order to study psycho-social mechanisms but rather that of witness-groups, which are close to real historical groups and which, both for their own sake and to satisfy the requests of the researchers, constantly behave as groups of militants responsible for the problems and the future of the movement within which they have participated in struggles.

3. Will the researchers, who are exposed to different experiences and, furthermore, led to oppose one another, arrive at the same conclusions? The likelihood of their reaching comparable conclusions, which is a factor that determines the confidence to be accorded to the intervention, depends on two causes. Firstly, the stipulation of the hypotheses and their introduction into a general theoretical approach; secondly, the appraisal of the entire body of documentation. It is easy to set one interpretation of a strike in opposition to another; it is far more difficult for each interpretation to account for all that the groups have said and done during the intervention. Uli Windisch and Alfred Willener,* with exemplary honesty, have offered a proof *a contrario* of the need for interpretation to be subjected to powerful documentary constraints. They conducted parallel studies on the Jurassian autonomist movement in Switzerland, Windisch aligning himself more directly with the separatists, whose anger and enthusiasm he shared, and Willener maintaining greater distance, studying documents such as television programmes rather than the actual militant action. At the end of the book, each evaluated the other's work, and these two texts reveal just how much each of the researchers – both very deliberately and very unconsciously – selected certain aspects of reality. By relaxing the constraints of documentation, i.e. of what must be explained in its totality, this type of participant intervention cannot help juxtaposing observations and interpretations which cannot possibly be integrated and between which one cannot choose.

It nevertheless remains that the researchers form part of the situation which they have to interpret, which endangers the value of their conclusions. In the future, it is likely that each team will have to be assisted by a *consultant* capable of analysing its problems and the effect of its behaviour on the group's life and on the interpretation given thereof by the researchers.

The idea has been expressed that this consultant should above all be a psychologist. If there is a price to be paid for the success of a group whose history might be almost completely interpreted through the problems of the movement is it not that the research team suffers the backlash of the psychological tensions that have been either thrust aside or neglected? This rebound can in fact be far better understood by an observer with an analytical training than by a sociologist. But it is not in this way that the research team should be examining itself. The researchers, like the interlocutors, should not be considered for what they are themselves but should be regarded merely as instruments of the intervention and of the subsequent interpretation. Since their role is to provide a sociological interpretation of the group's behaviour, they must move still further towards observing from the point of view of the theory of social movements in order to understand their own behaviour in the groups and between themselves. Interpersonal tensions should first of all be regarded as a sign of the weakness of the analysis, of the inability of the theory to account for observable facts. If the agitator identifies himself more with the group and the secretary with the movement, this may lead to tensions, and not merely interpersonal tensions at that. Similarly, rivalry may spring up between the two sub-teams of researchers: once again, one must first consider this fact as an indication of the difficulties of the movement. I mentioned that during the meeting of the student groups, the agitator from Amiens declared that he had felt the behaviour of the Bordeaux researchers to be aggressive. This feeling on the part of the agitator may be explained by his isolation, since the other researcher from Amiens – who was in charge of the research – wished to communicate with both the groups. But what his feeling above all reflected was the real domination of one group by the other, a domination of the word over action, of the desire of the movement over the experience of the struggle. Did not the feeling experienced by the researcher from Amiens indicate the powerlessness of those who were the most real actors, and their frustration at seeing that the student movement was taking shape only in the world of words? Here, the tension between the researchers disclosed the deepest fissure in the student movement. If the researchers were to approach their own behaviour as psychologists they would be tempted to view the groups with the same eye, or else, instead, they would place themselves outside of the groups: in either case, they would be drawn into contradictions which might lead to the splitting up of the research team. This, then, emphasizes the importance of the theoretical training of the researchers taking part in an intervention.

The agitators and secretaries must not only have a good knowledge of the situation in which they intervene, but they must also consider each intervention as the submission of theoretical ideas to the test. It is by no means desirable that there should be a sharp division of tasks between researchers involved in the same research programme, for this would mean that each would be given the main responsibility for an intervention, with the others merely playing the role of assistants. This would rapidly destroy the interventions, for the tension between the agitator and the secretary corresponds to the tension between the struggle and the movement. The research team will need gradually to expand, but by continuing to give all the widest possible research experience. Permanent sociology must also involve the constitution of a body of knowledge which develops by accounting for all the interventions and all the experience surrounding these interventions.

Demonstration or interpretation

All that has thus far been said of the researchers leads us to the question: are they the agents of the groups' self-analysis, who impose their conclusions upon the group, or do they interpret a collective experience in terms of their personal characteristics? At the time of writing, I am debating how to give final form to a book discussing the intervention on the students: could these conclusions be different; would others, or would we ourselves at other moments have interpreted the event differently?

I use the word event deliberately: intervention aims at reaching a movement through an event, at constructing a social field of action from a history. We do not grasp a structure directly as the anthropologist does when reconstructing a kinship system; nor do we define an evolution as a historian would. We are working at both levels at the same time and must therefore agree to bring a double judgement to bear upon ourselves. During the intervention, we analyse a *movement*, and hence a social field, but at the same time we judge an *event* by locating it more or less explicitly in an evolutionary order, and this interpretation, no matter how deeply considered it may be, cannot be of the same order: it is a *historical* judgement, far more deeply marked by the interpreter's scrutiny and by his situation. These two sides of analysis must be specified before one reflects upon their relation. The demonstration consists initially in formulating a hypothesis, concerning not only the historical nature of the struggle but also the social movement that may be present in it. This hypothesis is introduced sufficiently early into the group to be able to contribute towards its conversion, to be worked upon by the group and to guide it in its self-analysis. Thereafter, more concrete hypotheses are constructed in order to account for the distance between the struggle and the movement, and for the degeneration or splitting up of the movement. Every struggle is the split and fragmentary image of a movement, and can be analysed as an attempt to reduce the clashes or contradictions caused by this splitting. It is from this point on that one must account for the whole body of documentation, the group's behaviour, its evolution, and the relations between the actors. The group's reaction to these hypotheses, when they have been communicated, is a further and very important element in the demonstration of the hypotheses, for the group's reactions must accord with the predictions.

The *first hypothesis* on the nature of the movement depends on the researcher's orientation and corresponds to an 'idea', but the *concrete hypotheses* bearing on the life of the group and the movement should be able to be judged by their capacity to account for the documents. And they should not be confused with a *judgement on the historical situation* of a struggle. To see in the May movement the emergence of a new social movement does not amount to a historical interpretation of the May 'events', of an encounter between a student movement, a workers' strike and a political crisis. Likewise, in the student strike of 1976, we found reference to a possible social movement the stakes of which would be the social use of knowledge, but it is impossible to claim that this signification dominated the event. The crisis of the left and its anti-capitalist analysis of University problems was more crucial to the interpretation of the event. But this crisis may be viewed in many ways, and the political evolution of France between 1978 and 1980 may deeply alter the perspective in which the events of 1976 are viewed.

This discussion of sociological analysis and historical interpretation cannot be complete, but one must be aware of the distance separating the two. For, while a movement has the right to refuse a historical interpretation, it is difficult for it to reject a sociological analysis.

11

In the service of action

The principles of intervention

Before concluding, let us recall the principles of intervention and the way in which it sets out to explain collective action.

1. Intervention starts out from the idea that collective behaviour can best be discovered by interpreting the analytical work which a group of actors carries out upon its own action in conditions created by the researchers and jointly controlled by them and by the group itself.

2. A social relation is regarded as one of the determinants of collective behaviour if in the intervention group it is interconnected in a clear, stable and coherent manner with other determinants. This revelation of the problems of a movement in a group's life presupposes that at the beginning of the intervention the group should be confronted by both its partners and its opponents, for in being exposed to the opinions and attitudes thus expressed the group cannot remain enclosed within an ideology and must perforce undertake the analysis of its *raisons d'être* and of the problems involved in its action.

3. It is not possible to carry out complete separation of the directions of collective behaviour unless one sets out by according priority of research to the *highest direction*, i.e. the social movement, which is the collective action of a class actor against his class opponent for the control of historicity, which represents the cultural stake in this social conflict. The researcher's main role is to lead the group to consider its behaviour from the point of view of the movement therein embodied and intermingled with other types or levels of collective action. The researcher is primarily the mediator between a concrete struggle and the social movement that is present in it.

4. Struggles and, even more, other types of collective behaviour –

insofar as they are not entirely the expression of a social movement – experience the tensions and contradictions generated by the disintegration or the non-integration of the social movement, and, without realizing it, work towards overcoming the tensions.

The researcher, therefore, performs three main analytical operations:

- he raises the group to the highest possible level of action, thus enabling the central principle of the analysis of the movement to be brought out;
- he exposes the nature of the components of collective action, and these provide him with information concerning the social situations in which this action occurs;
- he accounts for the internal problems, tensions, and contradictions of collective action whenever this action does not fully correspond to a social movement and, consequently, whenever its elements are weakly integrated.

This brief recapitulation reminds us that intervention does not only provide a corpus of documentary material which is generally richer than that available in historical analysis or sociological investigation; for the group's life also brings out the problems of collective action to such an extent that the analysis of a collective action, a struggle or movement, should be directly presented as an interpretation of the history of the intervention groups.

The books which will follow this volume – on the students' movement, the anti-nuclear movement, the Occitanist movement, trade-unionism, and the women's movement – will endeavour to implement these guiding ideas and to show the usefulness of intervention as the main method for the study of collective behaviour.

The raison d'être of intervention

One doubt remains in the reader's mind. Even though he may be ready to acknowledge the interest of sociological intervention, he will hesitate to entrust himself fully to it; he may not even believe that I myself am taking him fully into my confidence. Does not the association between general ideas and historical documents or studies already enable us to construct the analysis of social movements, even though intervention may actually bring us deeper knowledge of the movements, at least of those which can be subjected to direct observation and which accept this observation? One must, therefore, accurately define the place of intervention in research into collective action. A social movement or a struggle is not an event; each is constructed by analysis based on events. Intervention enables us to learn about a movement or a struggle, and the method of intervention consists in extracting the direction and meaning of social relations; by contrast, truly historical studies place the event within an ensemble which is defined in terms of principles or developments, but never in terms of actions. This historical approach has long been imposed on the social sciences and has finally culminated in the often repeated declaration by contemporary Marxist sociologists that one must emerge from the world of actors in order to reach the 'system', the sole explicator, which in practice means that one explains social behaviour through a state of the economic system or a mode of production, the structure of which is ultimately determined by economic organization. The superficial layer of events is contrasted with the deep-lying strata of the economic – or cultural – system. This form of critique of the event has served its time. The outworn image must be discarded. What is deep-lying is the system of social relations, hence of collective actions; at the surface lies the present set of events, the social situation. The locus of intervention is that of social action; the closer one moves towards the locus of politics, of conscience, of the state, the more intervention becomes overlaid by the study of documents created by political practice, by the control of society. This links up again with the central idea of the study of historical struggles. Because these struggles occur in a context of change, hence in the state sphere, they by no means readily accommodate themselves to intervention, but it is only intervention that can reveal the forms of disintegration of collective action, of its submission to state initiative or its transformation into state intervention.

Once one has separated the analysis of the social system from that of the change of concrete political ensembles, one must replace recourse to a decision-making authority or to an infrastructure by the representation of society as an ensemble of systems of action shaped by the conflict between actors for the control of a cultural or social field. Only analysis in terms of social relations and action can enable us to conceive of society as a system and free ourselves from the quest for casuality among various categories of social 'facts'. The appeal to the economic system against the actors is in fact the opposite of an analysis of society as a system. Sociological intervention is the only method which directly adopts as its object of study a system of social relations. It must therefore be given priority. As long as the possible applications of this method remain few, one will be tempted to interconnect ideas on social movements and documents on the control of society, passing over and above the hidden but central position of collective action. This impatience is excusable, and may even prepare the way for new conquests by intervention. But only intervention can achieve the reversal of approach which is today necessary: to cease believing that action is explained by situation and to rediscover that situations are no more than the projection in historical change of systems of social relations and collective actions. The method of intervention can be judged only as a practical instrument of this reversal, one which governs the formation of a wholly social analysis of society.

Assisting action

In analysing the nature of a struggle, intervention reveals to the actors their utmost capacity for historical action, thus helping them to raise the project level of their movement. Such is its function: knowledge and action associated. It does not inform the actor as to a situation, nor does it advise him as to a tactic; the intervener is not a chartered accountant of historical action. He even seems to criticize a movement, to separate the elements whose mixture gives action its historical existence. But in reality he is shattering the false independence of each of the components of a social movement as well as exposing their confusion in ideological speech.

1. First of all, intervention destroys the *universalist* illusion, the direct identification of the movement with a general principle, with the progress of liberty or justice, with the defence of the rights of man, or with national independence. This also brings out the fragility of the 'forces of progress' in which a social movement, particularly at the beginning of its existence, tends to become lost. To recognize that a movement does not struggle for a right or a principle but that it also struggles against a social opponent is to break down the fragile coalition uniting the modernizing elements – situated at a purely cultural level – the agents of a new rising class, and the new popular forces.

2. Conversely, intervention reacts against *activism* and the preference accorded to desire for breakdown over the always suspect counter-projects of reformism. This it does in particular by entering at the base of the movement, by refusing to identify the movement with the strategy of the leaders, and by causing the voice of the people to be heard rather than by describing the laws of a pattern of domination or exploitation.

3. Finally, intervention protects the movement from the pitfall of *identity* by reminding it that identity cannot be separated either from a conflict or from a stake. A dominated category tends to escape from its master and from imposed order by taking refuge in its identity. This identity may serve as a cave in which the cultural weapons of liberation

216

are concealed; but a liberation movement, by opposing only its identity to alienation leads not to a social movement but to the formation of a new power as has been demonstrated by the experience of most third world countries and by the dashed hopes of Frantz Fanon. Liberation, cultural and social movements, just as much as national movements, are constantly in danger of becoming the basis of the power of new ruling elites. The more directly a movement defines itself by appeal to an identity and by its desire for breakdown, the more it is swept towards its own submission to new masters who monopolize speech, prohibit discussion and give preference to new privileges. Social intervention also allows for the voice of the people to be heard against that of these new masters, even when these masters still assume the figure of protest leaders, liberators or general advocates of the oppressed. The transition is often so swift from prison to throne, from protest to power, that one must act as promptly as possible against the reduction of a social movement to an order, no matter how progressivist it may wish to appear.

These are the three chief dangers threatening a social movement with disintegration or destruction. To them may be added a fourth, less serious, danger: whoever confuses the social movement with its institutional expression reduces it to a political force or even a pressure group. In this case, too, intervention is useful; behind the strategy and negotiation it rediscovers whatever is conflict and counter-project, whatever cannot be entirely negotiated, even though the conflict may be largely treated by institutional mechanisms. In dominant societies, whether capitalist or socialist, intervention recalls the priority of cultural innovation and of social conflict over political strategy and statist control. Intervention is a challenge, the appearance of the historical actor amongst the regulations, the games and coalitions, not as the citizen's protest against the powers that be but as men's action towards the production of their own history. Will intervention be able to penetrate right through to the great social movements and to the most dramatic struggles, or will it instead be accepted only by the weak movements of secondary importance, glad to have their voice heard and to be given an ear? Can one imagine fighters in civil or guerrilla warfare, revolutionary unionists, or outlaws participating in intervention? Is it possible that intervention will reach as far as workers subjected to managerial or governmental repression, as far as the peasants of the Andes crushed beneath the heel of the great estate owners, or as far as the oppressed nations? These questions would seem to crush a method which first began to be applied but a few years ago; yet I hope they are questions to which the answer will prove positive.

We may, perhaps, not reach to the heart of history; but who has attempted to come so close? The bonded, the oppressed, the outcast, the exploited, the conquered, and the exiled do not easily manage to gain a hearing. It is not they who carve inscriptions in stone, raise monuments, write on papyrus, parchment or paper, who have their voices recorded their actions filmed. What we call history includes more *terra incognita* than the old maps of Africa or Latin America. Let us now allow ourselves to become imprisoned by the conjuring up of this almost eternal silence; it has halted all forms of knowledge. On the other hand, let us not be too fascinated by warlike and revolutionary movements. They have been brilliantly spotlighted, as has everything which encroaches on state power; but have the social movements in them often been analysed? A world of slaves and conquerors, of customs and states, not only resists a certain method of analysis; it prohibits and eliminates the social movements themselves. And it is precisely intervention which, because it does not occur at the level of the most organized powers and forces, is best able to approach these areas where the movement is no longer anything but suffering, rejection, or hope in far-off compensations. Is not intervention able to bring out speech, discussion, and project from what seems to have been crushed and reduced to silence? Is it not important because it causes the movement to reappear in what seemed to have been immobilized? Why does it not turn to the refugees, the deportees, the imprisoned? Its conquered presence could be an active protestation, a struggle for knowledge against terror, repression, and absolute power.

And in our own society, where the field open to speech is far larger, is intervention not indispensable in order to bring out again the historical actors who seem to have become dissolved in incessant change or to have been crushed by the impersonal mechanisms of manipulation which crush discussion and protest? Intervention places the actors face to face with their opponents; it brings out the field of their struggles; it enables us to rediscover that men make their own history.

We do indeed begin with the study of movements which seem weak and which occur in a protected environment, safeguarded by great public freedoms. But it should firstly be noted that these are not light ripples on calm waters. Even if they do not lead to serious breakdown – though why should they not? – they bring out the most fundamental conflicts of our society at the same time as they reveal its deepest cultural transformations. What place was held by the first typesetters' strikes, by the ideas of the Saint-Simonians, or the publications of certain Christian socialists in pre-1848 French society, a society of peasants, traders, and property-holders? Why might not the anti-nuclear campaigns of today herald a series of struggles as important as were those of the workers' movement, which inherited the impulse of those earlier, seemingly petty stirrings? Secondly, is not the essential concern to learn again to view our society as the product of its innovations and its conflicts?

After having proposed a representation of society, the principal elements of which were to be found in the first part of this book, it was indispensable to convert this representation into a research practice, to study social movements after having defined them.

These two, historical and methodological, preoccupations entail a third. For several years, we have no longer known what to do. Sociologists have learned to be mistrustful of the false simplicities of empiricism; they have also wearied of devising interpretative discourse relating to science, and have carefully avoided yielding to the simplest demands of research. They are confusedly aware that research will not become possible again until the relation between the researcher and his object of research has been transformed. This relation is not plainly visible; it is hidden, overlaid by the categories of order, crisis, or change. It must be discovered at the same time as being redefined as the production of society by itself. One must stop believing that one is observing situations, and recognize that one must first reveal the social relations that are hidden by what transforms them into order and disorganizes them. This implies a change of method, which should in no way subordinate knowledge to past experience, to ideology or to the pleasure of dominating or destroying, but which involves the researcher in a new relation with those he is studying and without whom he could not attain the object of his knowledge. It is for these three reasons that we are today undertaking this first research programme, in the hope of coming far closer than has ever been done to both the din of combat and the silence of the prison, the pride of the overlords and the fear of the oppressed. These hopes may, perhaps, seem excessive, but they do at least show that intervention is not a technique but the implementation of a conception of society and of sociological knowledge.

The sociologist's role

Does not intervention build up a sociological power which might be a peculiar form of technocratic power? Is not the defence of social movements an appeal – beyond organizations – to 'forces' or 'tendencies', the sole legitimate expression of which resides with the sociologist? Will we not find tomorrow that parties, trade unions or associations have been reoriented by sociologists, just as firms have already been reorganized by business management consultants? This fear is by no means new.

We are well enough aware that society is a system of action to be able to feel that those who orient the actors by giving them a political model of social organization and a moral model of behaviour can exercise greater power than the masters of the economy or of the government. But they hold this power only if they control the apparatus.

The intellectuals play an important role when they uncover historicity and the conflicts which accrete around historicity, but they have no power unless their ideas are embodied in an apparatus of control and management. It is not from the ideas but from the apparatus that the power derives. Not only does the sociologist acquire no power by analysing the most central social relations, but he cannot even carry out his analysis unless he refuses to be placed inside any power apparatus, whether it be that of a firm, a party or a state apparatus. The intervening sociologist must be an independent professional, even when he is a salary-earner, which it is particularly possible for him to be when he is working in a research centre. He does not work for an organization, not even – and particularly – if this organization regards itself as the expression of the movement under study; and in particular he remains controller of his own publications. The sociologist is a man without power, who may even be grudgingly accepted and who finds himself in the same ambiguous situation as historicity itself, i.e. at the heart of society, but hidden by the conflicts of which society represents the stakes. It is because he reveals social relations that he is attributed the power to create them, but his intervention must dispel this error since it demonstrates that the movements have an existence more profound than their organization and their ideology. His importance is of a different nature. If the sociologist's intervention exerted an influence, this would mean that the ideas of society and collective behaviour would again be interconnected, thus opening up the way for the renewal of social theory and the renaissance of social movements. Are we not dominated and threatened today by the division between thought and action, which can be explained both for the actors and for knowledge at the time of a great historical but catastrophic change? The instruments of analysis have aged, the old social movements are declining, social action is drawn towards rejection, denunciation and violence rather than towards new projects for social transformation.

It is all very well to denounce the growing empire – wherever it exists – of the state's omnipotence; it is encouraging to see protest movements freeing themselves from the excessive institutionalization of former conflicts; but it is disquieting to see them becoming blocked within revolt, above all through the lack of available analysis and hence of a fitting political orientation. The denunciation of the ubiquity of power cannot but lead to a widespread rejection of social organization, including conflictual action. This rejection may be revolutionary, i.e. it may give priority to the overthrow of institutions and to the assumption of power by the state, but it leads to regressive forms of struggle wherever such a perspective is not imposed by the general disintegration of institutions. The threat of crisis and decay appears whenever the rejection is unable to find expression through any other means than the revolt by which it itself is destroyed.

Intervention aims to reverse this tendency, to recompose social movements wherever possible, to raise the level of conflicts, and to revivify historical action. I should not have undertaken this research programme had I not believed it was necessary and possible to define the actors, the fields of struggle and the new stakes, and hence theoretically and practically to re-form the analysis of society. Today, social life seems to be crushed between absolute power and the laws of nature; this is what happens in the case of collective action and particularly of the social movements which will enable its existence to be rediscovered.

On the other hand, intervention rejects the idea that the direction and meaning of a movement appear when it abstracts itself from action and becomes associated with the affirmation of identity. Once one no longer perceives the social relations and their stakes, one encounters on the one hand the rejection of an unknown opponent and on the other a recoil towards identity. Many movements today claim that their main objective is to rediscover an identity which might be defined by a difference rather than by a relation or by a conflict. This is a tendency visible in certain aspects of the regional or femininist movements, and one which, detached from any social basis, flourishes in cultural movements directed towards rediscovery of the body and of the communication which the individual establishes with his body, beyond all language. Intervention, as a practice of the sociology of action and of social relations, proposes instead to burst the bubble of identity in order to rediscover the social relations and a definition of the actor through his double relation with his opponent and with the cultural field in which their conflict occurs. Intervention must be the place where reflexion and expression meet up in order to generate analysis and to produce action.

In more concrete terms, intervention is the method suited to the analysis of movements which are ultimately defined as actions and are no longer defined as the expression of a historical need or of economic contradictions. The movement of the industrial era, which sought their direction beyond their action, called for an analysis of the system of production and of the laws of capitalist domination. The nature of the struggles corresponded to the method of analysis. Intervention corresponds in the same way to the movements it studies and to the development of which it must contribute. Neither the actors nor the analysts believe any longer in the meaning of history or in the laws of society, but they do believe in a culturally oriented and socially conflictual action capable of transforming the social and economic organization and of making a breach in the established order.

After so many years dominated by the modernizing optimism of the technocrats and by discussion of the laws of capitalism, the social movements which are making their new voices heard are calling for a new type of analysis, a sociology of action, and a new method of study – sociological intervention. It is the same approach which lies behind the progress of those who invent the social history of tomorrow and those who seek to understand this history at the very moment of its production.

List of works cited

vvvvvvvvvvvvvvvvvvvvvvvvvvvvvvvvvvvvvvvvvvvvvvvvvvvvvvvvvvvvvvvvvvvv

1. Men make their own history and The social movements

Alberoni, Francisco, *Movimento e istituzione*, Bologna, Il Mulino, 1977.

Alexander, Christopher, 'The city as a machine for sustaining human contact' in Ewald (ed.), *Environment for men*, Indiana University Press, 1967, pp. 60–102.

Attali, Jacques, *La nouvelle économie française*, Paris, Flammarion, 1978.

Bercé Yves-Marie, *Croquants et Nu-pieds: les soulèvements – France du XVIe au XIXe siècle*, Paris, Gallimard/Julliard, 1974.

Birnbaum, Pierre, *et al.*, *La classe dirigeante française*, Paris, PUF, 1978.

Bourdieu, Pierre and Passeron, Jean-Claude, *Les Héritiers: les étudiants et la culture*, Paris, Ed. de Minuit, 1964; trans. as *The Inheritors: French students and their relation to culture*, Chicago, University of Chicago Press, 1979.

Braudel, Fernand, *La Méditerranée et le Monde méditerranéen a l'époque de Philippe II*, Paris, Colin, 1949; trans. as *The Mediterranean and the Mediterranean world in the age of Philip II*, London, Collins, 1972–73.

Castells, Manuel, *La Question urbaine*, Paris, Maspero, 1972; trans. as *The Urban Question: A Marxist approach*, London, Edward Arnold, 1977.

Cottereau, Alain, 'La turberculose à Paris 1882–1914. Maladie urbaine ou maladie de l'usure du travail? Un exemple de production de connaissances et de méconnaissances sur les modes de vie.' Communication at the conference *Aspects de la vie quotidienne*, Montpellier, 1978.

Crozier, Michel, *Le Phénomène bureaucratique*, Paris, Éd. du Seuil, 1963; trans. as *The bureaucratic phenomenon*, Chicago, University of Chicago Press, 1967.

Crozier, Michel, and Friedberg, Erhard, *L'Acteur et le Système*, Paris, Éd. du Seuil, 1977.

Dahrendorf, Ralf, *Class and Class conflict in industrial society*, Stanford University Press, 1959 (revised version of *Soziale Klassen und Klassenkonflict in der industriellen Gesellschaft*, 1957).

Douassot, Jean, *La Gana*, Paris, Julliard, 1958; trans. as *La Gana*, London, Calder, 1975.

Dubos, René, *So human an animal*, New York, Scribner's, 1968.

Foucault, Michel, *Surveiller et punir*, Paris, NRF, 1975; trans. as *Discipline and Punish: Birth of a prison*, London, Allen Lane, 1977.

Foucault, Michel, 'Vérité et pouvoir' in *L'Arc* no. 70, 1977, pp. 16–26.

List of works cited

Friedmann, Georges, *Le Travail en miettes. Spécialisation et loisirs*, Paris, Gallimard, 1958.

Galbraith, John, *The new industrial state*, London, Hamish Hamilton, 1967.

Germani, Gino, *Politica y sociedad en una epoca de transicion*, Buenos Aires, Paidos, 1962.

Godelier, Maurice, *Horizon, Trajets marxistes en anthropologie*, Paris, Maspero, 1973, Vol. I, pp. 7–25; trans. as *Perspectives in Marxist Anthropology*, Cambridge, Cambridge University Press, 1977.

Habermas, Jurgen, *Strukturwandel der Offentlichkeit*, Neuwied, Luchterhand, 1962.

Illich, Ivan, *Tools for conviviality*, New York, Harper & Row, 1973.

Laclau, Ernesto, *Politics and ideology in Marxist theory: capitalism-fascism-populism*, Atlantic Island, Humanities Press, 1977.

Lefort, Claude, *Les Formes de l'histoire*, Paris, Gallimard, 1978.

Marcuse, Herbert, *One-dimensional man. Studies in the ideology of advanced industrial society*, London, Routledge & Kegan Paul, 1964.

Marx, Gary, 'Issueless riots' in M.E. Wolfgang and J.F Short (eds.), *Collective violence*, Chicago, Aldine-Atherton, 1972, pp. 48–59.

Melucci, Alberto, *Lotte sociali e mutamenti*, Milan, 1974.

Melucci, Alberto, *Sistema Politico, partiti e movimenti sociali*, Milan, Feltrinelli, 1976.

Melucci, Alberto, (under the supervision of), *Movimenti di revolta. Teorie e forme dell'azione collettiva*, Milan, CELUC, 1976.

Moore, Barrington, Jr., *The social origins of dictatorship and democracy. Lord and peasant in the making of the modern world*, Boston, Beacon Press, 1966.

Pereira de Queiroz, Maria-Isaura, *Réforme et Révolution dans les sociétés traditionelles. Histoire et ethnologie des mouvements messianiques*, Paris, Anthropos, 1968.

Peyrefitte, Alain, *Le Mal français*, Paris, Plon, 1976.

Poulantzas, Nicos, *L'État, le Pouvoir, le Socialisme*, Paris, PUF, 1978; trans. as *State, Power, Socialism*, London, New Left Books, 1978.

Riesman, David, *The Lonely Crowd. A study of the changing American character* (with N. Glazer and R. Denney), New York, Doubleday, 1955.

Tilly, Charles, 'The changing place of collective violence' in M. Richter (ed.), *Essays in theory and history. An approach to the social sciences*, Cambridge, Massachusetts, Harvard University Press, 1970, pp. 139–164.

Touraine, Alain, *Production de la société*, Paris, Éd. du Seuil, 1973; trans. as *The Self-production of society*, Chicago, University of Chicago Press, 1977.

2. Sociological intervention

Anzieu, Didier, 'L'illusion groupale' in *Nouvelle Revue de Psychanalyse*, 1971, no. 4, pp. 73–93.

Anzieu, Didier, *et. al.*, *Le Travail psychanalytique des groupes*, Paris, Dunod, 1976.

Bales, Robert F., *Small Groups. Studies in social interaction*, New York, Knopf, 1965.

Bion, Wilfred R., *Experiences in groups*, New York, Basic Books, 1961.

List of works cited

Fals Borda, Orlando, 'Por la praxis: el problema de como investigar la realidad para transformaria' in *Critica y politica en ciencias sociales. El debate sobre teoria y practica*, Bogota, Punta de Lanza, 1978.

Foucault, Michel, *Histoire de la sexualité, I, La Volonté de savoir*, Paris, Gallimard, 1976; trans. as *The history of sexuality, Vol. I: An introduction*, New York, Pantheon, 1978.

Freire, Paulo, *Pédagogie des opprimés* and *Conscientisation et Révolution*, Paris, Maspero, 1974.

Jaques, Eliott, *The changing culture of a factory*, London, Tavistock Publs., 1951.

Lapassade, Georges, *L'Arpenteur. Une intervention sociologique*, Paris, Éd. de l'Épi, 1971.

Lourau, René, *L'Analyseur Lip*, Paris, UGE 10/18, 1974.

Mendel, Gérard, *Sociopsychanalyse*, Paris, Payot, 1974, vol. IV, *Sociopsychanalyse dans une institution psychanalytique*, vol. V, *La sociopsychanalyse institutionelle, pour qui? pour quoi?*

Sociologie et Sociétés, 'Psychologie, Sociologie, Intervention', Montreal, 1977, vol. IX, II.

Willener, Alfred, *L'Image-Action de la société ou la politisation culturelle*, Paris, Éd., du Seuil, 1970.

Windisch, Uli, and Willener, Alfred, *Le Jura incompris. Fédéralisme ou totalitarisme?*, Vevey, Delta, 1976.